BUT TIME AND CHANCE:
The Story of Padre Martínez of Taos

BUT

The Story of
Padre Martínez of Taos, 1793-1867

TIME AND
CHANCE

By Fray Angelico Chavez

"I returned, and saw under the sun, that the race
is not to the swift, nor the battle to the strong
. . .but time and chance happeneth to them all."
ECCLESIASTES 9:11
The Padre's caption for
his own life's sketch of 1838.

Sunstone Press

FIRST EDITION

Book Design: Mina Yamashita
Printed in the United States of America

Library of Congress Cataloging in Publication Data:

Chavez, Fray Angelico.
But time and chance.

1. Martínez, Antonio José, 1793-1867.
2. Catholic Church--Clergy--Biography. 3. Clergy--New Mexico--Biography.
4. New Mexico--Biography. I. Title.
BX4705.M412553C45   282'.092'4 [B]   81-27

ISBN: 0-913270-95-4, softcover edition
      0-913270-96-2, signed, limited, hardcover edition

Published in 1981 by The Sunstone Press
              Post Office Box 2321
              Santa Fe, New Mexico 87501

To

JULIAN GARCIA

and

FABIAN CHAVEZ, JR.

Lovers of New Mexico's Hispanic history
and, in their own distinctive ways,
current makers of it.

Contents

Part One: The Old Dispensation

Part Two: A New Testament

FOREWORD

What makes a man or woman stand out for long on history's stage, be it only the local scene, is sheer personality. Such a person's particular deeds naturally count, but more as the script or scenario for one whose genius is a thing apart. Anyone less gifted, even after having played a similar rôle reasonably well, comes to be forgotten eventually. But the one endowed with an extraordinary presence lives on in the limelight of actual fact and legend, and he or she might have shone as much, if not more, in another time or before a different backdrop. Nor do moral virtue or its opposite have anything to say about it. Personality in history, as on the stage, has scant regard for either.

Such appears to be the case with Don Antonio José Martínez, whose long identification as the Padre of Taos dims the memory of all the padres of that historic valley centuries before his day or since. His wider activities in fields other than the ecclesiastical also make him stand out well above his contemporaries of every stripe in 19th century New Mexico. Already during early Mexican times his person had begun making its mark on the local scene, from the moment he returned home from Durango in Mexico as an ordained priest in 1823 – just two years after that country gained its independence from Spain – to the annexation of his own native land by the United States in 1846. It continued to do so during the first two American Territorial decades that followed, again on both the church and socio-political stage, and here through a tragic denouement which was due as much to certain grave flaws in his personality as to the quirks of history dictating the plot. Both Time and Chance, as he had presaged early in his career, did have their say.

His was indeed a most poignant and colorful life-drama which neither his contemporary foes and partisans, nor yet his modern critics and admirers, ever fully understood. What they all agree on is that his was a personality to be reckoned with, whether as hero or villain, or both, depending on one's ethnic feelings or moral set of values. But one cannot deny that Padre Martínez of Taos was a sort of genius in many ways, and also wonder at the same time how such a phenomenon could have sprouted and bloomed under the most adverse circumstances of time and place. This alone was enough to prompt the present critique of his life and works.

Fray Angelico Chavez

PART ONE / The Old Dispensation

Genesis of a Gifted Soul / 1

New Mexico in 1793 was the northernmost of the Interior Provinces of New Spain in North America. But this high-sounding designation does not tell us the actual hard facts, that she was still a most isolated and therefore backward frontier of the Spanish New World after her founding two hundred years before. Her inland isolation far from any seaports, unlike the rest of Spanish America far to the south and English America about as distant to the east, had deprived her of the economic and cultural advantages associated with the constant arrival of new peoples and new ideas from the European mainland. During those two centuries, little had changed in the almost primitive pastoral life-modes of an originally rustic Castilian folk who, besides being practically abandoned by their motherland, had always been beset by the hostile Indian tribes which surrounded them.

It was in this year that Antonio José, the first child of Severino Martín and María del Carmen Santistéban, was born in the tiny northern outpost of Santa Rosa de Abiquiú. He was baptized in the main mission church of Santo Tomás Apóstol when four days old on January 20, 1793, by Fray José de la Prada who was the Franciscan *ministro* of the place at the time.[1] These specifics are being emphasized here because his future foster-son and biographer, Santiago Valdez, stated that Fray José de la Prada, as *párroco* of Santo Tomás de Abiquiú, had entered the following data in the baptismal book: namely that on January 20, 1793, he had baptized Antonio José, four days old, the son of Severino "Martínez" and María del Carmen Santistéban of the Plaza of Santa Rosa de Abiquiú. Besides, the baptizing friar had also recorded the child's paternal grandparents as José "Martínez" and María Micaela Valdez, and the maternal ones as Juan Santistéban and María Francisca Trujillo.[2]

Here it is plain to see that this Valdez "birth certificate" is a fake, whether he made it up himself or found it among the Martínez papers he inherited. Padre Martínez himself, when telling about his birth and parentage in his autobiographical *Relación de Méritos*, referred to a document marked No. 1; this could have been the made-up certificate which Valdez used.[3] For Friar Prada in his much briefer entry used the correct Franciscan term *ministro* (missionary), and would never have employed the secular priest title of *párroco* (pastor). Nor had he entered the grandparents' names. Moreover, the family did not come to use the Martínez surname until some thirty years later, after the newly-ordained padre had returned from the Durango seminary. There he might have decided that "Martínez," a distinct patronym derived from "Martín," sounded better than plain Martín or its original Martín Serrano. And yet he might have had a more specific reason for doing so. Curiously enough, there is a land grant document of the years 1710-1716 which some brothers and nephews of the already deceased Padre Martínez presented to the American Surveyor General in 1878, for the purpose of clinching their claim to Taos lands which had been occupied by the family for a long time, perhaps since 1804 when the father of Padre Martínez moved his family up to Taos.

According to the old deed presented, this grant had been made in 1710 to the family's purported ancestor, a man by the name of "Antonio Martínez." The document alleged that this Antonio Martínez was a native of Sonora who had put in his claim from that distant and out-of-the-way place, but had not come to New Mexico until 1716, when he took possession of the grant with all the quaint formalities employed in those times.[4] However, the entire document looks like a forgery on several counts, and evidently that fellow from Sonora never existed. Prospective migrants did not put in such claims ahead of time, and in a country they knew absolutely nothing about. Nor had any settlers been coming to New Mexico from Sonora at that early period. Since the first Oñate settlement in 1598, and again following the Vargas resettlement of 1693, they had all migrated north in a beeline from the Valley of Mexico and Zacatecas via Durango and El Paso del Norte. Moreover, other such grants issued during the term of acting Gov. Felix Martínez (1715-1717) are likewise suspect.

If Padre Martínez knew of this deed before he left for Durango in 1817, believing it to be genuine, it would explain why he then chose to "restore" the surname Martínez. It also shows why more recent members of the family had boasted to historian Twitchell that Padre Martinez' grandfather had not only been a later migrant from Mexico but as family sagas have a way of building up, had even been a general in a Mexican republican army which did not come into existence until more than a century after that purported deed was made.[5]

Padre Martinez' roots, in fact, go all the way back into New Mexico's long Spanish Colonial history, to some of the 1598 Oñate colonists, and to a greater extent to several families of the Vargas Reconquest of 1693. As far as one can tell, none of those Martín ancestors had been outstanding individuals in an intellectual sense, whereby one might trace certain strands of genes which many generations later spiraled and fused together to produce something out of the ordinary. One might compare it to the blossoming of a rare cereus – and this in an arid soil (speaking beyond the topographical) of a New Mexico for so long isolated from the rest of a culturally advanced Spanish America. That the extraordinary flower continued developing under such adverse circumstances of time and locale attests to its inherent genuineness and vigor.

At the time of his birth there were numerous moieties in the entire area north of Santa Fe which owed their origin, or at least their surname, to a pair of brothers from Zacatecas who had brought their families in the original colony of 1598. These were Hernán and Luis Martín Serrano who, with two sons bearing their respective fathers' full names, had played significant roles militarily, especially in connection with the Indians of the Salinas district in that first century; here and elsewhere the children of the elder Hernán seem to have had marital relationships with the Humanas and other tribes.[6]

Although there is no way as yet of tracing back Padre Martínez' paternal line from his Martín grandfather to those first Martín Serrano brothers, his immediate family status and other indications of this nature point to a direct descent from the younger brother Luis, and this distinguished his own family and similar ones from their Indian or mixed-breed neighbors who happened to bear the same name. The mission town of Abiquiú itself had been founded for a people designated as genízaros who owed their origin to nomadic Indian women and children who had been "ransomed" from heathendom, the term then in use. Their own children of mixed tribal parentage had then come to be designated as genízaros, as if they were a distinct genetic breed.[7] Such ransoming practices were still going on among the padre's immediate progenitors as we shall soon see.

Now to the immediate family, concerning which some scattered data provide several interesting details. Despite that grand deception, or amplification rather, by Santiago Valdez and evidently his master before him, the additional particulars furnished turn out to be correct with regard to both sets of grandparents and the entire family's original residence in Santa Rosa de Abiquiú. His parents, Antonio Severino Martín (his full baptismal name also used elsewhere) and María del Carmen Santistéban, were married in Abiquiú on March 25, 1787. The bride's parents, by the way, were among the Santa Cruz settlers who had founded the village of La Cañada de Cochiti, hence it is possible that she was born there. They were a very popular couple in the Abiquiú area, for in the extant baptismal records they constantly appear as godparents for all sorts of infants between 1787 and 1801. Earlier in 1779, Antonio Severino had stood as godparent with his mother Micaela Valdés (this name's correct spelling then in use), while the still maidenly María del Carmen had done likewise with her brother Julián Hermenegildo Santistéban in 1785. Just a week after their marriage, Antonio Severino and his Santistéban wife sponsored a child of his elder brother Antonio José Martín and Guadalupe Santistéban. If this Guadalupe was María del Carmen's sister, it points to a common practice among the affluent Hispanic families, of two brothers marrying two sisters – this uncle possibly being the one after whom the future padre was named.[8]

Going back to his paternal grandparents, we know from some mission scraps which have survived that José Martín and Micaela Valdez, españoles, were already living in Abiquiú when their firstborn son Antonio José (the above Guadalupe's husband) was baptized on July 11, 1756 – and with a Rosa Valdez, probably a maiden aunt, acting as his godmother. Their second child, named Rosa, was baptized on September 3, 1759. Five years before, on July 8, 1754, Micaela Valdez and Salvador Valdez, presumably her brother, had acted as godparents together, hence she was very likely single at the time, and then came to marry José Martín in 1755. On October 5, 1760, José Martín and wife Micaela Valdez were padrinos at a baptism and on January 13, 1761, there was the baptism of their third child, who was christened Antonio – when the friar also wrote that they were tenidos por españoles.[9] This Antonio could very well be the future padre's father, Antonio Severino.

On June 3, 1779, grandfather Don José Martín finds mention as the Teniente, or magistrate and militia head of Abiquiú. What is of much more interest, on this day there occurred the baptism of a María Gertrudis, the natural child of a Bárbara Martín, who was a *coyota* servant (half-Indian and half-white) belonging to an Andrés Martín; the baptizing friar here noted that the child's father, according to what the godparents confided to him, was none other than the *Teniente* Don José Martín himself! In this very same month his wife Micaela Valdez and their young son Antonio Severino were godparents for a Juana Gertrudis Martín, a legitimate Hispanic child; hence the first mixed-breed Gertrudis is to all appearances the adult female servant who was remembered as such in the 1827 last will and testament of the padre's father, Don Antonio Severino.

Had the *Teniente* Don José subsequently taken his bastard child into the circle of his Indian and *genízaro* servants, and perhaps with special privileges? Of these he most likely had several. For example, on October 23 of the same year 1779, Doña Micaela Valdez is recorded as both godmother and owner of Isabel, an eight-year old Comanche girl.[10] These ransomed servants, by the way (or "slaves" as American writers liked to call them), were emancipated from their adoptive masters when they got married, in the same way that the same master's own children were at marriage time. As for Doña Micaela's husband, Don José Martín was still the *Teniente de Alcalde Mayor* of Santa Rosa de Abiquiú as late as November 1804, when he endorsed a badly scribbled land sale with his own clear miniscule signature and fancy rubric.[11] This was the very same year when his son Don Antonio Severino Martín moved his family up to Taos, the future Padre Martínez being ten or eleven years of age at the time.

With regard to others of his ancestors, his family status points to his being a great-grandson of the *Sargento* José Luis Valdés of Oviedo, one of the "gentlemen soldiers" brought from Spain by Don Diego de Vargas in 1693 – as was a distant cousin of his, José Manuel Gallegos, another priest of the times whom we shall often meet again later on. Other progenitors on the maternal side can readily be traced to some early pioneer settlers of the Santa Cruz district, such as Andrés Santistéban Coronel, Nicolás Moreno Trujillo, José Antonio Montaño, and Martín Fernández Valerio, all Spanish Creoles who arrived some months after the Vargas Reconquest of 1693.[12] All of these individuals just named were of a relatively superior sort in their day, and this must have had something to do with one of their future scions' fortuitous assemblage of genes, over and above what the Martín Serrano line might have contributed.

Precocious Lad of Abiquiú / 2

L ittle Antonio José Martín was only five years old when he began learning to read and write and do sums, which he soon mastered. Padre Martínez himself did not dwell on this early phase in his *Relacíon*, published in 1838.[1] We have this item and others from his subsequent biographers. In an *Historia Consisa* of the padre's life published in 1861, a work heretofore attributed to him but most likely composed by one of his disciples, we learn that his education began in October 1797 when he was five; then in March 1804 his family moved up to Taos where he privately continued his studies when not hauling wood or herding cattle; at age fourteen he began learning farming chores firsthand while keeping up his private studies in the meantime.[2] Santiago Valdez, in his much more extensive papers found with his unfinished *Biografía* of 1877, began with the same statement, saying that his first schooling since age five had lasted until 1800; in 1804 his parents moved to Taos where there was no school; hence he was put to work doing domestic chores, while he continued his private studies until his marriage in 1812.[3]

Two much later sources have a variation on the theme. Pedro Sánchez in his *Memorias* of 1903 has the boy first attending school at age ten under his father's supervision; then, after the family had moved to Taos, he has him applying himself exclusively to domestic labors while continuing his education on his own. A contemporary of Sánchez was Benjamin M. Read who, in his *Historia Ilustrada* of New Mexico, stated from what he had heard that a certain Don Gerónimo Becerra had conducted a school in Abiquiú at the turn of the century, and that among the lads who availed themselves of it was the future Padre Martínez.[4]

Both Santiago Valdez and Vicente Ferrer Romero, who was the most likely author of the *Historia Consisa,* could have culled their information from the padre's large numbered collection of papers. Or they could well have heard it from the lips of their revered master himself, later forgetting about that Señor Becerra brought up by Read. For we also know that by the turn of the century, occasional individuals had come up from New Spain (soon to become Mexico) as governmental or private schoolmasters.[5] As for Pedro Sánchez, we can dismiss his statement about the boy's education beginning as late as his tenth year, about the time when Don Antonio Severino transferred his family to Taos. But we can credit Read with a lucky find when he took hold of that item about the Señor Becerra; there is an item in an extant Taos marriage book for August 8, 1815, when a Tomás Becerra, the son of Don Antonio Becerra and Nicolasa de Ovando (both non-New Mexican surnames) married a Taos girl.[6] Tomás later moved down to the Rio Abajo where, from indications in some matrimonial investigations of the times, he stood out as a better educated person among his peers.

We do not know if Tomás Becerra had come to New Mexico alone, or if it was his father Don Antonio who came as a teacher with his wife and son to Abiquiú. Whichever the case, schoolmaster Becerra's first name had trickled down to Read as "Don Gerónimo." Tomás Becerra could have moved up to Taos when Don Antonio Severino transferred his own family thither. Whether our suppositions have any merit or not, or whether or not little Antonio José Martín of Abiquiú was that precocious at age five as Valdez and Romero claimed, we have his own subsequent record in the seminary at Durango to give these latter two the benefit of the doubt.

As for the young lad's arduous training in husbandry at such a tender age, especially since he belonged to perhaps the most affluent family in Taos, it is not at all surprising. At the time he was the firstborn and only son who had been followed by two sisters. Hence his father saw to it that he learned firsthand what it took to conduct a prosperous hacienda based on the two rural arts of stockraising and farming. We may also presume that the young fellow did not do all these chores by himself, but rather while also supervising the household's several Indian and mixed-breed servants. It was still acquiring new ones, for at Taos on April 8, 1810, there was the baptism of María, an eight-year old Ute girl "ransomed by Severino Martín."[7] At least young Antonio José Martín had this advantage over poor Abe Lincoln in a faraway land to the east, who as a similarly precocious boy began educating himself under less favorable circumstances.

Then came the day which every bucolic patriarch looked forward to, the marriage of his firstborn. And it must have been in this same patriarchal vein that Don Antonio Severino arranged for a double wedding with an old *compadre* of his back in his hometown of Abiquiú. For here on May 20, 1812, Fray Teodoro Alcina witnessed the marriage of Antonio José Martín, the son of Severino Martín and María del Carmen Santistéban, with María de la Luz Martín, the daughter of Manuel Martín and María Manuela Quintana of the Plaza de los Martines in Abiquiú. In the same ceremony, the good Franciscan padre took the vows of the bride's brother, José Manuel Martín, and the groom's younger sister, Juana María.[8] Also of particular interest, the witnesses for the latter pair were Pedro Gallegos and Ana María Galbadón, the parents of the future Padre José Manuel Gallegos.

The biographers being cited are anxious to point out that the nuptial pair (here pairs) was not related at all by blood, and this was entirely possible; the Martín surname in the north country had become so widespread, even among families classed as *españoles*, that many of these were not even close cousins. Moreover, we have enough *diligencias matrimoniales* or pre-nuptial investigations which show that even the fourth degree of consanguinity (third cousins) was closely watched; we can be sure that Padre Alcina would have brought up any such close relationships, had any existed, in order to apply for the required dispensation.

This romantic episode came to an abrupt sad end some fourteen months after the wedding, with the death in childbirth of the young wife. The child, a girl, survived and was named after its mother. The biographers give 1813 as the year of the poor wife's death, Romero specifying that it was in the month of July, while

Valdez added that the young widower went to live under parental rule for the next four years. From this one can infer that Antonio José Martín had stayed with his wife and her parents in Abiquiú following the marriage, for the Taos baptismal register of this period, which also contains the burials, records neither the wife's death nor the child's baptism.[9] There are no Abiquiú parish records extant to support this supposition, but it throws light on Valdez' statement about the young widower's returning to parental rule in Taos.

Here we can only guess how much the bereaved young husband had taken the premature loss of his bride of little more than a year. Or had the marriage prearranged by his father been less than satisfactory in a romantic sense? That he did not marry again within the next twelvemonth or so, as was the general practice among his contemporary young swains — and if only to provide a mother for his infant daughter — could mean that his bereavement had been most heartfelt, or else that the precocity of his younger years had begun channeling his thoughts to other things.

The Young Presbítero / 3

What took place four years later, when Antonio José Martín was twenty-five, laid the foundation for what was to shape his subsequent lifelong ambition, as well as the restless activities which that same ambition would start bringing upon the unpredictable tides of history. Although he held himself emancipated from his father because of his marriage, he still must have felt the same strong filial attachment for his parents which had brought him back to Taos after his wife died. It was a trait among New Mexico families which the hard life of the times made more keen. But by this time he had three younger brothers who were already assisting his dear father as he had done these several years. Besides, his little girl was in the safe keeping and loving care of her mother's parents in Abiquiú. The thought might have also entered his mind that, by doing something daring and new, like going far away from home to pursue a distinct career, he could return better equipped to render greater honor to his parents, as well as to his *paisanos* in general, not counting a definite personal ambition which he already had in mind. His whole life bears witness to it.

As the year 1817 began, he was almost four years a widower when he left New Mexico for Durango in order to begin his studies for the secular priesthood. Valdez, at the start of his *Biografía*, says that it was his love for letters which prompted him to seek the priesthood. This was basically true, but we shall be seeing that his motives went far beyond this. No other natives of New Mexico had done so within the general memory of her inhabitants, although the leading families of the Pojoaque valley did recall among themselves that a granduncle of theirs, Don Santiago Roybal, had been a priest as well as the vicar of New Mexico in what seemed ages past. Actually, this had happened in the years 1730-1774, and no other native of New Mexico had been ordained a priest since then.[1] Otherwise, Creole and Spain-born Franciscan friars had continued administering the parishes and missions even after a handful of secular priests from Durango had been coming up sporadically, and for very brief periods, during the past eighteen years since 1798.

The two major parishes of Santa Fe and Santa Cruz were the ones which had first been "secularized" in 1797, only six years before Antonio José was born; the third one, Albuquerque, had followed some five years later. But Santa Cruz and Albuquerque were now being served by the same old friars for lack of secular priests. Don Juan Tomás Terrazas of Durango, who had recently been in Santa Cruz for a brief spell, was now the pastor of Santa Fe and the only secular clergyman in all of New Mexico at this time. Hence the blue-cowled Franciscans had been the only clergy with whom the young man had been familiar – especially Father José de la Prada when he was a boy, Father Teodoro Alcina who had performed his short-lived marriage, then his wife's funeral and his baby's baptism.[2] Then there was Father Benito Pereyro now at San Gerónimo de Taos who had recently built (around 1815) the pretty church of San Francisco in Ranchos de Taos.[2]

If he had ever entertained any idea of becoming a Franciscan himself, it is quite likely that these friar friends of his had told him that their Order was not destined to last for long in New Mexico, after an exclusive ministry of more than two hundred years; for their historic Custody of the Conversion of St. Paul was dying on the vine because her friars were seldom being replaced when they died, or when any of them returned to provincial headquarters in Mexico City. Anyway, he would have to go all the way down to Mexico City, only to discover that the motherhouse of the Province of the Holy Gospel was in a sad state of turmoil. This had been growing worse for more than two centuries, from a bitter rivalry which had always existed between those friars who had been born and invested in Spain and those who had been either born or invested in the New World.[4] Of late this bad spirit had been accented by civil revolutionary disturbances going on down in New Spain since 1810, only seven years before, since the unsuccessful revolt of a secular priest, Don José Miguel Hidalgo, against Spain's monarchical rule. The Spain-born friars generally remained avidly loyal to their mother country while the Creole ones were siding with their revolutionary compatriots.

In New Mexico later on, in 1828 for example, the Franciscan major superiors in Mexico City voted to replace with six "American friars" the Spain-born friars who had left the Custody.[5] As for Antonio José Martín, he could have been told that there were no assurances that he would be sent back to his homeland as an ordained friar; nor, from what we learn about him later, did he have the vocation or inclination to make any vows of complete obedience, poverty and chastity. Moreover, since the revolutionary Hidalgo had been a secular priest, and, if a social consciousness had already been stirring in the young man's breast, this alone would have prompted him to become one himself.

Besides, in this very year of 1817, there was a General Visitor in New Mexico for the diocese of Durango who was now scouring all the missions and loudly criticizing the few Franciscans left for what he considered their ineptitude, while also commenting on the sad state of affairs in an impoverished land beset by fierce enemy raids.[6] This priest, Don Juan Bautista Ladrón de Guevara, might have told him when in Taos that three youths of the outstanding Ortiz family in Santa Fe had left, or were about to leave for the secular seminary in Durango. It would not be surprising if Antonio José Martín did set out for Durango with the twins Fernando and Rafael Ortiz who were almost four years younger than himself, and their cousin Juan Felipe Ortiz, a few months younger than the twins – and who someday would become his superior as vicar in Santa Fe for the bishop of Durango. He had no way of knowing, of course, that someday this quiet and more urbane fellow would become a thorn in the side of his own ambitions.

He entered the Tridentine Seminary of Durango on March 10, 1817, as he himself tells us in his *Relación*. Hence he did not leave Taos in March as Valdez has it in the place just cited. One cannot help but imagine that he presented a seedy gangling appearance in comparison with the more cultured and younger students of New Spain, and even his younger compatriots from Santa Fe who had never herded cows or laid a hand to a plow. All this could have spurred his innate mental and physical capacities to greater efforts, for soon all of his fellows found themselves being left behind in scholastic grades and honors, as well as in the genuine esteem of their professors. Nor did he modestly belittle these triumphs, but began hoarding the documented proofs as if foreseeing a practical use for them in a future glorious career. This can plainly be seen in his *Relación* two decades later when he outlined, along with further commendations of his work in New Mexico, all of these scholastic and other citations he had received in Durango up to the time of his ordination four years later. The better part of this biography is filled with a detailed description of his text-books and their contents, which are no longer of particular interest, but with which he meant to impress later adversaries back home who seldom saw a book.[7]

Santiago Valdez was to use all this material and amplify on it, as we shall be seeing all along. However, Padre Martínez was also proud of other more prosaic accomplishments. Almost from the beginning, he wrote, he was charged with the internal vigilance of the classrooms and his younger schoolmates, while sometimes acting as surrogate teacher. In the year 1819 the rector even placed him in charge of kitchen expenses and building repairs, as well as the seminary sheep which the herders brought in daily from the pastures. He was also charged to see that the younger boys were properly dressed and attended chapel in an orderly fashion. By 1821 he was the prefect or "under-minister" of all the seminarians, a duty which he discharged to the complete satisfaction of the college authorities, and for all this he made reference to documents he had on hand.[8] All of this, when he published it twenty years later, was meant to impress both his friends and his political foes with his gifts as a born leader as well as a practical man in economic affairs.

Valdez, as mentioned before, went into fuller details with regard to his master's scholastic triumphs by citing the documents which were simply referred to in the *Relación*. On January 16, 1820, Martinez' Latin professor issued a high commendation on both his scholarship and his deportment, stating that he had passed his examinations in grammar and rhetoric after his first seven weeks in Durango, and while coaching other students besides. On November 5, 1821, there was another certification on all of his studies as having been accomplished extraordinarily well. Similar laudatory ones followed on February 1, 1822, with regard to his course in theology. Here Martinez had boasted that he had read the entire Scriptures twice in concentrated meditation, over and above countless passages connected with the theological courses. Lastly, one thing that stands out is that, after having paid his own way at first, he was endowed with a royal scholarship by Bishop Juan Francisco Castañiza on March 9, 1820; this *beca real* had first been bestowed on his fellow New Mexican, Rafael Ortiz of Santa Fe, who evidently had not lived up to its requirements. On October 8 of this same year he received further written encomnia on both his talents and his application.[9]

The following year of 1821 marked Mexico's independence from Spain, and undoubtedly the republican ideas it espoused, and no less the exciting military events preceding it, had made the profoundest impression on the young man, as we gather from his subsequent ardent patriotism. Then, after having attained the highest scholastic honors mentioned, while also having given the utmost satisfaction to his superiors through his deportment, business acumen, and application to studies, he entered the clerical state at last. He received minor orders from Bishop Castañiza on March 16, 1821, then subdeaconship the following day, and the order of diaconate on December 22 of the same year. Here Valdez gives May as the month of the first ordinations, going on to say that on November 5 he received a written commendation on his having completed his studies remarkably well. On February 1, 1822, just prior to his final ordination, he got a similar certification from another professor.

On February 10, 1822, he was ordained to the priesthood, and he chanted his first Mass on the 19th. On the same day he received the faculties to preach and hear confessions at the seminary as well as in the *Sagrario* or parochial chapel in the cathedral of Durango. Then the bishop extended these faculties to the entire diocese.[10] All this was most unusual for what we call a *simplex* priest, one ordained a year before he had completed his theological studies.

This premature ordination could have been prompted by what was then considered his advanced age of twenty-nine, if not also by his superior scholastic record and other achievements. But it also might have been due to something else, whether real or feigned. Prior to it or around this time, Martínez had begun suffering from what he called "a certain palpitation" which greatly impaired his breathing, and hence, said he, his superiors granted him permission to return to his parents' home until he recovered his health. At the same time he was granted all the faculties for performing parish ministrations during this period of recovery.[11] According to him, it was in January of 1823 that he started back toward his native land, after his seminary tour of "five years, ten months and some odd days." What he proudly brought back with him, along with his new surname "Martínez" and his newly-acquired Mexican nationality, was the high-sounding title of *Presbítero* – "same Presbítero of this account is by nationality Mexican...his parents also Mexicans." To this he added, "and noble by class."[12]

What he also brought back with him, and this is of paramount importance to keep in mind, was an unbounded admiration for the most famous *Presbítero* of his day, Don José Miguel Hidalgo. This Padre Hidalgo, as mentioned before in passing, was the first revolutionary hero of Mexico since his aborted insurrection in 1810. He had been executed in Chihuahua the following year, only six years before Martínez went to Durango. He had been a prodigious scholar since his youth, and for his advanced social ideas had drawn to himself the suspicious eyes of the royal Spanish authorities and the Inquisition. His morals, at least later on, were also suspect. After having been exiled from his teaching posts to some obscure parish, he began taking the part of the oppressed and now restless Indians and *mestizos*, to the point of starting a revolt which he carried out as their actual military head. Following a series of defeats, he was fleeing toward the United States when he was captured in Chihuahua, publicly defrocked by the hierarchy, and finally executed by the royal troops. The highlights of his life may be found in the better encyclopedias.

By the time Martínez was in the midst of his studies in Durango, Mexican independence had arrived, and Hidalgo now stood high above all subsequent revolutionary leaders as the Father of his Country. Whatever Padre Martínez afterward proposed or tried to carry out as a self-designated priest-politician in his own homeland can be traced directly to his unbounded admiration for this man.

As mentioned before, Martínez still had a year of theology to complete when he was granted leave to return home to recover from his cardiac or pulmonary condition. It was on April 14, 1823, that he came back to el *Ranchito de abajo*, also called *de los Martines*, and on April 20 he preached his first sermon in the Guadalupe chapel of Don Fernando de Taos, which was still an *ayuda* or mission of the old Taos Pueblo church. On this day, says Valdez, the new padre made an *oferta* to the people of Taos, something about modeling his conduct on the gospel. Valdez also relays the entire sermon as found, along with other data he used, among his master's carefully hoarded and numbered papers.[13]

Soon he began assisting old and sickly Fray Sebastián Álvarez, who was the Franciscan in charge of Taos until July 1823; two other friars were to follow him briefly until Martínez eventually took over. On July 13, Padre Álvarez wrote a certification on Martínez' fine qualities and the excellent parochial assistance which the young cleric had afforded him.[14] For the latter, as he had done in Durango, kept on requesting and filing such certifications from priests and laymen everywhere he went, like building-blocks for a great career which he already seemed to be envisioning for himself. Then he temporarily replaced the absent secular pastor of Tomé in the Rio Abajo. This was Don Francisco Ignacio de Madariaga, who was a native of Mexico. Here he stayed from November 23, 1823 until March 29, 1824, according to the parish records, and here again he got another certification on a job well done from the village council of Tomé.[15]

At this period there also appears his first recorded civic act, when sometime during 1823 he had gone down to Santa Fe and there, with Padre José Francisco Leyva, likewise a native of Mexico, had joined others under acting Governor José Antonio Vizcarra in signing a pledge of loyalty to the latest Mexican Constitution. In June of the following year he is reported to have asked the New Mexico Deputation to declare his hometown of Taos a "villa," and thus have the parish secularized so that he might take it over from the Franciscans.[16]

Sometime during the year 1825 according to the biographers, or 1824 as Martínez stated in his last will, his little daughter María de la Luz died around the age of twelve. Romero gave November as the month of her death.[17] Her burial is not recorded in the extant Taos parish books, nor had her birth and baptism for that matter, and hence the supposition is that she had remained with her maternal grandparents in Abiquiú even since her mother's death a dozen years before. This must have made it all the more easy for her father when he left for Durango. And again, the burial records of Abiquiú have not survived to support this reasoned supposition. Once again, as when his young wife died, we can only guess as to the nature and extent of Padre Martínez' grief, or the memories which the sad event had evoked.

After this, and throughout the entire year 1825, we have no record of Padre Martínez except for his regular parish ministrations. He himself stated that on January 18, 1826, he had received additional priestly faculties from Durango, such as those of celebrating two Masses on Sundays and on festive days, absolving from sins reserved by canon law to the bishop, revalidating faulty marriages in the secrecy of confession, performing blessings in which the holy oils were not required, and so forth. He also declared that in this same year he was placed in charge of Abiquiú by a new Visitor from the Durango chancery, Don Agustín Fernández San Vicente. The latter made him pastor of Abiquiú, which he served from May to September, while also attending the parish of Taos since July 18. As we shall see, he resigned the Abiquiú parish in September 1826 in order to take full charge of Taos, and by orders of the same visitor.[18]

Bishop Castañiza had died sometime in 1825, leaving the See or *Mitra* of Durango vacant for the next seven years. The next year the Cathedral Chapter in charge sent Fernández San Vicente to inspect the churches of New Mexico when, like his predecessor Ladrón de Guevara, he began lashing out at the few remaining Franciscans right and left. In April he secularized the parish of Abiquiú, with Martínez as its first secular pastor. Evidently, having his eye on Taos from the beginning, Martínez had declined the office but was ordered to accept it.[19] The visitor had appointed him on April 15, and on May 6, following his arrival in Abiquiú as its pastor, Martínez wrote a friendly note to Franciscan Father José de Castro of Santa Clara, advising him about his new post and offering him his cooperation as his closest neighbor; he also gave a brief general census of the place.[20]

Before leaving Abiquiú after he had been appointed pastor exclusively of Taos, he once again got a formal certification from the Abiquiú civic council; these laymen praised him most lavishly for his pastoral work and for having aided the needy from his own private resources.[21] On April 30 he requested and received a similar document from the Taos village council, which also applauded him for his having given his all since April of 1823 when he had assisted Padre Álvarez, as also in more recent times when he had been ministering to the Taos people from Abiquiú.[22]

Valdez adds that a goodly number of the Taos citizens also formally petitioned the Durango Chapter to make their Guadalupe chapel a parish church, and with Padre Martínez as its *cura propio* or irremovable pastor. But it was learned afterward, Valdez goes on to say, that the petition had been approved but was not carried into effect by Don Tomás Terrazas (the pastor and vicar in Santa Fe). Then the same people elected Don Rafael Luna to go to Santa Fe and inquire about the whole matter, and he discovered that it had been referred back to Durango – the results of which were not known. At this very time, also, the folk of Ranchos de Taos wanted to have their own separate parish with Martínez as their pastor, while other settlements of the area wished him to establish his residence among them.[23] Here Valdez quotes the original petition, and it is quite possible that the Durango Chapter had at first rendered a hasty decision and approval, only to recall it when Terrazas must have reminded it that Martínez was a recently ordained priest who, moreover, had not taken the necessary synodal examinations for enjoying such a post. Nor does Martínez say a word about this incident.

What counted for the moment was that he was already the pastor of his beloved Taos, even if only as *cura encargado* or pastor in charge. The *cura propio* title could be worked out sooner or later.

Padre of Taos At Last / 4

From what we have been seeing all along, Padre Martínez had long aimed his sights on the pastorship of Taos, perhaps from the day that he had left his hometown for Durango years before. After Visitor Fernández San Vicente had proposed to New Mexico's Assembly that the old Franciscan missions of San Juan, Abiquiú and Taos ought to be secularized, he received the Assembly's assurance of June 10 from Don Santiago Abréu on July 13, 1826. Then he appointed Martínez as pastor in exclusive charge of Taos as of July 23, to succeed Franciscan Father José Mariano Sánchez Vergara, who turned over the parish books to him on that day. While at Abiquiú on August 7, the same Visitor wrote his disapproval of all the church records as kept by the former pastors, at the same time heartily approving those of Martínez and Sánchez Vergara.[1]

On July 27, Fernández San Vicente also urged Padre Martínez to establish schools at the Indian Pueblo of Taos and its satellite Hispanic villages of Don Fernando and Ranchos de Taos. By this time Martínez had already fixed his residence on inherited property by the church plaza of Guadalupe, and here by November he had opened his first school. Here, incidentally, Valdez' formal *Biografía* ends abruptly.[2] However, this Taos school was not the first one of its type as has often been claimed, for we know that already in 1819 Fray Sebastián Álvarez had been running one in Taos, and in which he supplied as teacher when the schoolmaster (Becerra?) happened to be absent.[3]

Although the ancient mission church of San Gerónimo at the Indian pueblo continued as the official parish headquarters, Padre Martínez established his residence and rectory, as just said, on the Guadalupe plaza of Don Fernando de Taos, on a plot inherited from his parents where he also bought a (contiguous) house and enlarged it into a simple *plazuela*, or house with its enclosed patio. Valdez prefaced this statement by boasting that the new native pastor had declined much better offers to remain in Durango because he had been "inflexible in his intention [to return home], since he felt himself destined by Divine Providence to illumine his native land."[4] All bragging aside on Valdez' part, it does seem to echo the proud sentiments which Padre Martínez must have had from the start.

By this year of 1826 the population of the entire Taos countryside had grown considerably, and it steadily continued to do so with the influx into the valley of people from other parts of New Mexico, as the parish registers and the extant *diligencias matrimoniales* amply show. It also marked the more frequent arrivals of such aliens as French-Canadian fur-trappers, most of whom married local women; soon they would be followed by Americans from the eastern states who did the same. The Taos area, by the way, kept getting the vast majority of such foreigners entering New Mexico from this time on, as shown by the registers of baptisms and marriages. These will be treated more fully later on when such migrations became more common. At the same time, Padre Martínez was witnessing the steady growth of the main town of Don Fernando, founded shortly before his father had brought his family there in 1804. But he always mistakenly designated it either as *San* Fernando or Guadalupe de San Fernando – extremely proud that he was of its church bearing the title of the Mexican Virgin of Tepeyac – and sometimes Fernández de Taos.[5]

He was wrong on both counts, of course. The correct name was Don Fernando, after the little stream called Rio de Don Fernando which had marked the 17th century property of the *Sargento Mayor* Don Fernando de Chávez prior to the Pueblo Indian Revolt of 1680. In this year this man's family had been massacred by the Taos Indians while he and a son were away, and these two men never returned from El Paso del Norte, having moved further south with others of their kin to become the first settlers of the Chihuahua region. Nor is this Don Fernando to be confused with his first cousin, the *Capitán* Don Fernando de Chávez of the Rio Abajo, who did come back to New Mexico in 1693 to continue this family name and strain in New Mexico.[6] This aside is purposely made here to show that Padre Martínez and his contemporaries knew precious little about their homeland's past history; this same kind of ignorance also affected many a statement which he and his later biographers were to make with regard to church-state affairs in New Mexico's Spanish Colonial past.

Somewhat older than Don Fernando was the nearby village of Ranchos de Taos, originally called Trampas de Taos after its little stream. It had been founded shortly before 1776, and at this time rivaled Don Fernando in population. But its now noted church of San Francisco de Asís, as we have already seen, was several years younger than the one of Guadalupe at Don Fernando. The license for this Guadalupe chapel had been granted by Bishop Francisco Gabriel de Olivares on November 18, 1801, on the petition of Juan Cristóbal Cortés and his fellow first settlers. The main reason given for its construction was the danger of its people's being ambushed by hostile Indians in the *bosque* between Don Fernando and the mission of San Gerónimo at the Indian pueblo. The chapel was most likely begun the following Spring, even though the civil approvals by the Commandant General in Chihuahua and Governor Fernando Chacón in Santa Fe were not issued until March 3 and May 18, 1802.[7] On November 2, 1815, the chapel was made an *ayuda* ("chapel of ease") on the petition of Don José Gabriel Martínez, the *teniente* of Taos, and Don José Romero, the syndic or treasurer of the chapel. Fray Benito Pereyro, who was building the church at Ranchos de Taos in this same year, likewise gave that same excuse of 1801 concerning the dangers of ambush in the *bosque* lying between Don Fernando and Taos Pueblo.[8]

Besides the localities just treated, the following village names appear in the registers of the period: Arroyo Seco, Arroyo Hondo, Ranchito de San Francisco, Las Trampas, Rio Chiquito, Ranchito de la Purísima Concepción, La Cieneguilla, Cruz de Chamisal and El Llano.

Two random papers of this period also tell us that on March 17, 1826, Padre Martínez certified that a certain José Manuel Salazar (a first cousin mentioned in his father's will?) had complied with some religious obligation; then, on May 8, 1827, the people of Rio Chiquito advised him through their spokesman, Bernardo

Durán, that they had selected "Nuestra Señora de San Juan" as the patronal title for the chapel which they were about to build at their own expense.[9] Here it is quite likely that Padre Martínez himself had suggested the title in his undiminished Mexican patriotism, after having told those people about a popular shrine of this name in the town of Talpa down in Mexico. Consequently, Talpa came to replace the original name of Rio Chiquito. In this same year, an American traveller by the name of George C. Sibley wrote that he had met with the *alcalde* of Taos (Don Severino Martín) and with his son who was the pastor of the place.[10]

In this same year, also, the federal government in Mexico City had issued an order for all the provincial authorities in the republic to keep en eye on Spaniards who had not left the country. As Valdez put it, Mexico had recently been freed from "the iron yoke of Spain," obviously echoing what he had heard from the lips of Padre Martínez. Hence New Mexico's Gov. Antonio Narbona, confiding in Martínez' staunch patriotism, wrote him on April 10 to investigate any such cases in his northern district. However, we doubt that there were any natives of Spain living north of Santa Fe at the time – except for two good friends of his, the Franciscan Fathers Teodoro Alcina and José de Castro, both of whom were incapable of any acts of subversion even if they had so desired. They had been automatically separated from their Province of the Holy Gospel when Mexico expelled all Spaniards who would not accept the republic; after having sworn their allegiance to the new government, both friars had continued laboring as Franciscans under the bishop of Durango. The first died soon after 1830, and the second one in 1840.

On June 29, 1827, and surely to the great sorrow of the young new pastor of Taos, there occurred the funeral of his dear father, Don Antonio Severino, who had passed away after receiving all the last rites. The exequies in the Guadalupe church were conducted by Martínez' fellow seminarian, Don Juan Felipe Ortiz, who had been appointed to his first parish at San Juan. When recording the burial, Martínez referred to his deceased father as the "benefactor of said church."[12] Filial pride aside, this could mean that Don Antonio Severino, as a pioneer settler of Don Fernando de Taos, had much to do with its interior and sacristy furnishings, alone with any repairs the structure had undergone. The good man had previously drawn up his last will and testament in which, among the many particulars of legacies, we find the following salient points, with some pertinent data inserted in parentheses.

He declared that he had married María del Carmen Santistéban at Abiquiú, where he himself had been born. Then he named as executors his son Padre Martínez and a son-in-law, Manuel Martínez (the one who had married his daughter Juana María on the same day that the future padre married Manuel's sister). Besides his widow, he left six children, all living: *Antonio José* (the priest); *María Estéfana* (born in Abiquiú, January 6, 1795, and married to José Ignacio Lucero); *Juana María* (born in Abiquiú, July 28, 1799, who married the above executor); José María de Jesús (born in Abiquiú, ca. 1800-1803, and who married María Carmen Sánchez in Santa Fe, November 11, 1833); *José Santiago* (born in

Taos, July 29, 1804, and who married María de la Luz Lucero); *Juan Pascual Bailón* (born in Taos, May 22, 1806, and who married María Teodora Gallegos).[13] Also mentioned by name was a nephew, José Manuel Salazar, perhaps the man previously referred to.

Remembered also in the will were two former household servants who were now married and emancipated. One was *María Gertrudis* (the natural daughter of Don Antonio Severino's father, the *Teniente* Don José Martín?). The other was *Dolores* (a Ute Indian and *"fámula* of the late Don Severino Martínez" who had married a José Miguel Martín, and had a son on November 11, 1827).[14] As one can see, these two females must have enjoyed very special status, since none of the other Indian and mixed-breed servants are remembered by name in the will. If we have gone into all these family details, it is because they later mesh with important events in the subsequent career of Padre Martínez, and help to clarify them as well.

Two years later, Padre Martínez buried his mother, Doña María del Carmen Santistéban, on April 25, 1829. Because her final illness had been cut short, her son wrote in the burial entry, she had not finished making her last will, but had managed to make an oral disposition of her property. She was interred in the nave of the church, he wrote, because her family had reserved the space and because her late husband was buried there, and also due to the fact that she was the pastor's mother.[15] Here, behind the expressions of solicitude and family pride, one can almost detect a feeling of deepest sorrow on her son's part, for this and his father's passing two years before ended a period in his life which had been marked with the truest of filial devotion.

We can now close the year 1827 with an item which is more than an interesting aside. The unstable Mexican government had been making efforts at establishing schools throughout New Mexico, over and above the solicitude shown by the churchman Fernández San Vicente, as we have seen. At this time there was a general superintendent of education, Trinidad Barceló, whose rare surname was later made famous in New Mexico's annals by his elder sister, Doña Gertrudis (Tules) Barceló and her gambling bistro in Santa Fe.[16] This Don Trinidad, while at Santa Cruz, sent a set of Ten Regulations on Education to Taos as recently prescribed by the Mexican republic, and they were endorsed by the Taos village council on December 2, 1827.[17] Evidently the rules were directed at Padre Martinez' school, since in his own and in the popular estimation his educational venture went beyond what we know as purely parochial schools today.

Then he must have continued keeping himself as busy as ever during the next two years with his ever increasing parish duties and the new school, but ever with his Mexican patriotism behind it all, as when on February 2, 1828, he transmitted some matrimonial papers to another patriot, the Creole Friar Sánchez Vergara, appending the republic's slogan: *Dios y Libertad!*[18] In March of 1829 he was also given charge of the vast vacant parish of Picuris with its several mountain villages, among them the new settlements east of the sierra at Lo de Mora (all of which he attended from March 1829 to April 1831). On April 14, 1829, Don Juan

Rafael Rascón, a new Visitor from Durango who had loaded him with the extra burden of Picuris, tendered him a most greatful appreciation, and here Valdez goes on to describe the great fifty-mile extent, from north to south, of difficult mountains and valleys which Martínez had to cover; his fold consisted of seven thousand souls, all of whom became enchanted with the force and clarity of his sermons, and likewise by the fact that he was a fellow native. "Never," said Valdez, "had they heard any native of New Mexico speak in such fashion." [19] Nor was this any empty boasting, for, sad to say, preaching as such had died long ago in New Mexico, due principally to the fact that the former Franciscans, as Indian missionaries, had confined themselves to simple catechetical instructions outside of Mass. The secular clergy who had come after for brief periods had apparently followed the same custom. Hence the oratory of Padre Martínez came both as a surprise and a treat.

The same sources tell us that on April 10 he was sent additional ministerial faculties by the Cathedral Chapter of Durango, the diocese still remaining vacant since the death of Bishop Castañiza. The continuing vacancy was due to Mexico's vaunted republican form of government which, despite its criticism of Spain's monarchy in this regard, kept meddling in the appointment of bishops and other purely church affairs. Martínez himself was to declare in 1837 that he was still only a "pastor in charge" of Taos because the political situation (down in Mexico) forbade the appointment of *curas propios* or irremovable pastors; anyway, said he, he would not have gotten such an appointment in 1830 because, since he could not find a priest to take care of Taos and Picuris during his absence, he could not have gone to Durango for this purpose. (Pedro Sánchez, wrong as usual, has him attending the synod in this year and acquiring the title.) Here Padre Martínez also went briefly into details outlining his priestly ministrations in the many communities he had to attend, his personal donations to the parish church, his distribution of farm seeds and clothing to the needy – all with reference to numbered documents which he kept on file, and which Valdez much later used in great detail. [20]

In connection with the above synod and another one to come ten years later, Valdez wrote that Padre Martínez privately pursued his studies with this end in mind – induced besides by his great love for *las bellas letras* – reviewing his theology between January 1829 and October 1839, and supplementing this from 1836 to 1839 with studies in canon law and the civil laws of Spain, along with the current ones of the Mexican republic. [21] All this is no doubt true, as Martínez was seriously looking forward to the next Durango synod of 1840. For to any secular priest of his day, his being constituted a *cura propio* was the highest attainment he could aspire to, short of being named a canon or a bishop. New Mexico, as we know, had no episcopal See with its cathedral chapter of canons, nor did anyone even dream in those times – not even Padre Martínez – that his homeland would ever have one.

Here is when Valdez, and Sánchez long after him, go on to say – appending their own comments at great length – that by 1829 Padre Martínez, after a studious glance over the deplorable conditions in New Mexico, had discovered their cause to be the ignorance in which Spain and Mexico had kept the common people, simply by letting the clergy exert their powerful influence over their temporal or economic interests and development. New Mexico, Valdez wrote, had been governed by theocratic laws, while the clergy imposed, besides the hard fees of the *arancel*, the full payment of tithes and firstfruits from farm products and livestock, which were the sole source of livelihood in the region. The people blindly obeyed the clergy, a foreign clergy which showed no mercy! Often the poor had to bury their dead in the "deserts" because they could not afford to pay the fee; they could not have their children baptized for the same reason, while couples had to live in concubinage! They were even obliged to steal in order to pay for the priests' services![22]

This, of course, was the anti-clerical propaganda of Valdez' own day. What might have been true in varying degrees with regard to colonial New Spain and Mexico did not apply at all to an isolated New Mexico where neither the old Franciscans over two centuries, nor the few secular clergy in the past three decades, had ever affected her economic or whichever other status one way or another. *New Mexico's almost total isolation from New Spain and the rest of the world had been the one and only reason for her backwardness and poverty in every regard.* Padre Martínez himself, almost completely ignorant like all of his contemporaries of New Mexico's Spanish Colonial past, and which he naturally looked back upon with a romantic eye, extended the Mexican revolutionary propaganda he had absorbed in Durango to his own poor homeland. To this, both Valdez and Sánchez added a kindred Anglo-American and Protestant propaganda of their own times, exactly the very same erroneous notions which had been spread about by such writers as Josiah Gregg, W.W.H. Davis and many others, who failed to distinguish between the conditions prevalent in Mexico and those which had existed in New Mexico proper.

Valdez also tells us that around this time Padre Martínez wrote an "Exposition" of all the foregoing evils. It was submitted to New Mexico's Assembly in Santa Fe, which approved of it and then forwarded it to the National Mexican Congress. It was this very paper, he said, along with other such Expositions submitted by different patriots throughout the Mexican republic, which had contributed to the abrogation of church tithes in 1833. He also states that Bishop Zubiría (installed the year before) had refrained from chiding Padre Martínez for it, simply because the latter enjoyed the full right to state his views as a free citizen.[23] Padre Martínez himself did not even hint at any such Exposition in his *Relación* of 1838; but twenty-eight years later, in the pages of a Santa Fe newspaper, he seems to allude to such a document, giving 1826 as the date of composition. This was only three years after his ordination and seven years before Bishop Zubiría became bishop of Durango.

Then the new decade of the 1830s began. According to Valdez, this is when Padre Martínez, after noting that the very first Mexican democratic laws had not favored religious liberty, declared himself in favor of the "toleration of cults" as a most necessary measure for insuring a free and prosperous government; thereby

32

outsiders (of every faith) could come in and contribute greatly toward the nation's prosperity. In fact, says Valdez, he wrote a book on it which had not been published.[24] While we may admit that these were Padre Martinez' views as far as religious liberty was concerned, the prosperity arising from the beneficent influx of such foreigners seems to reflect Valdez' own sentiments (and also Sánchez' later on) during subsequent American Territorial times. Because of this, more recent writers attributed Protestant ideas to Padre Martínez in this regard, but, as we shall be seeing much later on, our Padre of Taos, while he came to appreciate and approve of religious freedom as practiced in the United States, never for a moment wavered from the faith in which he had been born and nurtured.

It was in January of 1830, again according to Valdez, that his master began his preparations for attending a *concurso* in Durango. This was a competitive series of examinations which were required for his nomination as *cura propio*. With this in mind, he requested a certification from the Taos council, not only as to his ministerial services and private studies, but also with great emphasis on his material aid to the poor; it was issued on February 2, 1830.[25] As we have been seeing all along, the past four years of his pastorship of Taos, and of Picuris for a time, had been replete with activities of every kind, and his efforts were likewise rewarded with another major commendation which he added to his cherished collection. While inspecting the Taos books on August 24, 1830, Visitor Rascón recorded that Martínez was one New Mexico padre against whom he had never heard any complaints, and then praised him highly for his fidelity to preaching, and for having taken such good care of the additional parish of Picuris with its many farspread missions.[26]

Meanwhile, something else was taking place in Taos which would enter most intimately into the private life of Padre Martínez. It would also presage events of a related nature in the near future, not to speak of all kinds of wild speculations in much later times. On February 14, 1830, he baptized *José Santiago*, three days old, the natural child of young Teodora Márquez of El Rancho, she being the daughter of Vicente Márquez and his wife Guadalupe Trujillo. What promptly raises an eyebrow is the fact that the padre, in the space reserved for the father's name, entered this phrase: "Of his natural father, notice will be found in a secret tablet on the matter."[27]

Right away a person will assume that Padre Martínez himself was the father, but this is highly unlikely since he himself had baptized the infant – something to be elucidated a few pages hence. Nor would he have made such an incriminating notation, were he the actual father. What seems to have actually happened is that the girl in question had confided to him that her baby's father was one of his married brothers, the one named José Santiago who was married to María de la Luz Lucero. (For the name she gave the child follows a not uncommon practice, then as now.) Hence, Padre Martínez could not bring himself to record this adulterous fact, for the curious to discover in the future – as had happened very long ago with his grandfather in Abiquiú. Studious man that he was, as well as curious, he could well have come across that Gertrudis baptism of 1779 while he was pastor

33

there. But what is more significant to us as of now is that this infant Santiago is none other than our frequently quoted biographer, Santiago Valdez.

According to the Taos registers, on October 29, 1849, Padre Martínez performed the marriage of this Santiago Valdez and a María Agustina Valdez, but without entering the parents of either party; the banns had been dispensed with, wrote the padre, for reasons contained in the *Diligencias Matrimoniales* (which have not survived). But at the baptism of their son José David on December 1, 1854, the padre did record the child's paternal and maternal grandparents in a very significant way. Santiago Valdez' surname, he wrote, was *transversal y pasasivo* (the same as his wife's but one which was not permanent), as the adopted son that he had been of José Ignacio Valdez and the latter's grandmother, María Estéfana Madrid. Santiago's wife Agustina Valdez, however, was the legitimate daughter of the same José Ignacio Valdez and his wife María Manuela Sánchez, residents of El Rancho de la Purísima (where Santiago's mother Teodora Márquez had also lived.)[28]

In other words, Santiago Valdez had married his blood-unrelated foster-sister. As for his surname being *pasasivo*, this would indicate that Padre Martínez had always had an understanding with the Madrid woman and her Valdez grandson that their adopted Santiago was his own special ward, no doubt contributing toward his support. He was to declare in his last will and testament that he had always regarded Santiago Valdez as though he were his son, not his real son, at the same time specifying that Santiago's children were to carry on the Martínez surname, which they did afterward. This is a good indication that Santiago Valdez had been shown the "secret tablet on the matter," and thus was apprised of his being a true member of the Padre Martínez clan.

Years after the padre was dead, in 1877, a Teodora Martínez, the daughter of Santiago Martínez (Valdez) and Agustina Valdez, married a Larkin G. Read, who was a brother of historian Benjamin M. Read.[29] Here one can see how Larkin had interited the Valdez *Biografía* with its related papers.[30] His wife Teodora was then being referred to as a granddaughter of Padre Martínez, with the questionable pride current in her day of being directly descended from the now famous Padre of Taos. Evidently, Teodora did not know that she had been named after her real grandmother, Teodora Márquez, and not after a different Teodora about whom we shall be hearing soon.

For, as said before, the birth in 1830 of this little Santiago – *pasasivo* Valdez – was the harbinger of more serious things of this nature which were soon to come.

P adre Martínez' vastly increasing pastoral duties, and even the birth of that Santiago, could not distract him from his other interests. On October 4, 1830, he had been elected one of the seven deputies to New Mexico's Departmental Assembly for 1831-32; there he found certain inadequacies which he wanted reported to the federal Mexican Congress for correction. Valdez, amid paeans of praise on his civic patriotism, stated that his Taos constituents gladly elected him through the years 1830, 1831, and then in 1836 and 1837. Padre Martínez himself, when referring to his services as deputy in Santa Fe, as well as to the sessions of 1837-38, declared that he had helped pay the expenses of his office as well as those of his secretary, as shown by receipts he had, while he had never been paid for his attendance or for his travel expenses.[1]

At this time he had asked to be relieved of the extensive Picuris parish which he had been administering since March 1829.[2] Yet he had time and energy left to meddle in another, and perhaps politically tinted, area well outside his own parish jurisdiction. On April 6, 1831, upon his request, Visitor Rascón cautiously allowed sixty brethren of the Franciscan "Third Order" of Santa Cruz to hold their "exercises" in Taos, *so long as no abuses arose* that would call for correction during Rascón's visitation.[3] Hence we might ask why such a permission was so necessary, if necessary at all. This brings up that much misunderstood subject of *La Santa Hermandad*, the so-called Penitentes and their origin. Both Catholic and other writers in the past, totally ignorant of the roots of Franciscanism, have confused the New Mexico Penitentes with the Third Order of St. Francis of Assisi, believing that these strange flagellants were either a branch or degeneration of it – and here eveything points to Padre Martínez as the originator, or at least the perpetuator, of this misconception among the penitential brethren themselves. As we shall see, there was no connection at all between the two altogether dissimilar groups and their particular aims.

The good St. Francis in the 13th century was the first founder of Religious Orders to append a third one to his First Order of priests and laybrothers and his Second Order of cloistered Poor Clare nuns. By means of this third group, which he called "The Third Order of Penance," Francis affiliated onto himself married and unmarried men and women "living in the world" who wished to participate in his apostolate of peace. The original members ranged from such pious kings as St. Louis of France and his first cousin St. Fernando of Castile and León, as well as sainted queens like the two Elizabeths of Hungary and Portugal, to thousands upon thousands of townsmen and peasants throughout all of western Europe. It was the very first peace movement in history. As such "Tertiaries," these lay brethren of Francis promised not to carry mortal weapons on their persons as was the medieval custom, and to promote harmony among all with whom they came in contact.

Their pious practices consisted in fasts during Advent as well as Lent, and the reception of the sacraments of Penance and Holy Eucharist on stated feast days. As such "Franciscans in the world," they participated in the good deeds of the preaching friars of the First Order, and in the prayers and merits of the cloistered nuns of the Second Order. Underneath their regular clothing, both the nobility and the commoners wore a coarse gray robe girt with the distinctive knotted Franciscan cord, and they enjoyed the privilege of being buried in it as true Franciscans. This humble "habit" was also worn outwardly at chapter meetings and in public religious processions. All of this information may be found in encyclopedias, but the inner core of it comes from a person's many years of study on the subject, all the way from primitive Latin and Old Italian sources to modern treatises.

In New Mexico's earliest years, there had been this or that individual who referred to himself as a Tertiary of St. Francis, but no chapters of the Third Order were established in the three Hispanic parishes of Santa Fe, Santa Cruz and Albuquerque until well after 1700. This is when the Franciscan Padres were at their peak locally; with their decline in numbers, the lay Third Order suffered a decline as much as did the mission Custody. It was not until more than a century later, between 1800 and 1821, that the idea of the flagellant Penitentes was first introduced somehow from southern Mexico, initially at Santa Cruz and its villages; here, it seems quite possible, a remnant of the genuine old Tertiaries had joined the new Penitente brotherhood among its first recruits. However, this novel and distinct society was composed of males only, men who, unlike the true Tertiaries, did not wear the Franciscan habit and cord underneath their clothing at any time, much less in public processions. Instead, they stripped themselves down to a pair of drawers on the Fridays of Lent, and especially during Holy Week, in order to scourge themselves to blood and carry heavy timber crosses during their "exercises."

No doubt, the official name of the Franciscan Third Order as "The Order of Penance" had much to do with the confusion that had arisen, not only among the crassly ignorant but in the minds of much better educated men like Padre Martínez. For the true meaning and pious practices of the Third Order were not part of the curriculum in secular seminaries. As we shall see further on, Padre Martínez did get a written authorization two years later, from the Custos or regional superior of the Franciscans, to supervise whatever Tertiaries of St. Francis were to be found in the country north of Santa Fe – just as some secular priests have likewise been authorized down to this day in parishes other than those in care of Franciscan priests. But, as we shall also see, what the Custos and Padre Martínez had in mind were two altogether different things. What Martínez was referring to was a sizeable group of men confined to the parish of Santa Cruz who called themselves *Terciarios de Penitencia*, but whose practices, while well described by the second word, had nothing to do with the first term denoting the Franciscan Third Order.

Hence, in his total ignorance of Franciscanism, Padre Martínez, too, confused the spirit and practices of the genuine Third Order with those gory ones of the new Penitentes of Santa Cruz. Visitor Rascón himself, perhaps not quite as

36

ignorant in the matter, was nonetheless leery about the "abuses" he suspected among these Santa Cruz brethren who deemed themselves Franciscan Tertiaries. According to a notation by Ritch in the Huntington Library, Padre Martínez had composed a defense of *La Orden de la Santa Hermandad* – here employing a strictly Penitente self-designation; unfortunately this document no longer exists.[5] But it would not be at all surprising if his defense's contents did not reflect his confusion of the centuries-old and most venerable Franciscan Third Order with the upstart Santa Cruz Penitentes of his day. Whatever, it stands out clearly that, by assuming the leadership of the fast-increasing flagellants in the north country, Padre Martínez was finding another way of extending and solidifying his personal influence over the entire countryside north of the Capital.

At this time there also began a very dark period in the private life of Don Antonio José Martínez, the particulars of which he guardedly recorded in the baptismal books of Taos, yet fully and clearly enough each time for us to decipher and confirm what up until now has been undocumented hearsay or confused family tradition. If we now treat this shady episode at all, and also go into its most intimate details, it is to forestall any misapplications of the same data by others far less grounded in the technical niceties involved.

On May 1, 1831, there took place the baptismal ceremonies in church for *George Antonio*, nine days old, the "legitimate" child of *Antonio Martínez*, who was the son of Don Severino Martínez and Doña María del Carmen Santistéban, both now deceased. The infant's mother was Teodora Romero, also of Don Fernando de Taos, and the daughter of Don José Romero, deceased, and María de la Luz Trujillo. The baby, wrote the padre, had already been baptized "in case of necessity" – as though it were dying and there was no priest available – by Don Santiago Martínez (the padre's brother). The latter and his wife, María de la Luz Lucero, then stood as godparents when Padre Martínez supplied the other rites of prayers and annointings.[6]

In recording this supplementary ritual, the padre thinly but effectively disguised his paternity, not only by calling the child legitimate, but by entering his own first name as plain "Antonio," as if foreseeing that someday the interested investigator would conclude that he had such a brother named plain Antonio, which he did not. In short, he wanted his progeny, as he likewise did in subsequent entries, to appear before posterity as having had a legitimate and nonsacrilegious conception and birth!

As for the mother, Teodora Romero, she was twenty-two at the time, while the father was thirty-seven. She had been baptized in Don Fernando de Taos on April 1, 1809, as María Josefa Romero. Evidently, the old Franciscan baptizant had overlooked entering the additional name "Teodora," for Padre Martínez himself years later made this correction on the margin.[7] She was later mentioned as a widow at the baptism of a subsequent natural child, but thus far no trace of a previous marriage has been found. With regard to George Antonio, he was actually reared like subsequent siblings under the mother's name, Romero. This we know, first, from the fact that a certain Bernardo A. (Abad) Romero, who was the son of George A. (Antonio) Romero and María D. (Dolores) Medina, was decades later reputed, like Read's wife, to be a grandchild of Padre Martínez.[8] In this same connection, we find that Padre Martínez himself, in a small baptismal booklet which he kept after he had been suspended by Bishop Lamy, recorded the baptism in August 1863 of a Bernardo Abad who was the child of Jorge Antonio Romero and Dolores Medina. (The entry is almost illegible from water damage.)[9]

Now, we may legitimately ask, how could Padre Martinez have gotten himself into such a fix prior to this year of 1831? Had the birth of that illegitimate José Santiago, the adulterous child of his brother of the same name, turned back his thoughts more and more to that bride of his nineteen years ago, and whose love he had enjoyed for slightly more than a year? Did the untimely death of his one little girl, who had been the cause of her mother's demise and who herself had died just as she was reaching marriageable age, awaken in him a desire for new progeny of his own? This we shall never know. Whether for these reasons or simply from a strongly awakened passion during the months following the birth of that José Santiago, the natural child of Teodora Márquez of El Rancho, he must have begun having his secret trysts with another young Teodora next door to his house in Don Fernando, and whose surname was Romero, living alone with her widowed mother at the time.

What is of utmost importance to emphasize here is that Padre Martínez could not bring himself to pour the waters of baptism on his own child. Not only was this forbidden by canon law and proscribed by much more ancient Church custom, even in the case of legitimate parents, but it had taken on an aura of superstition which was more compelling than any Church laws or dogmas. Hence he got his brother Santiago to pour the baptismal waters on George Antonio beforehand. Evidently this subterfuge seemed far less baneful to him than his own really most serious breaches of the Lord's commandment and his violations of his clerical oath of celibacy. Moreover, unlike the Franciscan padres he had known, he had not made a solemn vow of chastity, hence he could have assured himself, as a canon law hair-splitter, that his secular priest's promise of celibacy was not that binding; or else his scrutinies of the Scriptural patriarchs had reminded him that those favorites of the Lord God, while their women were stoned for adultery, had freely gone a-whoring and had kept concubines. Impelling lust can readily produce such examples of self-justification, just as avarice does in business matters and other human affairs. Perhaps also in the back of his mind lurked the memory of his great hero of Mexican Independence, Padre Hidalgo, who was reported to have sired children himself.

Since we are on this subject, and because Padre Martínez kept repeating these same subterfuges, we might as well finish this chapter with them. On May 9, 1833, there again occurred the supplementary rites for little María de la Luz, six days old, and having the same "legitimate" parents and grandparents as George Antonio. She, too, had been baptized previously "in case of necessity" by a Don Antonio Ortiz (an in-law within the general Martínez clan); now the latter and his wife, María Dolores Lucero, stood as godparents when Padre Martínez again supplied the other rites of prayers and annointings as before. This child must have died because, on September 4, 1835, a second María de la Luz was baptized when eleven days old, and the event was likewise recorded with the same legitimate set of parents and grandparents. But this time Padre José Francisco Leyva happened to be visiting from Abiquiú, or else might have been summoned for the purpose, and he performed the entire ritual, water-pouring and all. Yet, and most surprising to say the least, on this very same day Padre Martínez himself performed the entire baptismal ritual for another María de la Luz, this one the child of his brother Santiago Martínez and wife María de la Luz Lucero![10] His superstitious dread of baptizing his own offspring stands out most clearly here.

This, on the surface, seems to have ended Padre Martínez' secret liaison with Teodora Romero, but past performances compel one to doubt it. Besides, she continued in cordial familiarity with his brothers' families, for on July 30, 1837, she stood as godmother for a child of José María Martínez and wife Carmen Sánchez. Teodora is subsequently mentioned as a widow when she had a natural daughter, María Soledad, when no father is given; this child was baptized on June 1, 1842, by a young assistant whom Padre Martínez had at the time, Padre José de la Cruz Vigil. But it was Padre Martínez who recorded the event later on as an "entry that had been overlooked." The inexperienced Vigil might well have forgotten to record the baptism, but certain suspicions arise nonetheless. Then on April 20, 1844, there was the baptism of *Vicente Ferrer*, again a natural child of Teodora Romero without a father being named; and yet the godparents were none other than Padre Martínez' youngest brother, Pascual Martínez and his wife Teodora Gallegos. Padre Martínez did not state in the entry what priest or lay person had baptized the child, but made another extraordinary notation like the one for Soledad – saying that the record should have been written the day before![11]

No other such baptisms were recorded thereafter, but all this leaves us in a further quandary. Were George Antonio and the two girls named María de la Luz the only bastard children of Padre Martínez and Teodora Romero? Or were the "widow's" two subsequent children, María Soledad and Vicente Ferrer, his also? The unusual circumstances surrounding their baptismal entries, and other indications many years later, do point this way. What we learn in this connection from the Territorial Census of 1850 is the following:

Antonio José Martínez, clergyman, 58, resident of Taos and a native of Rio Arriba (Abiquiú), and with real estate valued at $1,000.00; no others are listed in his household. The next entry is that of *Teodora Romero*, 42 (living next door), with real estate valued at $400.00. The members of her household are: *George Antonio Romero*, 20, *María de la Luz Romero*, 15, and *María Soledad Romero*, 9 (her three children born in 1831, 1835, 1842 respectively). Then come María de la Luz Quintana, 18 (probably an orphaned relative) and *José Vicente (Ferrer) Romero*, 7 (Teodora's youngest, born in 1844). All of these are natives of Taos County. The last person listed, María de la Luz Trujillo, is no doubt Teodora's mother, and born in Rio Arriba County. Of particular interest is how the census taker filled in the last column calling for handicaps like blindness, deafness, idiocy and so forth. This space is empty for everyone except George Antonio Romero; here the census taker entered the word "idiotic."[12] But since we know that George Antonio was quite active in later life, it could be he had retarded features, or that he suffered from the *petit mal* of epilepsy which used to be wrongly associated with idiocy.

Likewise in this same connection, it is worth noting that both George Antonio and Vicente Ferrer Romero were close to Padre Martínez after the latter had been suspended by Bishop Lamy. In a little burial book which the padre kept, and where his own burial is recorded by Padre Lucero in 1867, both Romero siblings continued recording a few interments in the Martínez private graveyard between September 1869 and September 1870. Some such by Padre Lucero are found in-between, and Pascual Martínez, the padre's youngest brother, entered the last one on May 1, 1872.[13]

Long after Padre Martínez was dead, a slew of individuals began claiming their descent from the subsequently "famous" Padre Martínez, as folks do elsewhere in similar situations when they have nothing else to crow about. There is the Larkin Read-Teodora Martínez example mentioned previously. But none can do so with complete certainty unless they can trace their ancestry to George Antonio through the Romero surname, as did Bernardo Abad Romero, or to María de la Luz Romero if she had any children. Less certain, but still possible would be a descent through Vicente Ferrer Romero and his sister Soledad. However, Martínez-surnamed people descended from Santiago Valdez have a collateral and not a direct connection with the Padre of Taos.

Still another thing to ponder amid the same perplexities is that the padre did not remember George Antonio and Maria de la Luz, much less Vicente Ferrer and Soledad, in his last will and testament. Evidently, he had provided beforehand for one or both pairs, so as not to reveal this well-kept secret outside the immediate clan. And a well-kept secret it must have been indeed, otherwise Padre Martínez' political foes in years to come would have made capital of it – and most of all, as we shall see much later on, an indefatigable scandalmonger named Machebeuf. As we know, it was only that first illegitimate Santiago of 1830, the son of Teodora Márquez who had been adopted by José Ignacio Valdez, whom Padre Martínez designated as his foster-son and sole heir of his private papers. Could this have been, we may ask, a red herring to draw away attention from his clandestine real progeny? It does look that way.

The foregoing clandestine relationships failed to exercise any restrictions on Padre Martinez' tireless pastoral, civic and social activities. According to Valdez, on April 23, 1832, Bishop Zubiría of Durango, who had assumed the Mitra in this year, sent him a renewal of the extra pastoral faculties of 1826, the ones already detailed.[1] It was in this connection, and with his having been elected to New Mexico's Departmental Assembly, that Valdez wrote that his master was enjoying the highest regard among all his fellow citizens for his unfailing zeal and exemplary conduct, but here we cannot even hazard a guess as to how the padre himself felt in the depths of his conscience.

At the Assembly, according to Pedro Sánchez, he was looked up to as a dictator, in the sense of his being a strong leader among his colleagues, but any such statements by him have to be taken with a grain of salt unless they are backed up with more definite data.[2] Padre Martínez himself later wrote that, during all his terms since 1830-31, he had defrayed all of his expenses, including his secretary's, out of his own pocket, and referring to receipts that he still kept.[3] Then his cherished Mexican patriotism was furnished with a signal outlet when, on September 16, 1832, he went down to Santa Fe for a civic celebration which was held in honor of Mexico's prime hero, Don José Miguel Hidalgo. He sang the Mass in the old parroquia de San Francisco, and also delivered the panegyric. Valdez gives us the entire lengthy sermon, which contains nothing historical with regard to New Mexico; it is a typically Mexican impassioned oration, quite intellectual in composition, reviewing "America oppressed since the days of Cortés."[4]

Thereafter came the significant year of 1833 when the new bishop of Durango arrived in New Mexico for his first of three visitations. He was the first prelate to visit the region in more than seventy years, since a famous one of Don Pedro Tamarón in 1760. Don José Antonio Laureano de Zubiría y Escalante made his grand entry into Taos on July 6, according to Valdez. However, the episcopal visitation officially began on July 1 with a Pontifical Mass, as we learn from a long entry by the bishop's secretary in the Taos baptismal book on July 5. Here this clerk included a comment in the bishop's name which, because of the particular interest it will elicit today, is here reproduced in its original Spanish. The bishop, he wrote,

> hallandose muy generalizada en el Territorio la propagacion de Ymagenes de toda clase de Santos muy deformes, y que por lo mismo no pueden ser espuestos a la adoracion de los Fieles...manda al Señor Cura que es ó en adelante fuere...que sobre esto instruya a sus Feligreses, para que no compren tales imagenes a los Escultores ó Pintores, y le prohive expresamente que los vendiga, si no estubieren medianamente regulares aunque no pueda darseles el nombre de perfectos.[5]

In other words, Bishop Zubiría thought that the locally made bultos in the round and the painted flat retablos were actually "very hideous," and for this reason not to be exposed to the veneration of the faithful. Hence he commanded the present and all future pastors of Taos to instruct the faithful not to buy such objects from the *santeros*, and expressly forbade the priests to bless them, unless they happened to be "middlingly acceptable while even then far from perfect." How Padre Martínez took this ukase we do not know. Perhaps he judged that all of these native *santos* were at least "middling," or even masterpieces as when he decried their removal from the chapels during a very serious crisis decades later. Or else he brushed aside the bishop's order on this score as he would very soon disregard the same prelate's much more vehement condemnation of the Penitentes.

In his conversations with the bishop, Padre Martínez most likely showed him both his scholastic commendations in Durango and the pastoral ones he had been collecting all along, thereby requesting to be constituted a *cura propio*. For Valdez, from a hazy statement in the padre's *Relación*, tells us that Bishop Zubiría himself examined Martínez, since he had been unable to attend a previous *concurso* in Durango. But for some unknown reason, he says, the bishop did not make him an irremovable pastor then and there, "although he deserved it," and that it was for this reason that Martínez, after immersing himself in those studies previously described, went to Durango in 1840. Valdez then relays Bishop Zubiría's confirmation on July 13, of the faculties which Martínez had received, along with his granting of further such privileges.

Here he also quotes a new certification by the Taos town fathers, who once again reviewed the good deeds of Padre Martínez since the year 1826: his strict compliance with all his duties in saying Mass at the various settlements, his unflagging preaching, his exempting the poor from paying the required fees, his dispensing of grain to the needy from his private granary and, to cap it all, his sterling personal qualities. It was signed by Alcalde Juan Antonio Lobato, Juan Antonio Aragón and Pedro Vigil.[6]

But there was also one unpleasant bit of news at this time, and the Taos padre must have been cut to the quick upon learning that this fine new bishop had confirmed Don Juan Felipe Ortiz of Santa Fe as his personal vicar for New Mexico. For it intruded into his own ambition, to stand out foremost among his fellow clergy besides the laity, as will be seen later on in his relationships with Ortiz and some others of the native padres. Moreover, the wealthy Ortiz people of Santa Fe, as long residents of the Capital and thus closer to its politics, had for this reason cast a shadow over what could be considered the more rustic Martínez clan in a frontier settlement like Taos. Padre Martínez, who was four years older and much more experienced in every way than Vicar Ortiz, had also surpassed him in grades at the seminary; in fact, he had received a royal scholarship which the new vicar's cousin, Rafael Ortiz, had been unable to honor. Hence, in his estimation, it had to be the long prestige which the rich and haughty Ortizes had enjoyed with former bishops by building or restoring the *parróquia* and other chapels in Santa Fe, besides endowing them with Chihuahua silverplate and silken vestments. Both his Hidalgo complex and his future conduct toward Don Juan Felipe Ortiz lend a firm basis to this observation.

Nonetheless, it did not deter Padre Martínez from taking another tack in which he would be the chief actor. At this time some local youths of humble status were making known their desire to follow in his footsteps and become priests, and so he broached the subject to Bishop Zubiría. When the latter brought up the sorry fact that these young men had neither the means nor the prerequisite education to attend the diocesan seminary, Martínez offered to prepare them scholastically as he had once prepared himself, and even subsidize them from his own resources. To his great joy the bishop readily assented, and this is how Martínez' "preparatory seminary" began at Taos in July of this same year, by way of a superstructure on the school he had been operating. Since there were no textbooks on hand other than his own, each student had to copy his own set of books by hand – not a bad system of pedagogy imposed by necessity. Martínez himself tells us that he started out with four clerical students on July 15, and three more were added in November. By August 1835, three of them were on their way to Durango.

Two of these were ordained early in 1836, these being Juan de Jesús Trujillo who became pastor of Santa Cruz, and Eulogio Valdez who was now the pastor of Abiquiú; both of them had been entirely subsidized by Martínez because they were poor orphans, Valdez likewise being a close relative of his as Santiago Valdez tells us. The third student, Mariano de Jesús Lucero, had been ordained in October 1836 and by 1838 was assisting Martínez in the combined parishes of Taos and Picuris. By this time, Martínez boasted, he had prepared ten men, five of whom were still studying in Durango.[7]

What we may think of these hasty ordinations is another thing. Surely, a couple of years' study under Padre Martínez in Taos, and only one or two in Durango, were far from sufficient toward providing the necessary education and training in strict disciplines which the priesthood required. As we have seen, even Martínez himself, what with all his superior talents and verve, had put in almost six years before he was ordained, and this prematurely. What one has to consider here, lest we blame Bishop Zubiría too much, is that other prelates were doing the same when finding themselves desperately short of priests in a vast territory that was largely primitive. A few native priests laboring among their own people was better than nothing, and these poor folk would be provided at least with the consolation of the sacraments and Holy Mass as well as catechetical instruction. This same practice, we may add, has prevailed in latter times in pagan lands where the majority of the people are more or less primitive according to our Western standards. Bishop Zubiría, well aware that most of his own cultured and well-educated Mexican clergymen were loathe to be sent to the boondocks, as the saying goes, had no other choice.

Santiago Valdez can then be pardoned for boasting that the little seminary of Padre Martínez had indeed been a most outstanding accomplishment, since on less than eighteen alumni of those who had graduated between 1833 and 1845 had been ordained by Bishop Zubiría. Sánchez said they were sixteen without naming them.[8] However, Valdez was somewhat mistaken in his estimates, and so we list here his eighteen native padres, followed by our comment: Eulogio Valdez, Mariano de J. Lucero, Juan de J. Trujillo, José Manuel Gallegos, José de J. Luján,

José (Antonio) de J. Salazar, José de la Cruz Vigil, José Vicente Montaño, José de J. Baca, José Antonio Otero, a certain Varela and another Gallegos, both of whom remained in Durango, Vicente Saturnino Montaño, Ramón Salazar, Tomás Abeyta, a certain Valencia, Rafael Chávez and, finally, a certain Bustos who also stayed in Durango.

However, it is highly improbable that several of these men had begun their studies under Padre Martínez. Those from the country north of Santa Fe must surely have, but not the rest necessarily. Then there is José Vicente Montaño who had come from Mexico as an ordained priest, and it is possible that the second Montaño, Vicente Saturnino, was likewise a native of Mexico. José de J. Baca (Cabeza de Baca), José Antonio Otero and Rafael Chávez, all three from affluent families of the Rio Abajo, had parents who saw to it that their sons were educated locally at an early age – as Padre Martínez himself had been, and also the Ortiz brothers and cousins in Santa Fe. Hence they had not needed Padre Martínez' services in this regard. Lastly, there was that Valencia fellow, whose first name was Nicolás, and whom we shall meet again under not too favorable circumstances; so far we have no complete knowledge about his origins.

But when all is said and done, there is not the least doubt that Padre Martínez was most sincere in giving his all toward providing his homeland with a large number of native clergy, as well as many more educated future leading citizens in the bargain. While he was secretly making himself a carnal father, he publicly strove to become the ghostly and scholastic father of new priests and, as we shall see later on, of solid citizens from other parts of the region who got their start under his tutelage in Taos. Still, and this is something to note with more than mere curiosity, he discouraged members of his own immediate Martínez clan from studying for the priesthood, as Valdez also tells us. The reason Padre Martínez gave them was that it was a "burden which he considered extremely heavy for man." Hence he did not want any of his close blood-relatives to follow his own career.[9]

One wonders then if he not only had his own secret carnal detours in mind, but was also well aware of the fact that, if and when his "nephews" (including Santiago Valdez) applied to enter the seminary in Durango, their illegitimacy would have to be disclosed. For the canonical laws decreed that any illegitimate aspiring to ordination had to have a special dispensation all the way from Rome – and that no *figlio di prète could be ordained at all!*

Another thing that Padre Martínez could well have had in mind in his assiduous production of both religious and civic leaders was a future reserve of loyal followers when the great moment of truth arrived. This alone, without detracting from his merits in this regard, cannot help but make one conclude that he envisioned himself more and more than ever as the future Gran Señor of his native New Mexico in every respect, and clad no less than with the mantle of his one great hero, Don José Miguel Hidalgo. For this he had all the talents, and these supported by his inexhaustible ambition and tireless energy.

I n the same year of 1833, no sooner had Bishop Zubiría left Taos than Padre Martínez turned his attention once more to a humbler field, the same one he had begun cultivating two years before when he invited sixty brethren of the "Third Order" of Santa Cruz to hold their so-called exercises in Taos. Now he persuaded the Franciscan Custos, who was the lone missionary far south at Sandía, to appoint him the spiritual director of all the Tertiaries left in New Mexico. Fray Manuel García del Valle was one of the handful of the old friars left, and would soon pass away; knowing nothing about what he was authorizing on August 1, he started out by saying that, "since it is so many years that the third order brethren lack a commissary, and there being the remotest chance that *[more]* friars will ever come, it behooves us to appoint a secular priest..." He now made Martínez the *comisario interino* (temporary director) of the *Terciarios de Penitencia*, with the faculty of accepting new members and receiving their simple vows thereafter.[1]

Obviously, the poor moribund friar did not know that he was applying the hallowed Franciscan name and identity of his Third Order to a disparate movement of "penitential" flagellants which had come up from Mexico while Martínez was a student in Durango, and in the meantime had both displaced and replaced the real Third Order at Santa Cruz. What is most surprising and baffling is the fact that, only nine or ten days before, Bishop Zubiría, while inspecting the parish of Santa Cruz after that of Taos, had soundly condemned the Penitente movement in no uncertain terms. On July 21, 1833, he wrote the following strong admonition for the present and all future pastors of Santa Cruz. It, and an extract from his Pastoral Letter on the same subject, are reproduced here in their original Spanish for the same reasons that the bishop's judgment on the native *santos* was cited. Not only has it been a highly controverted subject among natives and outsiders alike, but it involves Padre Martínez himself in no small way.

> Ympuestos á no poder dudarlo de que en esta Villa hay una Hermandad de Penitentes, ya de bastantes años atras, pero sin autorizacion ninguna ni aun conocimiento de los Ordinarios, que ciertamente no habrian prestado su consentimiento para semejante Hermandad, aun quando se hubiera solicitado, por ser tan contrario al espiritu de la Religion, y á las determinaciones de la Santa Yglesia, el exceso de penitencias corporales muy indiscretas que suelen practicar en algunos dias del año, aun con publicidad, que entre otras cosas ó incombenientes de mucha gravedad que puede traher, no es nada conforme con la humildad Cristiana, por lo que no debieran haberse dejado introducir tales practicas y mucho menos permitirse por ningun Cura la construccion de Pozada destinada a la custodia de instrumentos de mortificacion, y de reuniones de Penitentes...mandamos estrechamente encargando la consciencia de nuestros Curas Parrocos de esta Villa, el actual y venideros, que no se permitan en lo succesivo tales reuniones de Penitentes por ningun pretexto: que la Pozada en que han guardado sus cruces, etc., quede para el servicio de la Santa Iglesia Parroquial, y que dichos instrumentos se saquen y pueda cada uno llevar el suyo a su Casa sin constarse mas en lo de adelante por congregante ó Hermano de tal Hermandad de Penitencia que anulamos y deve quedar istinguida.

Furthermore, Bishop Zubiría instructed the pastors of Santa Cruz, should they get wind of any other such *Hermandades de Penitencia* in any other parish of the territory, to notify its pastor of this decree.[2] To put it briefly, the bishop was amazed to find in Santa Cruz a Brotherhood of Penitentes, existing several years since, which no former prelates would have authorized for its being so contrary to the spirit of Religion and the pronouncements of the Church. The indiscreet penitential excesses publicly practiced on some days of the year, with all other consequences they could bring about, were the least conformable with Christian humility, hence such practices should never have been allowed to be introduced in the first place, much less the erection of the meeting-house (*posada*, later called *morada*) in which the "instruments of torture" were kept and the Penitente reunions held. Therefore, he laid it upon the consciences of the pastors, the present one and those to come, never to permit such reunions of Penitentes. The meeting-house which had held the crosses and other things should remain for the use of the parish church, while each member could take home the "instruments" belonging to him, but never again considering himself a member or brother of such a Brotherhood of Penance, which he now made null and which must remain extinguished.

This grave problem must have kept rankling in the poor bishop's mind, for, three months later, he returned to the subject in his very long Pastoral Letter of that year, written in Santa Fe on October 19 at the conclusion of his visitation. This letter reveals the sad state into which the parish churches and missions had sunk through centuries of neglect, such as the condition contrary to liturgical laws of such sacred objects as the altar-stones, the Eucharistic tabernacles, the confessionals – and here, when dwelling at length on the sacrament of Penance, he dived once more into something related to the sacrament by name only, and which had kept bothering him in the extreme. As a conclusion, he started out, of this heading:

> En conclusion de este articulo para atajar otro grande mal que puede ser mallor en adelante proibo esas hermandades de penitencia ó mas bien de Carniceria, que ha ido tomando cresimiento al abrigo de una tolerancia indebida. Cada Parroco ó Ministro en todo el distrito de su administracion, cuidará de que no quede ninguna de estas hermandades, y que no halla en parte ninguna recogida ó guarda de esos grandes maderos, y otros instrumentos de mortificacion con que algunos medio matan los cuerpos, tal bez al tiempo mismo que no hasen caso de sus almas, dejandolas estar años enteros en la culpa. No se prohibe la penitencia moderada que es tan saludable al espiritu, pero hagase sin reuniones malamente llamadas hermandades que no han tenido autorizacion ninguna legal.[3]

Again, briefly, the greatly worried bishop, to forestall another great evil which could become worse in the future, proscribed forever those penitential brotherhoods which he now classed as sheer butchery! Strictly private but moderate disciplination could be salutary to the spirit, he allowed, but not in assemblages, and by brotherhoods formed for the purpose like a shambles or a meat market, which is another meaning for *carnicería*. Soon thereafter, the pastor of Santa Cruz, who was Don José Francisco Leyva, was transferred to another parish, although we do not know if it was precisely because he had tolerated the Penitentes. Nor could he be blamed for their introduction; as the bishop observed, the brotherhood had been in existence for a goodly number of years, whether a mere dozen or a couple of decades.

However, it is certain that the idea had been introduced from southern Mexico or Guatemala during the present century, brought in most likely by some late immigrant, or by some *familiar* in the household of one of the first secular priests from Durango. There was Don Manuel Rada, for example, the Mexican secular priest who had served the longest in Santa Cruz, from 1821 to 1828; among his servants might have been the first *penitente* as well as the first *santero*. For the two phenomena are somehow connected, in spirit as well as with regard to timing. Or the idea could have been introduced twelve years before by some servant of Don José Vibián Ortega, who was the very first secular priest to serve the Santa Cruz parish in 1798. He himself was also a devotee of *Nuestro Señor de Esquipulas*.[4] This Guatemalan image of the so-called miraculous Crucified Christ of Esquipulas, which gave the impetus to the now famous Santuario of Chimayó, appears intimately connected with the Penitente movement, historically as well as by way of devotion.[5]

And, as we shall be seeing soon, someone in Taos had more than a cursory affinity with both.

Padre Martínez soon came to learn about the bishop's strong condemnation of the Penitentes. If his friend Padre Leyva had not advised him of it immediately, he most certainly did find out a few weeks later, when he transcribed Zubiría's Pastoral Letter in a new Patente book, or record of official communications, which he started at Taos on December 13, 1833.[6] What now puzzles us is the fact that he chose to ignore the ban as he seems to have disregarded the bishop's prohibition of the native-made *santos*. It had to be something endemic in his nature, of letting nothing stand in the way of his own private goals. For he continued cultivating the Penitentes and, as mentioned long before, he later wrote a defense of *La Orden de la Santa Hermandad* under his care. The historic Third Order of St. Francis needed no defense, and this alone tells us that Martínez, whether deliberately or not, had come to confuse that venerable institution with the flagellants condemned by Zubiría.

As if these and his many other activities were not enough, Martínez received a message from Vicar Ortiz in Santa Fe as of October 26, telling him that the bishop had left an order for him to take over once again the vast parish of Picuris, this time from Fray José de Castro. Here his signed entries run until October 1845, along with those of Padre Lucero after the latter was ordained in 1836.[7] This additional burden disconcerted him perhaps, and more so because the order was relayed through Vicar Ortiz. But then, three days later, Ortiz forwarded a much more welcome message from the bishop, one which surely must have made his chest swell with pride. It was a five-year faculty to administer the sacrament of Confirmation, a rite ordinarily reserved to bishops. As the official decree went, it had been granted by papal privilege to Vicar Ortiz in Santa Fe and its environs, and only anonymously to present and future pastors of Taos for the Rio Arriba and those of Tomé for the Rio Abajo. These were the two main divisions of New Mexico north and south of the Capital.[8] But Padre Martínez himself, and his biographers after him, wrote about it as though he had been the sole recipient of this signal honor.[9]

It also may be noted that on July 4, Bishop Zubiría had designated the Guadalupe church of Don Fernando as a regular place of worship as distinct from the original old mission of San Gerónimo at the Indian pueblo. However, it does not seem as though it began enjoying full parochial status for the entire area, not even after a second decree of this nature was issued on July 12, 1845. This took place as late as 1850, when Martínez made much of the fact.[10] The only certain item that we have for the following year of 1834 deals with some complaints which Vicar Ortiz received from Taos against Padre Martínez, but they were not specified by the vicar when he requested an explanation on the following day.[11] Nor do we know if the Taos padre ever replied; from what we learn later, it had to do more with politics than his parochial administration.

The following year of 1835 marks another great stride, a most important landmark one must say, in Padre Martínez' unflagging efforts in behalf of both his students and New Mexico's population in general, while still allowing for his personal ambitions. Deeply conscious of the great scarcity of books in the region, wrote Valdez, the zealous padre bought an *Imprenta Manualita*, or small handpress, which happened to be in Santa Fe, "the first one ever in New Mexico." When transferring it to Taos he also brought along its operator, a man by the name of Jesús María Baca. Then the first thing that the padre did was to donate it to the community of Taos, at the same time inviting literary contributions to be printed on it. This was on November 27, 1835.

The first works printed at the padre's own expense, again according to Valdez, were the following titles: *La Cartilla de Primeras Letras* (a primer), *La Ortografía Castellana* (a speller), *Aritmética y Retórica* (numbers and syntax), *El Catecismo de la Doctrina Cristiana* (the catechism of Jesuit P. Ripalda referred to later), *El Catón Cristiano* (on oratory), besides some points on *Lógica* which he translated from the Latin. Evidently all these, except for the last points, were full or partial reprints from among the many books which he had originally brought from Durango. These editions were followed by various small prayerbooks and a multitude of pamphlets, the latter containing counsels and exhortations toward a good life, while also reprehending vices. All of them he distributed throughout the territory, reserving enough copies for his students, who received them gratis.[12]

The donation of the press to the people of Taos, and the above date of November 27, 1835, suggest an *Aviso* which was printed on this same date, and hence this *Aviso* was the very first piece to issue forth from the small press. Three days later on November 30, there came forth a certification on the press itself, and loaded with the signatures of the Taos council and many others of the citizens.[13] As for the books and lesser works listed by Valdez, and in that sequence of issue, we have no way of checking. Two very scholarly articles published many years ago, based on all the extant samples which have survived both before and after Padre Martínez bought the press, cover its short-lived history.[14] The titles which

Valdez gives are not among those samples, but these studies do help in correcting two erroneous claims which have long been made concerning Padre Martínez and his famous press. One is that it was he who first introduced a press into New Mexico, and the second, that he published New Mexico's very first newspaper on it.

Although sundry writers in the past have contended that Padre Martínez is the one who brought the first printing press from Durango, along with its operator, Valdez clearly states that both were already in operation in Santa Fe. Padre Martínez himself makes no mention of this in his *Relación*, which he printed on it three years later, something that would not have escaped his prideful list of accomplishments in that same book. Nor did he ever make any such claim in subsequent occasions whenever he brought up what he had accomplished during his long career. The facts are, as proven by the studies just mentioned, that the little hand-press already existed in Santa Fe in 1834, having been brought there from Mexico by Don Ramón Abréu, whose father had brought his family from Mexico.

Others have been claiming, ever since Pedro Sánchez wrote his *Memorias* on Padre Martínez, that he published the very first newspaper in New Mexico under the bannerhead of *El Crepúsculo* (The Dawning). Sánchez called it the first west of the Missouri. But neither Padre Martínez himself nor Santiago Valdez, who had all of his papers, ever made any such assertion. Again, the fact is that Don Antonio Barreiro, a barrister and governmental deputy from Mexico City did publish a short-lived newspaper at Santa Fe in 1834 and its name was *El Crepúsculo de la Libertad*. Its only four issues came out during August and November in that same year. And again, neither Padre Martínez nor Valdez ever boasted, as they certainly would have done, of any such *El Crespúsculo* being published in Taos at this early period. It is true that Benjamin M. Read did relate many years later that, when Santiago Valdez gave him some of the padre's books, he had also given him a copyu of *El Crepúsculo*.[15] But this, if published in 1834, had to be Barreiro's publication. If Padre Martínez published a similar sheet of this name, it belonged to a much later date.

One certain fact in connection with the small press is that Padre Martínez did publish the very first book in New Mexico, his *Cuaderno de Ortografía* of 1835, not at Taos, but on Abréu's press while it was still at the Capital.[16] This work is most likely the Castilian speller which Valdez lists among the books published in Taos. There is also sure evidence that some fourteen years later, around 1858-1861 or earlier, the padre did publish – or rather his ward Vicente Ferrer Romero – what the latter referred to as a "literary publication" in Taos, and perhaps it did bear *El Crepúsculo* for its title. This could have led Sánchez to confuse it with Barreiro's much earlier publication. This latter Taos periodical will be treated later on in a much more hectic period in the life of Padre Martínez.

Then there is another first, as we now say, in the padre's printing of the standard forms for the *Diligencias Matrimoniales*, or pre-nuptial interrogations. These were of most serious obligation throughout Europe and Latin America, and the large body of such handwritten investigations extant proves that such interrogatory practices had been taken most seriously by both the old Franciscans and the secular clergy who followed them. The use of such forms had not been observed in the United States until about four decades ago, and so Padre Martínez has the distinction, for whatever it is worth, of having printed the first pre-nuptial interrogatory forms in this country. However, this our modern preoccupation with "firsts" need not distract one from the much greater credit which the Padre of Taos deserves, first for his foresight and sagacity in having purchased that small press which had been in Santa Fe for only a year, and then for the many publications which kept pouring out from it for years to come.

In doing so he enriched his poor homeland with a most necessary and helpful luxury it had lacked heretofore. What is more, he was the author of most of the publications, while they were printed at his own expense. Nor was this a venture for mere worldly profit, for, like those of farming and stockraising which he had learned from boyhood, the fruits were plowed back into the overall single grand venture of helping his fellowman – even if all this was also meant to promote his dream of personal greatness.

But the best of dreams do not develop quite as they have been planned, and they themselves can bring on surprises from their interplay with circumstance, as the ambitious Padre of Taos would soon learn. Dreams often have a rude awakening.

T he year 1837 thrust Padre Martínez into a field of most violent action, something which was not at all foreign to his favored image of Padre Hidalgo of Mexico. But it was something he least expected. Valdez emphasized this when starting his account of an uprising in this year by certain rustic elements in the area of Santa Cruz and Chimayó, and which soon spread to Taos. Here Valdez went on to class the insurrectionists as belonging to the lowest class of most ignorant peasants, who were alarmed by rumors of certain taxes about to be imposed by the government in Santa Fe.[1]

But one might say that the underlying cause was the example of Padre Hidalgo and subsequent famed revolutionaries far down south which had brought on the independence of Mexico from Spain in 1821, and more so the new nation's *Plan de Iguala* of 1822 which had decreed that henceforth all the classes of people were to be designated as *Ciudadanos Mexicanos* (Mexican Citizens) in all civil and church records; that is, no longer were they to be divided into *españoles* on the one hand, and on the other as *mestizos, castizos* (and in New Mexico *genízaros*) and such other castes as had been the practice under Spain.[2]

However, these unlettered rural folk alluded to by Valdez had no way of knowing about any such decree of racial equality unless they had been told about it, and here is where Padre Martínez comes in. His openly vaunted Mexican patriotism had not been a mere idealistic one, much less a pose; his writings, as we have seen, centered on human rights, the equal rights of all men without distinction under their common Creator. Hence one can safely assume that his preaching and conversation throughout the north country often touched upon these matters, and with impassioned references to Padre Hidalgo and the Iguala laws on equality and freedom. But since New Mexico, unlike the rest of the republic far south, had continued quiet and peaceful for the past sixteen years since the republic was born, he had not realized how much the ideas he had implanted had taken root, both among his own Taos parishioners and among others in the large district of Santa Cruz during his cultivation of the Penitentes.

The first part of the year had been ordinarily peaceful, with Padre Martínez absorbed in his widespread pastoral activities and other multiple projects – like his school, his farming and stockraising interests, and more recently his printing press. In the area of politics, he had attended the Departmental Assembly in Santa Fe where, on May 1, he with Padres Leyva and Madariaga had been among the seven electoral members who unanimously chose Vicar Juan Felipe Ortiz as New Mexico's next deputy to the national Mexican Congress.[3] Whether he was all for it or merely went along with the majority, we do not know. One would think that he, despite his many projects at home, had wished to be elected instead of the vicar, for whom he had little esteem. Surely, he must have dreamed more than once of hearing his voice resounding through the congressional halls in Mexico City.

Meanwhile, that restlessness spoken of by Valdez had been brewing in certain parts of his northern district, or Rio Arriba, among the *coyote* and *genízaro* elements, and it suddenly burst out in violence during the month of August at Santa Cruz and Chimayó. According to Valdez, it was a revolt against the Mexican government, or more specifically a war of the "Chimayoses" against the "Villeros," the civil officials in the "Villa" of Santa Fe. These, the rebels were claiming, were not only enemies of "Religion," but they were planning to tax every little thing among the poor – from irrigation waters and firewood to the very sunlight streaming through the windows, and down to the killing of a chicken for food. And hence their motto was: *Defender la Religion y la Fe de Jesucristo!* Then, when the movement reached Taos, and Padre Martínez opposed it with all his might, he was not only called a traitor to *Dios y la Nación* but was even threatened with death.[4]

These are Valdez' own recollections and expressions made up partly from hindsight and from local lore, and from what he must have heard from the padre himself. He was only about seven years old when all this happened, but it must have made a deep impression on the bright lad that he seems to have been, later prompting him to make further investigations. Nevertheless, while the immediate cause of the revolt consisted of rumors which had spread from Santa Fe, about taxes to be imposed on things that had never been taxed before, one can also discern, from the conditions of the times, that at bottom lay a certain resentment among the lower social and economic classes for their still being looked down upon as such by those in governmental circles in Santa Fe. These high officials, while publicly asserting their Mexican Citizenship, kept considering themselves as superior *españoles*.

Many years later, Pedro Sánchez gave a more detailed, and in places a rather different version, of both causes and events. He had been born far south in the parish of Tomé in 1831; then his parents had moved up to Taos in 1837, in the very year of the rebellion. Hence he was about seven, the same age as Santiago Valdez, when the uprising took place, and just as impressionable when we take his subsequent career into account.[5] His, too, is an account built on childhood impressions and from later hearsay, along with what he recalled from Padre Martínez himself.

According to him, it all started with some debt which two Santa Cruz individuals owed a Victor Sánchez of Taos; when Diego Esquibel, the magistrate of Santa Cruz, ruled in his subjects' favor, the case was appealed to Don Ramón Abréu in Santa Fe, and he overturned Esquibel's ruling and suspended him from office besides. This is what promptly assembled into a bomb other alleged grievances of long standing against the elite leaders in the Capital, coupled with rumors of impending taxations on the poor people's harvests, from their *punches* (native tobaccos) down to the most recent egg laid by a hen, as they put it. *Pension!* (taxation) then became the rallying cry among the lowest classes of Santa Cruz under the leadership of two Montoya brothers. Ultimately it was being heard as far north as Taos, and southward to the Keres Indian pueblos of Cochiti, Santo Domingo and San Felipe. It was an alleged war of *la nación* (the common folk) against the elite suppressors who ran New Mexico's government.[6]

Benjamin Read's version of the affair varies somewhat, and he quotes the rebels' own platform, which was written on August 3, 1837: To be on the side of God and the Nation and the Faith of Jesus Christ; to defend the homeland even to the shedding of the last drop of blood in order to attain the desired victory; not to admit the Department's plan or any form of taxation; not to tolerate the evil ways of those wishing to carry them out.[7] As one can see, there was a literate person among them, but his thought processes reflected the wild yearnings of his constituents. Here Read calls the magistrate of Santa Cruz "Juan José" Esquibel instead of "Diego," and who might have been the writer of the declaration.

Padre Martínez, as we shall see later, was to receive the blame for it all. In his printed *Relación* of the following year, which he evidently composed to defend himself against charges of sedition by reviewing all his procedures in every field since the very start of his public career, he made some brief allusions to the rebellion of the year before, but not as if coming from his own experience. What we do have in this regard is contained in a poem which he composed on the affair, on February 2, 1838, and which Valdez copied in its entire length. It is what was called a *décima*, ten sections or stanzas in trimeter which are doggerel at best. This is not meant to downcast the padre in this field; versification in the Romance languages is so facile, due to the inherent cadences of the multi-voweled words, that such *décimas* and *corridos* can be composed at the drop of a hat, and with the rape of the Muse of Poetry much of the time. No matter, Padre Martínez in these verses gives us a good peek into what he experienced himself.

It was for certain in August of '37, he began, that the "inexpert Cañadero" (Santa Cruz valley native), after straying from the fold, broke into riots. It was by orders of El Chepón (Little or Big Joe as the case may be, referring to José Gonzales who was the leader) that the "Cura Antonio Martínez" was apprehended (while he happened to be in Santa Cruz). On the seventh day this priest returned home in haste, loudly beseeching God to forgive those lawless unfortunates, thus displaying his genuine charity toward all men. Then, at the invitation of a certain Esquibel, he went down to Chimayó in order to celebrate Mass.[8]

This Mass, we interrupt the poem here, had to take place in the Santuario of *Nuestro Señor de Esquipulas*, and, since Padre Martínez took such pains to celebrate it far away outside of his own parish, it could well have been for the Penitente Brotherhood, which was his pet extra-parochial congregation. Padre Trujillo was the pastor of Santa Cruz and he, as we learn later on, strictly adhered to Bishop Zubiría's condemnation of the society; but, as a former Martínez student, he must have refrained from saying anything to his former master on this score. As for that Esquibel individual, he seems to be the Santa Cruz magistrate mentioned by Sánchez and Read, and who could have also been the Penitentes' *Hermano Mayor*. In his *Relación* of the following year, Padre Martínez still made much, if only in passing, of his having been made the supervisor of the "Penitential Third Order of St. Francis."[9]

Going back to the padre's poem, he tells us that from Chimayó he went on to Santa Fe in order to attend a departmental meeting. Then, upon his return to Taos, he received a real *rebato*, a most startling surprise – for a goodly number of his own parishioners were up in arms. On September 2, he found himself obliged to flee back to Santa Fe with his brother Santiago. Following this, his rebel Taos people wrote him with tender love to come back, but on his return they threatened him with imprisonment; they even demanded the parish funds which he was forced to turn over to them. At the same time they imprisoned his brother Santiago, treated him very cruelly, and made the fellow sign an oath of fealty to their cause.

Here, the poem goes on to relate, the rebellion in Taos ceased for a brief spell, but then the priest's life was threatened anew by the *Coyote* Antonio Vigil, in spite of the many favors which this man had received from the clergyman in the past. This second phase of the rebellion continued and, because of the priest's unrelenting exhortations for it to cease, he was dubbed a traitor. Here and in a subsequent long *décima*, which lacks a relation of events, Padre Martínez dwelt exclusively on the poor *Coyote* Vigil, who later was hanged on a gibbet for his crimes and was denied Christian burial, simply because the lowly *coyote* had tried by his howling to be a wolf! *Un Coyote huyaba / deseando ser lobo* – not a bad poetic metaphor.[10]

Now, the man who had emerged as the rebels' overall leader was not Antonio Vigil of Taos, but a Taos fellow who had been residing in Santa Cruz. He was José Gonzales, whose full baptismal name as it often appears elsewhere, was "José Ángel." Thus, as we learn from Pedro Sánchez, he was nicknamed *El Angelito*, which is the diminutive of his second name, and evidently applied to him as a descriptive epithet aimed at his physique and not any spiritual qualities of his. For in the nuances of the Spanish language this bit of sarcasm could denote either a small chap or a giant of a man, as in Padre Martínez' poetic reference to him as *El Chepón*. In either case he was a brave and sturdy individual who was already a celebrity among his fellows as a great bison hunter. Valdez, who mistakenly called him "Señor Francisco Gonzales of Taos," says that he was a good hunter of bison, as dexterous with the lance as he was a good shot with the carabine, while Sánchez calls him an illiterate who was only famous as a bisonslayer, and for this one reason had been elected governor by the rebels on the banks of the Santa Cruz river. According to Read, an eyewitness had written that José Gonzales was a *ranchero* whose only talent was knowing how to kill *cíbolos*.[11]

Thus, we may add, fate was to cast Gonzales briefly in the rôle of Governor of New Mexico, to provide modern Anglo-American writers and observers with an opportunity to gloat over the fact that a pure-blooded Pueblo Indian of Taos, warpaint and feather-bonnet and all, had broken up the centuries-long roster of rapacious Spanish royal governors and more recent crooked Mexican *jefes*. However, a minute tracing of his ancestry reveals that Gonzales was not a Taos Indian, properly speaking, but a true *genízaro* by birth and upbringing. His baptismal record, April 14, 1799, identifies the infant José Ángel, the child of José Santos Gonzales and María Dominga Martín Listón, as a *vecino* (Hispanic settler or mixed-breed observing Spanish ways). His parents had been married on June 18, 1788, when his father José Santos was identified as the son of José Antonio Gonzales, *coyote*. His mother María Listón (Ribbon), however, was recorded as a native

Indian woman of the pueblo of Taos. This couple had eight other children, among whom José Ángel was the fifth; their respective baptisms occurred between 1790 and 1808, mostly about every other year. In some of these baptismal records, the children's parents are designated as *vecinos* residing in the community of El Rancho in the Taos valley.[12]

And so the future governor was a true *genízaro*, both by his mixed Indian blood and his upbringing away from the pueblo. All of this is corroborated by José Ángel's three marriages. On June 10, 1817, his parents are actually designated as *genízaros* of Taos, the day he married María Josefa Fernández, an orphan girl from Santa Barbara (present Peñasco) in the parish of Picuris; hence she was not a Picuris Indian, but most likely a mixed-breed like the groom. The pair lived in Taos valley, according to the baptisms of two children of theirs in 1818 and 1823. Widowed the following year, José Ángel Gonzales, *vecino* and of Taos Pueblo origin (through his mother) married a widow, María Ignacia Martín, whose first husband had been a Taos Indian named Romero. She died some months later, for on December 15, 1835, José de los Angeles (sic) Gonzales, thirty-nine and widowed of María Martín, married another young widow, María Ramona Bernal, in the Villa of Santa Cruz de la Cañada.[13]

It was here in Santa Cruz that he resided when the insurgents of 1837 selected him as their "general," to install him soon thereafter in Santa Fe as rebel governor.If we have dwelt so much on this man's racial and personal identity, it is because they both come into the current adventures of the Padre of Taos.

Now back to Padre Martínez. Among the lengthy paeans of praise for his master, Santiago Valdez tells us that the "symptoms" finally reached Taos. According to Sánchez they were carried thither by *Coyote* Vigil and José Gonzales. When the padre fearlessly exhorted his rebel parishioners to desist from their foolhardy actions, they called him a traitor "to God and the Nation," and began persecuting him to the point of threatening his life. Obviously, Valdez got this from the padre's poem. Then, he continues, it was at this crucial moment that the chief magistrate, Don Juan Aragón, and a considerable number of the sensible citizens of Taos, banded together in the padre's house, set up a row of fire-arms at the ready, and from there tried to restore order somehow. The rebel mob of Indians and others, which had only bows and arrows, refrained from attacking them, and this is how, Valdez goes on to say, the life of the good Padre Martínez came to be saved.[14]

Then the *Cantón*, as the Santa Cruz rebels designated themselves, began its advance on the Capital. Near Pojoaque or Santa Clara (Valdez is not sure), it ran into a small force which Governor Albino Pérez (himself a native of Mexico) had put together for the purpose of quieting the disturbance. It was promptly routed by the much more numerous insurgents, who proceeded toward Santa Fe, now having been joined by Indians from some of the northern pueblos as well as others from the pueblo of Santo Domingo. Just outside the Capital they brutally murdered Governor Pérez and some of his aides, the three Abréu gentlemen named

Santiago, Ramón and Mauricio (Mariano?), and perhaps some other such citizens of Santa Fe. (Sánchez lays the blame on the Santo Domingo and other Indians.) Right after this the rebel troup entered Santa Fe, seized the reins of government, and installed Gonzales as governor.[15]

Referring back to the padre's verses, Valdez has Padre Martínez fleeing down to Santa Fe where Gonzales sat as governor. This was in the beginning of September 1837. While there he was thinking of going on to Durango, presumably to report the matter to his bishop, but at this juncture his brother José María arrived from Taos, sent by the rebels there to beg him to return home; he would not be persecuted any more, they promised, for his presence was needed to restore order. This is when he returned to Taos, and accompanied by none other than Governor José Gonzales himself, who assured him that he would get the *Cantón* to treat him with all respect. And it was during this absence of Gonzales that Manuel Armijo retook Santa Fe with his force of seven hundred men from the Rio Abajo. The insurgents there were dispersed and their leaders hanged, but this did not mean that the revolution had come to an end.[16]

As the new year 1838 began, Padre Martínez, fearing a resurgence of all these troubles, sent a message to Manuel Armijo on January 2, through a Manuel Martín. Armijo replied on the 8th, saying how glad he was to learn where the padre stood in the matter, and praising his good disposition. Evidently, he had suspected all this while that Martínez had been behind the revolt. Now he confided to him that on this same day he was expecting the arrival of regular troops from Mexico, a vanguard of two hundred men under Lt. Cols. Justiniani and Muñoz; the headquarters company was to follow under General José Joaquín Calvo. He reiterated his trust iin the padre's patriotism, as a man whose counsels would be heeded by his people. A few days later Armijo called a meeting of the Assembly members, and Martínez, who was one of them, left for Santa Fe on January 15. But as soon as he left Taos, a good portion of the people resumed the rebellion and dispatched a troop to Santa Cruz, where José Gonzales was preparing an advance on Santa Fe like the one of the previous August. When informed of this, the padre promptly placed himself at Armijo's disposal, offering himself as chaplain for the forthcoming engagement with the insurgents, and Armijo gladly accepted the offer.[17]

Read's version of the entire affair varies as usual, and perhaps is more authentic. But its details do not particularly concern us here except for what Armijo wrote on January 24, saying that in that very morning he had decapitated Juan José Esquibel, Juan Vigil, Desiderio and Antonio Abad Montoya.[18] Evidently they had been caught in Santa Fe when Armijo took the Capital, if Read has the correct date.

Going back to the Valdez account, we learn that Armijo began his march northward on the 26th with his native militia and the Mexican regulars under the two lieutenant colonels he had named. Early next morning he discovered that the enemy, supremely confident of its own strength, was already waiting for him atop the hills of El Puertecito de Pojoaque. He promptly launched an attack and, during the bloody battle that ensued, his chaplain went heroically about attending to the wounded and consoling the dying with the last rites. After the rebels were defeated, Armijo went on to Santa Cruz with his forces and there, after Padre Martínez had heard their confessions, he executed José Gonzales and other lesser leaders (cabecillas). Antonio Vigil had been killed in battle, and Armijo had his corpse hung on a scaffold as a warning and deterrent to the rest. [19]

Besides his descriptive poem, as said before, Padre Martínez has only some brief references to the affair in his Relación of 1838. First, he said that he had contributed a sum of money for the upkeep or relief of the troops employed in downing the public disorders of the preceding year, besides smaller amounts which he refrained from mentioning, and that he had a receipt from a lieutenant named Don José Silva. Secondly, he himself had been persecuted by the rebels when trying to prevent those disorders. Lastly, he had been gladly accepted by Armijo as his chaplain. During the battle of Pojoaque, he had "deported himself as a brave and charitable soul, hearing the confessions of the wounded and others who died in action, which duties he discharged with the bullets whistling over his head and all around him, while surrounded by the other horrible apparatuses of war." Now he also took credit not only for having forwarned the governor about the outbreak and for having prevented a larger assemblage of the rebels, but even for both the timing and the tactics of the military engagement. [20] Of course, he was defending himself against prevailing rumors about his having been an instigator of the revolt, and for this reason one might here overlook the bravado and the bombast.

Here Pedro Sánchez has much the same account as Valdez, except for his confusion of dates. He also said that Padre Martínez continued as Armijo's military chaplain until the end of 1838, having misread a passage in the padre's Relación, where the latter wrote that he had been in Armijo's service "until just lately," but actually referring to a letter from the Taos magistrate of January 30, 1838. This shows that Padre Martínez was composing his book during the first months of the year. Sánchez also says that Vigil's corpse was hung on a post where the roads of Pojoaque and Jacona join, and this seems more likely than the gibbet or scaffold mentioned by both Padre Martínez and Valdez in trying for literary effects. Lastly, Sánchez is the only one who gives one short and sharp detail about Armijo's execution of Gonzales at Santa Cruz. He wrote that Armijo, turning to Padre Martínez, curtly said: "hear me the confession of this Genizaro before they give him five bullet-shots." [21]

This last item has captured the public imagination ever since it was first published. However, there is a contemporary one in the Taos burial records which, somewhat like a surprising codicil to a will, nullifies this particular historical bequest by Pedro Sánchez, and hence also Santiago Valdez' own testament concerning the execution of Gonzales at Santa Cruz. What is of utmost importance here is that Padre Martínez himself does not treat about it either in his poem or his Relación. The item in question is a burial entry by Martínez himself, in which he states that on September 27, 1838, he buried José Ángel Gonzales in the graveyard of the Indian mission church of the pueblo of Taos. He wrote that he was survived by a daughter, and by his widow, whose name he did not know because she was "from San Juan y Miranda," while the deceased was "an Indian of Taos whose confession I did not hear because he did not summon me."[22]

Had poor Gonzales, severely wounded in the fray at Pojoaque, effectively hidden himself from Armijo then and there, or later on at Santa Cruz, and then had found his way to Taos? Or had Armijo, if Gonzales did approach him at Santa Cruz for a parley, spared him because of his pitiful condition, a man who was about to die anyway? This does not sound like Armijo's way of doing things. What appears to be the actual fact is that Gonzales, who was thirty-nine years of age at the time, had strength enough to find his way up to Taos, if by slow stages with the assistance of some of his aides. Another possibility is that he had not been wounded at all, and, upon realizing that his cause was lost for good, had sneaked away from Pojoaque in the direction of the pueblo of Taos, and here he had died prematurely from some serious illness nine months later. Whichever the case may be, he had sought his mother's native pueblo because there Armijo would never find him within its intricate adobe honeycomb. Also, completely disillusioned by his lost efforts in trying to remedy the sad lot of his fellow genízaros and Indians, and no less by his brief if glorious venture into the white man's sphere of government, he had been drawn back to his mother's people – by the pull of her Tiwa blood in his veins, besides that of his father's Plains Indian mixed ancestry.

Hence, as he lay dying, he had not sent word for the padre's last ministrations either because he no longer believed in the religion brought by the Spaniards or because the ancient chants of the medicinemen proved more consoling. Since the women were not that radical, his daughter had called Padre Martínez to perform a proper Christian burial.

The Taos padre must surely have known José Ángel Gonzales in days gone by, having witnessed his second marriage to María Ignacia Martín in 1834. Yet it is quite possible that this fellow from among the prolific genízaro families of the Taos valley had not made any particular impression on him, especially since he lived away from Don Fernando at El Rancho and was away a great part of the time, out on the distant great plains in pursuit of the bison. Curiously, when recording that marriage of 1834, Padre Martínez called him both a vecino and a native of the Indian pueblo as though he were a pure Taos Indian.[23] This is how he now designated him in the burial entry also, a good indication that he did not know the man any too well. As for the daughter he mentioned, it looks as though she had married back into the pueblo, as had his second wife on her first marriage, and it was in her house where he had been staying and where he died. As for the widow likewise mentioned by him, his third wife Ramona Bernal, Padre Martínez did not know her at all. Nor did this daughter of his, who must have told him that she was a woman her father had married a couple of years ago down south, somewhere around San Juan y Miranda. This last was the general mountain area directly south of Taos and northeast of San Juan, called Lo de Miranda ever since the 17th century. Had Ramona Bernal been present, she would have told him her name, and that she was a resident of Santa Cruz.

And yet, it is entirely possible that Padre Martínez did know who the dead man was, if only from his very distinctive full name. It could well be that he deliberately chose not to allude to Gonzales' important rôle in the 1837 rebellion, just as he had failed to mention him in his poem except as *El Chepón*, and not at all in his *Relación* which had just come out or else was in press at this very time. It had been a most unfortunate episode in his life, and charges continued to be circulated at the Capital that he had been the real culprit behind it all.

According to Valdez, Governor Manuel Armijo – made so by the President of Mexico when authorized to quell the revolution – wreathed Padre Martínez with honors, *con laureles*, upon the army's return to Santa Fe after the victory. But the padre did not dare go back to Taos until he received a message on January 30, 1838, from Don Juan Antonio Aragón, who told him that on this same day civic order had been restored; the former rebels had now promised to obey the laws, he wrote, especially those of El Rancho (José Gonzales' former home) and the Indian pueblo of Taos. Thereupon Padre Martínez returned to Taos, and bearing a general amnesty for all the guilty ones, something which Armijo had conceded him in view of his personal merits and recent service. In doing so, Armijo charged him to keep a sharp eye open for signs of any future troubles.[1]

Among these same unpaginated papers which have been designated as *Notes*, there is a snatch of an account composed by Padre Martínez, perhaps a sermon, in which he states that his office as *cura encargado* continued apace, while he recalled all the good that he had done for the people in the past, and now exhorting them to a better and more fruitful life. Valdez uses it to append his own lavish encomnia on the padre's meek and humble virtues.[2]

Two weeks prior to the Pojoaque battle, Padre Martínez had received some most gratifying news, dated January 2, from Padre Leyva in Santa Fe who was in charge of that parish while Vicar Ortiz was away in Mexico City as federal deputy. The letter had been written on the same day that Martínez had advised Armijo about his fears of an uprising. What Leyva sent was a renewal, just received from Durango, of his faculties to administer the sacrament of Confirmation. This one, like the first issued by Zubiría on this subject, did not mention him by name, again referring anonymously to the present and future pastors of Taos and Tomé. Here Valdez goes on to say that the revolution of August and September in the preceding year had caused the harvests to be lost throughout the Taos district, and that Padre Martínez – despite his having been forced to surrender the parish funds to the rebels, and also having suffered the loss of his own livestock to Navajo rustlers – most generously distributed grain from his storerooms to the needy and starving, over and above what he had been able to glean from his fields that Fall.[3]

On August 7, 1838, Padre Martínez had another of his typical personal commendations drawn up. Young Padre Eulogio Valdez, his relative and former student who was the pastor of Abiquiú at the time, had been visiting his mother and brethren in Taos when he requested a very special certification from him. As Santiago Valdez cites it, this young padre reviewed all the previous commendations which the padre of Taos had received since the visitation of Fernández San Vicente in 1826 to the present year. It was notarized with Don Eulogio's signature and that of Vicente Saturnino Montaño (who was teaching in Padre Martínez' school and appears several years later as an ordained priest).[4] This makes it look as though Martínez' penchant for such commendations was still going strong;

nevertheless, the present one must have been prompted by certain political charges against him emanating from Santa Fe.

For on May 30, 1838, Governor Armijo had accused him of complicity in an uprising of the Utes and Apaches, the Cochiti Indians having also made a complaint of this nature.[5] We do not have the details, and all this could have taken place in 1834, when Vicar Ortiz had requested an explanation from him.[6] There is also mention in the same source of a suit brought against him by one of Armijo's party, Don Juan Bautista Vigil y Alarid, a man who was to accuse him of complicity in the 1837 Gonzales revolution; while it dealt with the Durango chancery concerning the question of tithes, it also appears as part of a scheme to embarrass the Taos padre.[7]

Whether or not the 1834 sedition charges have any foundation at all, Armijo's resurrecting of them does point to a break which had been taking place between himself and Padre Martínez – as does Juan Bautista Vigil's suit. The governor had been engaged during this period in parceling out enormous vacant tracts of land to some foreigners, open country which had always been a common hunting ground for the New Mexicans, *vecinos* and Pueblo Indians alike, and not excluding the Comanches and other Plains Indians. This unusual largesse to foreign "developers" went against the grain of Padre Martínez, naturally, and it could have some connection with that uprising of the Utes and Apaches brought up by Armijo. And so rumors became more widespread that he had been the main instigator behind the Gonzales revolution.

As said before, all this seems to have motivated the certification by Padre Eulogio Valdez, just as did the Martínez printed *Relación* of this year, and which Valdez thought had been composed for the sole edification of his students. Also, as we have already seen further back in the passages dealing with his birth and origins – with strong emphasis on his Mexican nationality and patriotism – and then on his struggles in behalf of the poor among his *paisanos*, he was likewise alluding to his innocence with regard to the uprising of the year before. However, we must say that this biography is also an unabashed disclosure of his inner self and character. It is a marvel of self-revelation, starting out with the preamble which he headed with a passage from *Ecclesiastes* 9:11, about the race not going to the swift, nor the battle to the strong, but rather to time and circumstance. While he meant this as a general allusion to the war of the previous year, he was holding up his own great genius for all to see.

Here he referred to himself as Don Antonio José Martínez y Santistéban, as if in rebuttal to that double-surnamed Vigil y Alarid fellow of Santa Fe. Although far removed from the more comfortable conditions existing in the Ecclesiastical Capital (Durango), "he considered himself happy in the possession of his talents, or endowments of his genius, and the use of them which he had made, and would make..." Although he might not attain a higher rank in his (clerical) profession, he went on, and had to depend on his sustenance as a farmer, which he had been since his first years and which he had never ceased to be as a clergyman, he believed that he could sincerely say – quoting *Acts of the Apostles* 20:33-34 – that he had never coveted gold nor silver, but with his own hands had labored for all his needs.[8] While all this was directed at his foes in Santa Fe, as said before, it does paint a vivid picture of a man obsessed with his own superior worth and gifts. It was an obsession which in a far-off day would end in madness.

We do not have a copy of the original edition of this *Relación de Méritos* of 1838, except for some poor photos of the title-page, and a handful of some pages following, in the library of the Museum of New Mexico. Hence our dependence on the imperfect but adequate translation by Cecil V. Romero in the *New Mexico Historical Review*. As Valdez described it, it was a booklet of fifty-three printed pages, which cited only by their assigned numbers the hoarded documents which he himself fully utilized in his *Biografía*, along with what we call his copied *Notes* and other papers.[9]

Then the decade of the 1840s began. The year before, says Valdez, Bishop Zubiría had convoked a *concurso* in Durango (sometimes referred to as a synod for both occurring at the same time), according to customary diocesan procedure. This was to provide ordinary pastors with the opportunity to compete for the status of irremovable pastors, *curas propios*. Padre Martínez had been assiduously preparing for it with all the studies previously mentioned – and, we might add, all the certifications he had collected and filed since his student days in that city. For this was the highest distinction which a pastor could aspire to, short of a prelacy, and here Valdez points out that it was not so much the distinctive title that Padre Martínez wanted, but the assurance that it brought of his remaining in Taos for life, so that all of his educational efforts would not come to naught.[10] This we can believe, while sure that he would glory in the title, too.

He left for Durango during August 1840, after getting Padre Lucero to take charge of Taos. He suspended the classes of grammar, logic and the rest, leaving only the one of "first letters" in the care of his printer, José María Baca. By this time, Valdez brings in as an aside, some of his best friends and other parishioners, through the evil influence of certain foreigners in Taos, had fallen into the vice of gambling with cards, and with the expected bad consequences. Over and above his previous spoken exhortations, he now left them some *décimas* on the subject, and which Valdez quotes. By far the best verse in the long doggerel runs as follows: *Los arboles vegetando/ cumplen el fin de su esfera/ pero el jugador esmera/ su fin propio irlo variando/ con imposturas viciosas/ que se atornan tenebrosas/ nada dejando en su ser,/ toda gloria y placer/ en perder todas las cosas.* – Yes, indeed, the trees accomplished their intended purpose by growing according to their nature, but the gambler, by straying from his own destiny in his vain search for glory and pleasure, ended up with nothing.[11]

The padre also took along some of his students who were ready to pursue higher studies, says Valdez. They arrived in Durango in September, and he remained there for five months, which included January of the following year. He left there early in February, and was back home in Taos on March 20, 1841.[12] However, we know that he left Durango much earlier, from a notation he made in the burial book on January 29, 1841: "I returned from my trip on the 22nd to continue as pastor." Also, the baptismal book of more frequent entries has his last signed one on August 19, 1840, while the last one by Padre Lucero on January 30, 1841, is signed by both priests. Here Padre Martínez explained the gap caused by his absence, "Don Mariano Lucero having remained in charge because of my trip to Durango for the *concursos*."[13]

But what elicits a bit of surprise, he did not come back to Taos as a certified *cura propio*. Valdez says that he was among those clergymen who got the highest marks in the examinations, and that, because of his abilities and character, he had been offered any of the best parishes he chose down in that rich area. Padre Martínez had turned down the offers, of course, desiring no other parish than that of his native region. As for his not having been constituted a permanent pastor then and there, Valdez says that it was due to some *trámites de estilo* – formalities of some sort for which he could not prolong his absence from Taos.[14]

In this connection, Padre Martínez must have come back to Taos with a flair, boasting before all his friends and peers about his triumphs at the synodal examinations. Or else he was instructing his fellows while regaling them with facts about a great city they had never seen. This did not sit well with Carlos Bent, an alien in Taos who had been his friend but who was now linked with Governor Manuel Armijo's land dealings in Santa Fe. In a letter written from Taos on January 30, 1841, Bent sarcastically referred to him as "the greate Literry Marteanes" who had just returned in triumph from Durango.[15] As we can see here, this sagacious promoter, and future territorial governor, was not too good at spelling.

Valdez, on the other hand, has nothing but praise for his master, declaring that ever since his return every village wanted him for its resident priest, not only for his being a fellow native, but because he was one padre who preached to the people. Of this we have not the least doubt, as explained long before. And how much his people had rejoiced, Valdez wrote, when they learned that he was coming back home, having heard rumors that he had been retained permanently in Durango. At the news of his approach, practically everyone went out on foot or on horseback to meet him at the ravines near the Plaza of Los Córdovas. From here they escorted him back to his house in triumph, all of them trying to see him close and to kiss his hand.[16] After this, one can confidently assume he plunged back into his many long-interrupted activities, and without letting up on the stories he had to tell about his sojourn in the faraway great city of Durango.

On November 1, after the harvest season was over, and which was the usual vacation time for his pupils, Padre Martínez opened his primary school to many other youngsters from various parts of the territory, and who were brought to Taos by their respective parents. Among the local ones were his many *sobrinos* of both sexes, his nephews and nieces, says Valdez. There were also his young *familiares* which included Santiago Valdez himself. We know that the latter belonged to both categories, and here we can include the perhaps not too bright-looking George Antonio Romero, who was of the same age. These and their schoolmates were placed under a teacher whom Padre Martínez had brought from Durango, by the name of Vicente Saturnino Montaño. (He was already in Taos three years before as we saw earlier.) For the formal opening exercises, two of the padre's (legitimate) nephews, José Manuel and Inocencio Martínez, who had been trained to chant at Mass, sang a "sonnet" composed by the padre himself. Valdez quotes it – twelve short uninspired lines in alternating trimeter and dimeter with a bow to teacher Montaño.[17]

Sometime thereafter, the padre composed and printed a set of moral *décimas* in 121 lines which Valdez also quotes in full. Then, after discussing the number and names of the seminary students who had attained ordination, which was already treated previously, Valdez goes on to say that Padre Martínez opened a class on Spanish and Mexican laws as they applied to New Mexico. This is when he printed a recopilation of *El Derecho Civil de España* in 168 pages, which also contained extra points on the matter from a work by a Dr. José María Álvarez and, at the end, some axioms which Martínez himself translated from the Latin. From the heavy tome on Law by Murillo he extracted everything having to do with last wills and testaments, which he also printed, and of which many copies were still circulating throughout New Mexico. He likewise extracted for his students, likewise for publication, the more important parts of four tomes by the same Dr. Álvarez, and this work was reprinted in Taos in 1842. Valdez quotes the padre's lengthy Prologue which contains nothing of historical importance.[18]

If anything, this and what Valdez detailed just before serve to show that, for Padre Martínez, every minute counted. And these were only two related facets on the many-sided gemstone of his untiring activities. Besides, even before the War of the Chimayoses not too long ago, his New Mexico had begun entering into a new phase in her life and politics which was being influenced by alien forces, as well as with threats to himself for his activities in this field.

Finally, Padre Martínez became the *cura propio* of Taos. He received the notification from Durango, dated November 8, 1842, which stated that Canon José Tomás Ribera down there, during the absence of Bishop Zubiría, had granted him the much coveted status of irremovable pastor. Martínez immediately wrote back his eager acceptance, suggesting a clerical friend named Don Gregorio Hernández as his proxy, and the latter officially received the high honor for him on May 16, 1843. Sometime thereafter, Valdez does not give the day, Padre Martínez took formal possession of his parish as *cura propio*, with Padre José Vicente Montaño acting as the official witness of this most solemn act.[19] This Montaño priest, whose family resided in Mexico City, first appears in the New Mexico mission records in 1842.[20] He might have come with Martínez from Durango the year before, and thus Valdez had confused him with the younger lay teacher, Vicente Saturnino Montaño, who had been in Taos well before this.

In this same connection, Bishop Zubiría sent Martínez a lengthy document, dated November 13, 1844, approving the preceding grant and solemn act, and outlining the specific duties and privileges of a *cura propio*, mentioning that by way of protocol the matter had passed through the desks of major civil officials in Mexico and of Governor Manuel Armijo in Santa Fe. The bishop also appointed

Martínez as the Vicar and Ecclesiastical Judge for the Taos or northern Rio Arriba district.[21] Here we can see the supreme regard with which the hierarchy and clergy held the office of *cura propio*, and why, in a different American hierarchical situation that was to come, the clergy of New Mexico so strongly resented and resisted what they had considered a rape of such a sacrosanct and inviolable office.

As for the last item mentioned by Bishop Zubiría, the high-sounding title of Vicar and Ecclesiastical Judge, both Padre Martínez and his biographers made much of it, as though it signified the most extraordinary powers. Martínez himself, and this was not through any ignorance on his part, was to use the title in challenging Vicar Ortiz' jurisdiction as vicar for all of New Mexico. Actually, this office, which was also conferred on some other pastors, merely empowered the recipient to judge on matrimonial cases, and to grant nuptial dispensations without having to recur to faraway Durango or even Santa Fe. It also gave him the powers of attorney when parochial matters touched on civil law. And all of this was restricted to his own parish or civil district. But one can imagine that both of these new titles spurred the Padre of Taos to greater efforts in his multiple projects, while making his head swell a trifle, were this possible in his case.

An interesting aside by Valdez at this juncture is that the place east of the sierra from Taos, still being called Lo de Mora, had been growing by leaps and bounds. Padre Martínez had attended the Mora valley for several years, whenever in charge of the Picuris parish to which it belonged. Valdez had discovered among his papers a license from Durango, dated May 5, 1837, for a cemetery on the southwest corner of its lower town of Santa Gertrudis, and he says that the padre solemnly blessed it after Mass.[22] He does not give the date for this ceremony, but it could have taken place sometime in 1843, the year Valdez was treating. The upper town of San Antonio de lo de Mora (now Cleveland) had been founded as early as 1818, and had been attached since then to the parish of Picuris. The lower settlement of Santa Gertrudis, the present town of Mora, had been started between the years 1835 and 1838.[23] These facts are brought in because Padre Martínez came to regard Mora as his own preserve.

A Dirtier War of Politics / 10

The year 1844 was replete with action for Padre Martínez in connection with governmental affairs in New Mexico, as he soon found out and no doubt had expected. During the last tenure of Governor Manuel Armijo, several things had been taking place which the padre, as a genuine patriot and ever under the spell of his Hidalgo dream, did not like and was both ready and eager to say so. There were those land deals with the foreigners which he disliked the most, and he had been holding meetings in Taos to discuss the matter and do something about it.

We know that on July 6, 1843, Governor Armijo had complained to Vicar Ortiz about secret juntas being held in Taos in the padre's own house. Ortiz had sent a copy of the governor's letter to Martínez requesting him to appear in Santa Fe with an explanation; but on August 3 Ortiz advised Armijo that he had not done so as yet. Young Padre José Manuel Gallegos, stationed at San Juan at the time, had attended such juntas and was evidently part of the cabal, for Armijo made similar complaints against him at this very time. Gallegos did write an explanation upon the vicar's request, but as in the case of Martínez, no particulars as to the nature or purpose of the Taos meetings are included in the correspondence.[1]

It was then that Padre Martínez composed what Valdez calls an "Exposition," which the military commandant in Santa Fe, Don Mariano Martínez (de Lejanza, and a native of Mexico) forwarded to President López de Santa Ana. The latter gave his hearty approval of its contents sometime before January 31, 1844, and Commandant Don Mariano, who had copies made of it in Santa Fe on April 8, sent one to Padre Martínez. Actually, as we shall see, the President had received the Exposition on December 2, 1843, and his wish was that the Department of New Mexico should seriously take its proposals into consideration in their practical aspects.[2]

This "Exposition on Affairs in New Mexico," as we learn of the full title elsewhere, had also been published on the padre's press on November 28, 1843. As Valdez treats it, the document dealt with the sad plight of the *indios bárbaros* of the eastern plains and western deserts and, we may add, of the mountain valleys closer to the padre's home. Although Padre Martínez does not refer to the distant past, ignorant as he was of New Mexico's Spanish Colonial history, we know that these uncivilized Indians (*bárbaros* in Spanish without a pejorative sense) had raided the Hispanic settlements and Indian pueblos for more than two centuries, killing and pillaging, and making off with their horses and sometimes their children. Of course, there had also been retaliatory forays by the Spanish militia with auxiliary pueblo troops. Moreover, the Plains Indian tribes had always been at war with one another, capturing each other's women and children, some of whom ended up as "ransomed" servants among the Spanish families and mainly through the hands of the Comanches during what were called *ferias* (trading fairs) during periods of truce.

Referring to his own times, Padre Martínez wrote that as late as the year 1843, the Navajo had raided some settlements, killing adults and taking children as slaves, while the Mexican government had remained passive. They were the worst of all the wild tribes, he said, and yet his heart went out to them as it had done all this while toward the more unfortunate among his own people. For he did not propose their total conquest or extermination by way of vengeance; rather, he wanted all of these nomadic tribes gathered into villages in their own territory, where they could be taught the advantages and virtues of civic policy through agriculture and industry. (Here Valdez remarks that, because his master's immortal idea could not be put into effect at this time, it had been left for "the magnanimous Government of the United States" to take the necessary steps, *as it was doing now* – an altogether different concept and procedure referred to these days as the inhumane "Navajo Long Walk.")

In this same vein, and by way of illustration, Padre Martínez in this same Exposition had complained that the local Mexican government, unlike the one of former Spanish times, had allowed foreigners (Bent *et al.*) to build forts on the Arkansas and Chato Rivers and some other places ever since 1832, to the detriment of those nomadic Indians who, because of the miserable conditions that ensued, had become thieves and robbers. They had deteriorated morally because they were being sold liquors by the foreigners; the great bison herds, which had been their plentiful supply of meat, were now almost a thing of the past.[3]

Here a person cannot help but admire the padre's humanitarian idealism, as well as his sage foresightedness, and at the same time regret the fact that the local government totally lacked the means, not to mention the corporate idealism, to carry out his dream. The attempt made later on by the American government through Col. Kit Carson had the most disastrous results because, contrary to Padre Martínez' idea, it was carried out by sheer force and by removing the Navajo from their traditional home and hunting grounds. Whatever, both were impossible dreams because of so many other problems involved. Nor could the Martínez proposal even have gotten off the ground so long as Manuel Armijo, who must have read the Exposition with its condemnation of his alien friends' forts, was in the way. This brings us to a dramatic encounter between the two as described by Valdez.

It was also around this time – in 1843 according to Valdez, while Sánchez gives 1844 – that the departmental electors assembled in Santa Fe to chose the next deputy to the National Mexican Congress. Padre Martínez was already being considered the unanimous choice, just as Vicar Ortiz had been in a previous election. They were all assembled under the *portal* of the Palacic Nacional, with Vicar Ortiz presiding, Governor Armijo appeared with a squad of soldiers. Pointing his *bastón* or batón of office at the president, he demanded the election of another man by the name of Diego Archuleta, and, of course, Armijo's decision was not questioned. However, Padre Martínez, greatly disappointed as he must have been, especially since his peers had offered to pay for his travel and other expenses, did not hold this against Archuleta. As Valdez explains it, he was a fine young man whom the padre liked very much for his staunch personal qualities, his good education in Durango, and his liberal views. And so Padre Martínez returned home to resume the many projects dear to his heart, which would have suffered by his absence while at Congress in Mexico City.[4] But he could not restrain himself from disseminating an article which he wrote against Armijo on this score, as we shall see.

Then, Valdez continues, Don Mariano Martínez de Lejanza was appointed governor at the beginning of the year 1844. He must have been an all-around man of culture, as we learn elsewhere, anxious to promote letters besides such things that make life more pleasant; he was the first governor to plant trees on Santa Fe's ancient *plaza de armas*, also ordering them to be planted, with an *acequia* for watering them, all along the street and road leading to the Rosario chapel northwest of town. Valdez tells us here that one of his ambitions was to publish a periodical for wide distribution, something which New Mexico sadly lacked at the time, and so he wrote to Padre Martínez on March 13, offering to buy the press which the padre had. Martínez refused to sell it, with the excuse that he badly needed it himself; but he lent it to the governor gratis "for the public good" until the 20th of August, by which time a press ordered by his Excellency should have arrived from Mexico.

Here Valdez also tells us that, well before this, a newspaper had been published in Santa Fe by a Don Felix Zubía (Barreiro's editor?), and on the very same press which the padre had lent the governor. He also remarks that the padre had already been attacked in the political field, quoting extracts from his correspondence with this same governor, in which he told him that he intended to counter those libels in the months to come, since at present he was too busy with his pastoral duties and his students.[5]

At first, wrote Padre Martínez, he had been calumniated by the lower classes (the Gonzales rebellion), and now by those of higher category. He also wrote the governor on August 22, 1844 that, just the night before, some trustworthy person had told him that Don Juan Bautista Vigil had already composed a libel impugning his honor, especially concerning his patriotism when referring to the years 1837-1838 (the Gonzales revolt again). What was worse, Vigil had done it at the urging of Don Manuel Armijo, who paid him to do it with the purpose of having it published, and, ironically, on the padre's own press. This was because Armijo was very much aggravated by an article which he, Padre Martínez, had disseminated with regard to the elections (the Archuleta affair), and which was ready to go to press. Hence he begged the governor not to have Vigil's libel printed.[6]

Valdez then relates how Padre Martínez had also written to the governor about certain actions taken by Armijo, during his term as governor, against the commonweal of the Mexican republic – *quitandole un poco de ella* – yanking off a portion of it to bestow it on foreigners. It was his feeling that, had not Governor Martínez de Lejanza replaced him at this time, he would have already squandered away the whole Department of New Mexico, or else that the circumstances would have been irremediably ripe for such an abhorrent development. That same bad spirit of Armijo's party, the padre continued, among the voters in the Assembly, was already evident when it surrendered El Cimarrón and Huerfano as if they were populated areas. As a matter of fact, the second place named was already occupied by aliens without his Excellency being aware of it. Valdez ends by saying that Armijo had been calumniating Padre Martínez because of his comments on that illegal election of 1843, when Armijo himself had boldly violated the law. [7]

When all is said and done, one has to admire once more the patriotic spirit of the Padre of Taos, and no less the stamina shown in his unrelenting struggle for civic justice and integrity as much as one has to render him due credit for everything he had thus far accomplished in the pastoral and educational fields. It denotes some sort of genius which cannot be denied. And yet, he also betrayed certain less admirable traits – his clandestine concubinage and past siring of progeny aside – on the ecclesiastical level, as hinted at long before in his sour relationship with his legitimate superior, Vicar Juan Felipe Ortiz in Santa Fe.

Sometime in April 1844, Vicar Ortiz had assigned young Padre José Manuel Gallegos to the parish of Picuris, but Martínez insisted that he could not have its attached villages of Lo de Mora, as if they were his own private preserve. They had never belonged to Taos. Then, during this contention, the people of the Picuris area told Ortiz that they did not want Gallegos, evidently egged on by Martínez; whereupon the latter went so far as to contend that Ortiz was not the bishop's vicar for all of New Mexico, but only for the central district around the Capital. Ortiz then wrote him two calm letters on April 21 and May 11, in which he proved his overall jurisdiction. On the following day he also wrote to Bishop Zubiría, stating that he had left Martínez have his way at Picuris in order to keep the peace, and until the bishop made his own final decision. [8]

This is not the only specific example of Padre Martínez' insubordination in this regard. Thus far he had evidently made use on his own of Padre Lucero's assistance in Taos and Picuris, ever since the latter's ordination in 1836, because four years before the Gallegos incident, he had also placed the young Padre José de Jesús Luján at Picuris without consulting the vicar. When by a direct order of Bishop Zubiría, dated August 23, 1840, Luján was transferred to Chihuahua, the people of Las Trampas in the Picuris parish had asked Vicar Ortiz to reconsider the change he had dutifully transmitted. The vicar knew that it was Martínez who was behind it, and so he wrote to the bishop, telling him that he was laying hands off the matter for the reasons stated. [9]

Another case in point is the underhanded way in which Martínez worked against the vicar, during a schism caused far south in Belén by Padre Nicolás Valencia, whom Bishop Zubiría had previously suspended for insubordination. This Valencia is also listed as one of Martínez' pupils, and this incident will be treated later in its place. All of this was a kind of dirty politics, too, but with the Padre of Taos on the culpable end. Hence one can say, from all the evidence, that Padre Martínez had always envied and resented Don Juan Felipe Ortiz in his superior status as his bishop's vicar of the entire Church in New Mexico. He had no excuses in this sphere about malfeasance in office or any kind of scandal, as he had with regard to Manuel Armijo in the secular or civic one. Nor had Ortiz caused him any harm whatsoever. But this all rankled within him nonetheless. It, too, intruded upon his Hidalgo dream of being the number one man in everything.

These internecine troubles could have been one of the several reasons why Bishop Zubiría, while urged primarily by his pastoral zeal, decided to make his second visitation of New Mexico in 1845. What might have been another reason, as some have supposed, was his concern about the growing number of Americans from the east coming into the region, but for Padre Martínez himself this posed no special problem.

The Padre and The Americanos / 11

For Padre Martínez, besides the impending visitation of his bishop which the latter's office had announced from Durango on February 5, 1845 – at the same time requesting prayers for his safety because of the wild Indian perils enroute[1] – there were other signal developments in which he would be involved in one way or another, and as much as ever before. Chief among them was the fast growing presence of what his people called the *americanos*, among whom they sometimes lumped as kindred aliens other assorted individuals like the French-Canadian trappers from the north and others of whatever other national origins arriving from the east.

The padre had long become well used to the whole gamut of such *extrangeros* since the great majority of them gravitated to Taos. The very first such strangers had come there even before he was ordained some twenty years before. Since his ordination, he had been marrying a steadily increasing number of such French-Canadians and eastern-state Americans to the native women of his parish. He had also baptized, with the proper religious instructions beforehand, some of the latter who had expressed their desire of becoming Catholics. All of this naturally entailed a close cordial relationship between himself and the newcomers, both before and after the baptisms and weddings. To all appearances, up to this time, Padre Martínez and his native flocks had gotten along very well with the strangers of every description who had been settling among them, and for this reason most of those who remained had practically become natives themselves.

At this juncture a different breed, called the *tejanos*, has to be brought in because of the impact which the term itself had made on the minds of Padre Martínez and the native people in general. None of these so far had come to New Mexico, but the word *tejano* had become a watchword of alarm in the past four or five years. During several years before this, governmental notices from Mexico to the officials in Santa Fe had told of some American colonists in Mexican Texas who wanted to form an English-speaking republic apart from the Mexican nation. There were reports of battles, but these made little or no impression on New Mexico's folk in their isolated northern frontier, just as similar reports about political turmoils within the Mexican government itself had left them cold. Padre Martínez of course, did pay attention to the latter, since it involved the shaky course of an inexperienced young democracy with regard to religion, taxes and education. But the Texan struggle itself meant little to him, as with the common people who knew about a post called San Antonio de Béjar, but nothing else about that faraway land where their own Rio Bravo del Norte was said to run into the sea.

But things had suddenly changed in 1840. Their civic leaders in Santa Fe had been telling them that those English-speaking Texans, by now an independent republic, were getting ready to invade their own homeland. The alarm grew when they heard the same from their church leaders. On July 22, 1840, Vicar Oritz sent out a warning to the clergy and the faithful, about an invasion by the Texans which was in the offing, earnestly begging their prayers so that it would not come to pass, or that it would be repelled when it did. The feared invasion did not come until a year later, and the people must have rejoiced with pride and relief when the vicar notified them on July 7, 1841, that the "Texan adventurers" had been summarily defeated on the 5th at 8 o'clock in the morning, and ordering a Mass of thanksgiving to be celebrated in each parish.[2] There is also an interesting letter in this connection as of October 4, of this same year, in which a Vicente Baca advised his pastor at Belén, Padre Luján, that he had participated in the campaign and was now escorting the Texas prisoners down to El Paso del Norte; mention is also made of the church *mayordomos* having been exempted from military duty.[3]

Padre Martínez, no doubt, had most willingly carried out the vicar's orders this time with regard to the public prayers and Masses. One can almost see him fanning his people's patriotism in his sermons and conversations, and it could be that he roused a goodly number of the men to join the militia voluntarily. What we know for certain is what he mentions briefly in his *Relación*, that he had contributed an amount of money "as a voluntary donation for the Texan emergencies."[4] Here he evidently included a second invasion made by the Texan invaders two years later. Again, on July 5, 1843, Vicar Ortiz had sent another message to his clergy and their parishioners about the same "Texan adventurers," once more requesting public prayers, and for the pastors to celebrate Masses to insure a second victory.[5]

The Texans came and were trounced again, and this was the last such attempt made by the Texas republic. It had harbored the mistaken notion that, because her treaty with Mexico had designated the southern bend of the Rio Grande as the dividing border between the two republics, it meant all the territory on the eastern south-to-north bank of the great river all the way to its source in what is now Colorado. To make matters worse, the politicians in Washington, and without any right to do so, had confirmed that error. This, of course, included practically all of New Mexico which had been a geographical and civic enclave under Spain even before the Texans' English ancestors had landed on the Atlantic coast. Ever since then, the published journals by the Texas survivors themselves, and scores of subsequent writings on the subject, have related the mitigating circumstances which contributed to the Texans' double defeat, as well as some unsavory actions committed by certain of the New Mexican victors in their treatment of prisoners. But this does not concern us here, only what the New Mexico clergy and their flocks had felt at the time, and with particular reference to the Padre of Taos.

Nevertheless, from this time on, *tejano* had continued to be a bad word in New Mexico's vocabulary, as we shall see later in Padre Martínez' own use of the term. Otherwise, as mentioned in the beginning, *americano* was the general word employed for the foreigners, unless they were specified by their origin. The term *gringo*, a very old corruption in rural Spain of *griego*, Greek – and later applied over there to any foreigner, especially the English for whatever reason – had become a pejorative epithet down in Mexico for the invading English-speaking Americans during the United States-Mexican War. In New Mexico at this time it was not in use as commonly supposed, nor does it appear in any record – as did *gavacho* far back with reference to Frenchmen only, again a very old term from rural Spain. It was the English-language Americans having recent personal experiences down in Mexico and Texas who were applying "gringo" to themselves as coming from the New Mexican people. One can see this in their writings of the times.

This is why we can say that to Padre Martínez the newcomers had always been simply *americanos* or *franceses*, as the case may be, and not *gringos* for the first or *gavachos* for the latter. One can see this in the many papers which he left with Santiago Valdez, and gather as well from the tenor of his baptismal and marriage entries in Taos. To him they were all human beings and children of the same Creator, just as were his dear native *paisanos* and his Pueblo Indians – and even the *indios bárbaros* who had been their common enemy for so long. All of this is brought up here, not only to emphasize one good basic quality in the far from perfect character of Padre Martínez, but because subsequent writers accused him of having been violently anti-American, which he never was. Valdez himself goes into these false accusations which were already rampant when he was writing in the decade following the padre's death; they had arisen, he said, because of his opposition to the covetousness of some Americans and others, referring to the land deals made by Governor Manuel Armijo with a few of them, and only because the padre was a staunch Mexican patriot at the time watching out for the best interests of his native land.[6]

Simply because this is the story of the Padre of Taos, and of Taos also for its being his beloved home and the stage of his long colorful career, a general glance over the foreigners who availed themselves of his generous services should not be out of place. A list of these non-Hispanic names, along with their pertinent data, has already been published.[7] Roughly between the years 1826-1850, there are over 130 such alien names in the church records all over New Mexico. Of the 87 or so French names, 77 are found in Taos alone. Of the 125 or so from the eastern United States, more than 75 are found in Taos, where there also appear two from Germany, one each from England, Ireland and Scotland, and one fellow by the name of Simon Levi (no origin given).

Except for the supposedly Catholic individuals with French names, most of the newcomers were not Catholics, and Padre Martínez, as just said, instructed a number of these in his Faith prior to their baptisms, while most of the others he united with local women by way of mixed marriages. Most of the Frenchmen are merely designated as such with no place of origin, while eight are recorded as having come from France, eighteen from Canada, seven from St. Louis and one other from New Orleans; the rest could have been French-Canadians. Years later, French Father Gabriel Ussel of Taos declared that the famed Jesuit missionary of the Northwest, Father Jean-Marie DeSmet, had once vainly tried to contact Padre Martínez for some reason.[8] This could have been for the purpose of inquiring about certain French-Canadians who, either as squawmen or married to Indian females ("of the North" as Martínez put it), had left their squaws behind, some of them bringing their natural or legitimate half-breed sons to Taos.[9]

Among the larger number of *americanos*, 26 are not given a place of origin, or else are called natives of the "States of North America," while 14 are designated as having come from Missouri, 11 from Kentucky, seven from Pennsylvania, six from Virginia, four each from New York and Tennessee and one each from "Carolina," Vermont, "Jersey," and Arkansas. Among those whom Padre Martínez instructed, as he fully noted down at good length, and then baptized, a young Missourian by the name of Cristóbal (Kit) Carson stands out. In this respect there are others who appear in Western annals, such as the brothers Stephen Louis and Joseph Elliot Lee, Richard Campbell, Joseph William Wolfskill and Joseph William Workman – the latter two being the leaders of families which later emigrated to California, some of them with their Taos wives and half-Spanish children.[10] Among those whose marriages the padre performed we also find David Alexander, who was to be another pioneer California settler, Richard or Richens (Old Dick) Wootten, Lucien Maxwell, Charles Hypolite and John Baptist Beaubien from Canada, and a certain Rowles (Rowland?) who could be the individual who led another party of settlers to the Pacific coast. There also appears the name of Carlos Bent, whose female Indian servant "of the North" he baptized, and with an Elfego Bent as her godfather.[11] Although Bent's wife was a Taos woman, their marriage does not appear in the Taos records.

In connection with all these people's baptisms and weddings, another thing stands out – a goodly number of these men were so illiterate that they could not even spell their names. Ironically, it was at the very time when American travellers were writing about the crass illiteracy of the Hispanic native of New Mexico. Hence Padre Martínez himself, totally unfamiliar with English vocal sounds and orthography, wrote down their respective names as they sounded to his Latin ear. Who would ever suspect that "Caquindó" stood for Kuykendahl, and that "Julian Gon" meant William Gordon? The latter was one of those good men who emigrated to California with their Taos-sired families, and came to be the first settlers of Montecito in California. This came to light some years ago when their descendants, about to celebrate the centenary of their town, requested the preceding data about their Taos ancestors.

One can readily imagine that when Padre Martínez blessed their American-made covered wagons prior to their departure, a most touching scene took place as relatives on the Taos plaza of Don Fernando wailed their lament of never seeing their loved ones again. If his generosity was as great as his collected commendations make it, and there is no reason to doubt it, he must have added all kinds of foodstuffs to his benedictions for their long and perilous trek to the far Pacific coast.

Going back to Bishop Zubiría's second pastoral visitation of New Mexico, we find Valdez telling us that the prelate commended Padre Martínez, as he had done in 1833, for his fine administration of the combined parishes of Taos and Picurís, particularly with regard to the parish records he kept. This is borne out by the registers themselves. On July 12, 1845, his secretary heartily approved of the marriage entries by a pastor "whose activity and efficacy is patent here and in the other branches." At the same time he disapproved of the ones by Padre Lucero from August 1840 until February 1841, when Martínez was away in Durango. This clerk likewise wrote much the same in the baptismal and burial books, further commending the pastor in the latter book for his zeal in visiting the sick and administering the last rites to the dying.[12]

As for Padre Martínez' current activities, Valdez refers to a note he sent the local justice of the peace, as of August 13, and starting with the patriotic motto, Dios y Libertad! It was a request for cooperation which, Valdez goes on to say, served to get the people to work together for the public good, while the padre himself continued with his works of charity and his own good example to everyone.[13] Here Valdez also notes that on September 18 of this year of 1845, Bishop Zubiría wrote Martínez from Santa Fe, extending his extraordinary faculties for the next five years. He also empowered him to absolve from "mixed heresy" (Valdez' misreading of the faculty to perform mixed marriages) and also to absolve in foro interno (in the secrecy of confession) any clergyman who should incur what canon law called the most serious censure of "irregularity."[14]

This last prompts a bit of speculation which is most apropos with regard to Padre Martínez. For he himself had certainly become "irregular" through his past concubinage with Teodora Romero. Had he now privately revealed it to his bishop in confession, and thus had been absolved from the censure along with his many years of sin? This meant the discontinuation of his liaison with Teodora, if it had not ended before this. The bishop, of course, could not act externally on this knowledge in any way whatsoever; his future judgments, as much as his lips, were completely sealed in this regard.

Padre Martínez had also begged the bishop to relieve him of the added burden of the Picuris parish and its distant missions in the Mora valley. Zubiría did so at the end of his visitation by appointing Padre Lucero to take full charge of both places. Also around this time, says Valdez, Martínez discontinued his Latin classes begun in 1833, so much fatigued was he by his many other projects as well as by his advanced age (fifty-two!). Here Valdez went on to name and comment upon his Latin students who had gone on to the priesthood, the passage already treated. This is also when Valdez tells us that the padre had discouraged his own immediate kin from pursuing that course. He also added that the padre's purpose in educating many other lads for a lay career was for the day when they could distinguish themselves as useful citizens. These men, Valdez said, were too numerous for him to count or identify.[15]

Returning to the civic scene, Valdez went on to say that there were new developments which were bothering both Padre Martínez and Bishop Zubiría, and here we ourselves return to the theme of the americanos. Valdez quoted part of a letter which the padre wrote the bishop on September 2, in which he told him that sooner or later New Mexico would come under the government of the United States. He was calmly resigned to it, he said, except for one thing. This nation, he now told the bishop, tolerated all religions, but he himself was prepared to continue as a faithful servant of the Church and would resist the propagation of sects which was being introduced by force. For example, he went on, the bishop himself already knew that some forty foreign families had arrived in one of the Mora settlements with the pretext of settling there, and not far from them were stationed some *gente armada* (people armed militarywise), and no one knew for what purpose. Perhaps, in the event that the New Mexico government tried to prevent those families from settling there permanently, these latter armed people would come to their aid – either because they were actually *tejanos* or else others bent on defending the families in question.[16]

As to the reference by Martínez about the toleration of cults by the United States, we already know that as a democratic liberal he had longed favored religious freedom. What he now wrote the bishop was in connection with rumors of its being propagated by a show of force, and under the guise of the feared and despised *tejanos* besides. Moreover, there seems to have been a definite connection, in the padre's mind, of those forty alien families with the land grants contiguous to the Mora area which Manuel Armijo had previously made to a handful of *americano* landgrabbers. Nor had the latter remained passive to his previous criticism of them. Already on March 30 of this year, Carlos Bent had again written most sarcastically about Padre Martínez, and with the same atrocious spelling.

This was in a letter from Taos to Manuel Álvarez in Santa Fe, who was an English-speaking Spaniard acting as U.S. consul at the time, and also one of Bent's associates in the landgrabbing syndicate. In it Bent quoted Álvarez as having written to another partner, Beaubien, that Padre Martínez had lent his press to the governor (Martínez de Lejanza) with the proviso that nothing was to be printed on it against his own person. But this was only a subterfuge, said Bent, since Padre Martínez himself had remarked at the time that it was to be used for exposing the wrong-doings of certain individuals – hence Bent wanted Álvarez to have an article of his own printed during the "chainge of Authoritys, if possible."[17] (Within a year, 1844-45, a triple change in the governorship did take place in quick order, from Martínez de Lejanza to José Chávez to Manuel Armijo once more.)[18]

In the same letter Bent made another charge against the Padre of Taos. He said that Martínez had wanted the governor to transfer a soldier guard (against wild Indian raids) from Ojo Caliente and El Rito to Red River; but his two attempts had failed because the arrogant priest cared less about the Red River settlements than he did about guarding his own people at San Cristóbal, as well as the large grazing and farming lands which the padre and his Martínez brothers owned between Arroyo Hondo and Red River. Bent also remarked with glee that the same padre, feeling quite merry at a certain American's wedding in Taos, had publicly said that the present governor was good for nothing and should be driven out of office.[19]

In connection with the land syndicate, there is a letter among the Valdez papers which is as difficult to decipher as it is to follow its line of thought. Valdez classified it as a vindication of his master following a suit which had been brought against him. The letter is addressed to the governor in Santa Fe, dated November 17, 1845, by Don José Benito Martínez, judge of the first instance of the district of

Taos. It starts with a request for information concerning crimes (against the padre) which the foreigner Carlos Beaubien had published on the governor's press, and of which he also had knowledge from two attached papers written by Beaubien as contained in an official act by Magistrate Don Mariano Lucero, president of the Council of the northern department. The said Beaubien, off since the end of October "toward the north," had not appeared when summoned. Now, to carry out his responsibility, Justice Martínez, from an *auto* which he had before him, referred to another cause which had been produced as evidence in the Rio Arriba court, as well as to a written decree of the governor, who was involved in the same cause. Here Beaubien had stated that he no longer preferred any charges, nor entertained any feelings one way or another concerning Padre Martínez and his brother Pascual. What is more, Beaubien himself, according to his own statement, no longer wished to pursue the matter.[20]

From everything about the land syndicate which has gone before, it can be seen that Padre Martínez harbored as much love and respect for all the *americanos* of good will, and that his particular enmity was reserved for those individuals in all ethnic categories – such as the American landgrabbing Bent and others, the Mexican Guadalupe Miranda, the Americanized Spaniard Álvarez, and his very own *paisanos* Manuel Armijo and Juan Bautista Vigil who had connived with them. To him it was the same raping of his beloved homeland which had been done down in New Spain by the rich *hacendados* under the Spanish monarchy, and was now being continued in Mexico under a supposedly republican government. Nor could his unyielding if heroic Hidalgo stance endear him further to his opponents, arrogant and intolerant as such messianism can be – and which has long since become apparent in the character of Padre Martínez, both in his proud statements about his own person and in his attitude toward anybody who crossed him, and more particularly in his relationship with the meek vicar of Santa Fe who had never done him any harm.

As for Padre Martínez' amicable regard for the good *americanos* in general, but most especially his admiration for what their nation stood for, this will soon become more evident in the months to come.

1846 — The United States / 12

On August 18, 1846, General Stephen Watts Kearny with his more modernly equipped Army of the West entered Santa Fe, when he promptly proclaimed New Mexico as a new part of his westward-expanding nation. Governor Manuel Armijo, who had loudly sworn never to surrender at the time he was assembling his civil and poorly armed militia of native volunteers, had abandoned his men just before the expected battle at Glorieta southeast of the Capital, and then had fled south toward El Paso del Norte with a company of regular dragoons from Mexico which he also had. Read's account of events, over and above Twitchell's own and the American military journals themselves, is of particular value for quoting the proclamations on both sides. He gives us Armijo's long harangue of bravado of August 8, 1846.[1]

However, one might credit Armijo with a wise and compassionate move, since his poorly armed irregulars would have been massacred by the much superior invading forces, although a subsequent rumor had it that he had also been bribed with a sizeable sum through an *americano* merchant in the Capital, and this was in keeping with his covetous character. Besides, the other native leaders in Santa Fe had not been against the invasion, and they very likely had persuaded him to take the course that he did. As for Padre Martínez up in Taos, we already know that he could not have been surprised by the turn of events, except perhaps for its timing. The year had started with New Mexico still safe as a Mexican Department when her twenty-fifth year under the Mexican flag began. On January 1, the padre had joined Padres Leyva and Gallegos in Santa Fe among the fourteen voters in the Assembly, and among several proposals discussed was a strengthening in military administration which all of them approved. Padre Martínez himself, like a good politician, proposed changes concerning local magistracies which would benefit his own district of Taos.[2]

The available Valdez papers in Spanish having run out by this time, we have to depend now on some faulty translations made by Larkin G. Read. According to these, the padre had written to Armijo on March 26 as the "Vicar of Taos," requesting to have himself licensed as a civil attorney. The long petition is replete with the involved niceties of old Spanish church-state law which the Taos padre always loved to cite, the conclusion of it all being that under certain circumstances a clergyman could act as a lawyer in cases which involved his ministry and his own relatives. Here he referred back to the year 1836 or 1837, when he had defended a niece of his in civil court. He gave no particulars, merely saying that he had included the case in a treatise on human rights which he had printed back in 1839.[3]

As we saw long before, he had been authorized by the bishop as a "vicar and ecclesiastical judge" to stand in civil court for cases involving parish matters. Perhaps this is why he now designated himself as the vicar of Taos, if Read's rendition of the term he used is correct. What he now wanted were also the powers of attorney to defend his relatives in court. To make it short, Armijo answered him briefly from Albuquerque on April 1, saying that he was forwarding his petition to the Assembly in Santa Fe. Then, on April 20, Don José Chávez and Don Miguel E. Pino gave their approval, but with the proviso that he did not exceed the limits of the laws he had so minutely cited.[4] It does look as though these two officials were no less dumbfounded than Armijo by the padre's pedantic citations, and so got the pesky priest off their backs with this hedging reply. Valdez, in his own continuing adulation of his master, used this incident as an unwarranted example of the padre's unbounded charity in helping his fellowmen without recompense.

There is also reference elsewhere to a meeting which Governor Armijo called for July 11, this one specifically to discuss the impending American invasion. According to it, the governor had summoned, through Padre Martínez' brother Pascual who was a colonel of militia, nine other men from Taos. Four of these were priests: Padres Martínez himself, Mariano Lucero, José María Valdez and Eulogio Valdez. Padre Martínez, however did not attend the junta.[5] Whether his absence has any significance or not, we do not know. Incidentally, Lucero was stationed at Picuris, and Eulogio Valdez at Abiquiú. There was no such Padre José María Valdez, unless this is a misreading of a Padre Jesús María Salazar, of whom there is only one single mention later on in 1850-51.[6]

Then came that momentous occasion when General Kearny took over New Mexico for the United States. Padre Martínez does not appear in the American military journals of the Kearny event, as did Padre Leyva anonymously when the army passed through San Miguel del Vado on its way to Santa Fe, as well as Vicar Ortiz after it had taken the Capital. Nor in Read or Twitchell for that matter, and other kindred sources. General Kearny had given his famous speech on civic and religious liberty on the 18th, and the next day Don Juan Bautista Vigil y Alarid had made a formal reply in the name of his people, all of them having now welcomed the new flag "with its stars and stripes." This man had been acting as governor since Armijo's flight.[7]

But, according to what Valdez wrote on his own, and as translated by Read, the American general had invited all the prominent natives of Santa Fe to confer with him shortly after his raising the American flag in front of the Palace; following this, he not only sent a special invitation to Padre Martínez, but dispatched twelve soldiers under "Captain Bent" to escort him back, along with some other Taos leaders. The padre came to Santa Fe with his brothers José María and Pascual, and all were sworn in as American citizens.[8] On the surface this looks like a forced invitation, but Valdez related it as a gesture of honor and highest esteem on Kearny's part. Then, after the padre had returned to Taos, General Kearny wrote to him personally, offering to buy or rent his printing press. Padre Martínez, as he had done before after a similar request by a Mexican governor, let the new government have it free of charge, and the first American work printed on it was what Valdez called "Kearny's Code" of military laws. After this the press was returned to Taos, and the padre continued with his own multiple projects during the peace which reigned after Kearny had appointed Carlos Bent as provisional civil governor under military rule.

This was on September 22, when four other Americans were made heads of the major departments, with one native, Donaciano Vigil, as general secretary. Of the three superior court justices appointed by Kearny was another native, Antonio José Otero, whom we shall meet again. This was also the day when Kearny's Code was promulgated. Despite what Twitchell says, Kearny left for California on September 3, leaving an infantry regiment with an extra batallion in Santa Fe, as well as an artillery battery.[9]

Around this very time, says Valdez, Padre Martínez began paying more attention to his law classes. Thoroughly convinced that the American occupation was to be a permanent one, he counseled his students to learn the English language. For this he purchased some books, which he himself began studying with the aid of a dictionary, while encouraging his students to do the same. Later on he was surprised to learn that the English pronunciation of vowels and consonants was different (from the Spanish) and so he started his studies all over again.[10] While there might be some truth in this, and whether it happened at this very time or not, one has to question Valdez as to Padre Martínez' surprising discovery at this late period. For a full score of years already, he had enjoyed the intimate acquaintance of his many American friends in Taos, at the very start conversing with them in a basic or pidgin-Spanish with innumerable gestures, as is the practice in similar situations everywhere, and writing down in his records the names of the illiterate as they sounded to his ear.

But in time, surely as the intellectual man that he was, he must have picked up many practical words and phrases in English, thus making it easier for him to converse with other *americanos* who came later, particularly when he instructed them prior to a marriage or baptism. We know that some printed material had been coming in with travellers on the Santa Fe Trail, one branch of which passed through Taos, and both his intelligence and curiosity must have told him that the English words as he heard them, while off-key from the straight Latin vowels, sometimes did not even sound as both the consonants and vowels were spelled. Even if he had not acquired any facility in speaking the language, his gifted brain must have come to grasp what the foreigners were saying. The French-Canadian trappers had to do the same, and we can presume that most of them lacked his brains.

What is of much more importance, Padre Martínez had long been acquainted with the principles on which his American friends' nation was founded, as we have already discerned in his utterances and writings. No doubt he had come to learn about the practical application of those principles from his conversations with them, but the solid knowledge that he had of the American federal system must have come from books, if not from Mexican ones which touched on the subject, from this or that treatise which had come over the Santa Fe Trail – the ones which Valdez says he had purchased. Whatever, Padre Martínez had already been definite sold, as we say, on the basic principles of American freedom, justice and equality. On the practical side he already foresaw a much better system of administration and a just application of its laws for everyone – in behalf of education, which had always been his chief concern, he envisioned all the children of the territory blessed with well-conducted schools; in the area of domestic life, there would follow a steadier import of household goods, conveyances and farming implements which the Santa Fe Trail had been introducing, and which had never been seen before; lastly, there would be a strong and dependable military force to protect the frontier villages and ranches from the wild Indian raids which had become more frequent and menacing than ever. These nomadic Indians, too, might then be brought to learn the advantages of civilized living.

All this might surprise those who have always held up the Padre of Taos as the staunchest of Mexican patriots. But the fact is that his nature and ideals went beyond mere national patriotism. He was first and foremost a humanist and humanitarian, not a chauvinist in its narrow sense. During his student days in Durango he had latched on to the ideals of the Mexican revolution which had promised a devoutly desired change from the despotism of the old European monarchies; and back home in his native New Mexico he had upheld them in order to produce a better life for his fellow citizens. But when he came to realize that all this had failed him through the unfortunate instability of the central Mexican government and the dictatorial antics of provincial governors which it could not stop, he began turning elsewhere even at the cost of giving up his long-cherished Hidalgo dream. If he intended it to continue, it was now more of a Jeffersonian dream.

Nor did his contemporaries understand this either, both among his native peers and the American newcomers. Besides lacking his vision, many were turned away by his own arrogant and overbearing ways when he thought himself in the right. And so he soon had to suffer the same arrows which fortune had let loose at him ten years before, during and after the War of the Chimayoses in 1837.

During the first fifteen weeks or so, following General Kearny's entry and his establishment of a provisional government under the military, peace and contentment reigned among the Hispanic New Mexicans and their newly-acquired fellow citizens who spoke English. As one gathers from the military accounts, Kearny and the men with him, while enroute to California, were well received in the towns of the Rio Abajo along the way. In Santa Fe, the military officers had little to do except attend parties and plays with the native and English-speaking citizens and their wives, Vicar Ortiz taking part in them. All of these males, including the ordinary soldiery, also found exciting recreation at a drinking and gambling salon (of Doña Tules Barceló), while Governor Bent tried to bring some semblance of puritanical sobriety by ordering the place and the merchant houses to close on Sundays.[11]

What then happened as December began reminds one strongly of the modern young terrorists throughout the world today. Whether around the first day or the twelfth, a cabal of hot-headed younger *caballeros* with their humbler followers hatched a plot to kill all the Americans, as well as the native leaders who were collaborating with them. The ringleaders were that Diego Archuleta whose election to the Mexican Congress had been forced by Manuel Armijo – and whom Padre Martínez happened to like – and Don Tomás Ortiz who was a much younger half-brother of Vicar Ortiz. Read adds a third fellow, Don José Manuel Gallegos (a Santa Fe layman who happened to have the same full name of Padre Gallegos, the pastor of Albuquerque). Tomás Ortiz was slated to be the next governor, while Archuleta looked forward to being the commanding general. Needless to say, it was a foolhardy plot, considering all the circumstances, but, like the terrorists just mentioned, they did not count the costs and that their attempt was doomed to failure. Midnight of December 12 was set as the fatal hour but, poorly organized as they were, the blow was postponed until the 24th. The reckless plotters must have been thinking that the Catholics, especially a third of the American soldiers, would be in church for *la misa del gallo*, while the rest of the *americanos* would be celebrating the Holy Night in their homes and at the barracks.

But the plot was discovered in time through the viligance of Colonel Sterling Price, and as a result some of the plotters fled south to Chihuahua and others north into the mountains of Rio Arriba. [12] Others say that Governor Bent himself first got wind of the plot, and still others that Doña Tules Barceló had learned of it at her bistro and then had warned the authorities. Whichever way the rebellion was discovered, it was a comic opera plot at best. There was absolutely no way for the plot to succeed. Yet, no sooner was the excitement over than rumor began implicating Padre Martínez as the mastermind. The rumor grew into certainty well into our century, as when Twitchell wrote that Padre Martínez had been behind it all, from what others had been claiming ever since the thing first happened. It had been the style of those earlier times among certain Anglo-Americans and even some of the native politicians to blame the native clergy for anything that went wrong. Vicar Ortiz had been likewise suspected, obviously because of his half-brother, and also Padre Leyva of San Miguel for whatever reason. Then there was Padre Gallegos, evidently because one of the plotters had the same name. However, in the military trials which had immediately followed, not the least evidence had been found against any of these padres, but, as just said, the same rumors had persisted, focusing more and more on the Padre of Taos. This was mainly because of what took place shortly thereafter up in Taos, during January of 1847, after the December Santa Fe uprising had been nipped in the bud.

Confident that peace had been entirely restored, or else heedless of rumors from the north, Governor Carlos Bent went up to Taos on January 14 in order to see about his family. For he and Kit Carson, who was away at the time, had married two Jaramillo women there years before. With Bent were Pablo Jaramillo, his brother-in-law, Narciso Beaubien and some others. Five days later Bent and these men were cruelly massacred by a Taos mob, along with (Stephen) Louis Lee, the acting sheriff, Cornelio Vigil, the prefect and probate judge, and James W. Leal, an American circuit-lawyer. [13]

Valdez gives his own version from the Taos point of view. After relating how, at daybreak of the 19th, Bent had been roused out of bed by the rebel mob of Indians and Mexicans who had besieged his residence, and then had been killed along with Jaramillo and Beaubien, he says that Padre Martínez was on his way to the church to celebrate Mass when he was halted by the screams and sight of a man running toward him. It was Elliot Lee (whom he baptized "José Elías" three days later!) being pursued by the mob. The padre asked the rebels what it was all about and, when they told him what had already happened, he began berating them vehemently as plain murderers. But they did not dare stop him when he took Lee into his house. They came back later to tell him that they had also killed the two Mexicans (Jaramillo and Vigil) because of "their adherence to the Americans." Valdez also says that the mob had burned the town's official records. [14]

Padre Martínez, of course, stoutly continued his harangue. He told the revolutionaries that there were many more Americans still alive (in Santa Fe and other places) whom they would have to deal with, but they answered that they were positive that every single one in the territory had been wiped out – since this had been the appointed day for the general massacre. Besides, a general called Urrea was on his way from Mexico with a force of 2,000 men! [15] From this one can assume that a lower class of terrorists at Santa Fe, because their high-born leaders had already fled, had now failed to carry out their own part of the bargain, no doubt realizing at the same time that they were no match for the American troops in the Capital. According to Twitchell and others, the Taos rebels had also destroyed a distillery in nearby Arroyo Hondo, killing seven Americans there, while at Mora over the sierra a number of American traders, who were well liked by the good Mora inhabitants, had also been cruelly exterminated by the same type of rebels. [16]

Coming back to Padre Martínez' fearless confrontation of the mob, a man named Pablo Montoya, who had been away from Taos for a long time, suddenly made his appearance. The rebels cheered him wildly and chose him as their commanding general on the spot, something which he accepted rather reluctantly. Meanwhile the padre kept chastizing the insurgents as Christian brethren gone paganly berserk, and warning them that their terrible crimes had provoked the ire of the American government. They had killed defenseless people, he told them, while they were asleep, but now they would find it much more difficult to attack and kill well-armed civilized troops. To this their leaders replied that they did not fear the cannons, confident that these would be blown away by the wind – what sounds like Indian talk – because they themselves were on God's side. It was then that Montoya ordered the mob to retire, and here Valdez adds that the insurgent leaders had been greatly disappointed because Padre Martínez was not with them. But, so great was their respect for his person, that they dared not harm him even after he had given safe harbor to an American. [17]

Just as Padre Martínez had warned the rebels, there was a quick military reprisal from Santa Fe. Twitchell and Read provide a succinct account of Colonel Price's Taos campaign. Setting out from the Capital's garrison with 480 men and four field pieces, he encountered some 2,000 of the insurgents at Santa Cruz under two leaders named Ortiz and Montoya; he defeated them during a fight which lasted toward sundown, and then caught up with those who had fled northward, routing them also. After arriving in Taos, Price marched his men to the Indian pueblo where the rest of the rebels had fortified themselves, fired a few artillery rounds, and then withdrew to Don Fernando with his troops. This was on the evening of February 3. The next day, at nine in the morning, he launched his now famous assault through which the rebels were completely defeated. The walls of the centuries-old mission church of San Gerónimo were also pounded down by the cannon balls.[18]

Again from the Taos point of view, Valdez tells us that Padre Martínez, as the head of the better classes of people, had gathered their families inside three private residences. These houses were the padre's own and those of Buenaventura Valdez and Raymundo Córdova, where they all remained huddled until Colonel Price arrived. (Pedro Sánchez, who condenses the Valdez narrative, claimed that Padre Martínez had previously sent a messenger to Price, notifying him of the insurrection.) Valdez goes on to say that the insurgents, upon realizing that not all of the Americans had been exterminated elsewhere, sent two companies in the direction of Santa Fe. The first contingent met Price's army at Santa Cruz where it was badly defeated, and where their leader Jesús Tafoya was killed. Price then came upon the second one at Embudo and promptly put it to rout, the individual escapees dispersing to their homes and their leaders into the mountains.

Those who were from the Taos valley came back to their homes and then began fortifying themselves in order to continue their resistance, and this is when, on February 1, a "general" named Pablo Chávez called on Padre Martínez, to ask him why he was sheltering all those people, contending that his own followers did not want to harm them or him. The padre replied that they were there because of the atrocities which had been perpetrated by his followers, telling him in a lengthy discourse that he and his men had to give a strict account to God for their misdeeds. Chávez himself was rendered speechless by this, as well as by the defiant yelling which followed from young and old within the padre's house. Padre Martínez then counseled him to go back and inform his men about their great folly, promising to intercede for them before the American commander who was on his way to Taos. However, he insisted, their leaders had to be turned in. Chávez promised to do so, but he did nothing of the kind.[19]

Colonel Price and his troops arrived on February 3 at 10 o'clock in the morning, Valdez continues, when Padre Martínez, Elliot Lee and other citizens went out to meet him waving a flag of peace. The padre, through Lee, informed the colonel of everything that had taken place in Taos, at the same time requesting him to pardon the poor families now wandering about in the mountains out of fear of being punished. Price did so, ordering word to be sent out for them to return to their homes. Then Price led his forces to the Indian pueblo but refrained from attacking it, bringing back his men to Don Fernando. This made the Indians and others with them believe that the American soldiers were afraid of them, and they began revelling after such an easy victory. Colonel Price, who had set up his headquarters in the padre's house, confided to Padre Martínez that this had been a ruse of his to keep the Indians from fleeing from their pueblo during the night. Next day, at nine in the morning, the battle of Taos Pueblo began. The Indians were strongly entrenched behind the sturdy adobe wall which surrounded their village. But Price's troops, by assaulting it all around with cannon rounds and dashes by the cavalry, while the infantry attacked the pueblo's front, had the enemy surrendering by one in the afternoon.[20]

After this, the colonel sent Padre Martínez to retrieve the vestments and other sacred articles from the pueblo church, which had been "burned down," and also to bury the dead. On the sixth day (after doing some reconnoitering elsewhere), Colonel Price stopped in to see the padre. A Carlos Ortiz also came in with Pablo Montoya as his prisoner, and now a court-martial was held in the house of Padre Martínez. Montoya was found guilty and then was hanged on the plaza – across from the courthouse of Valdez' day. Afterward, the rest of the rebel leaders were tried in district court, which was presided over by Judge Carlos Beaubien. All were provided with defense attorneys, and in the end some were judged innocent while those found guilty were hanged.[21]

When writing to Bishop Zubiría on October 4, 1848, after cursorily reviewing the American occupation of New Mexico from the very first rumors in 1845 to the accomplished fact in August 1846, Padre Martínez told his bishop about the latest uprising by a number of prejudiced Mexicans which was similar to the one of "37 and 38." The pueblo church had been completely destroyed, he said, and the American commander had delivered the vestments to him; these and other such articles were now in the church of Don Fernando. He went on to say that in January of this same year some American soldiers had broken into his Taos sacristy and had made off with most of the sacred vessels and vestments. But as soon as he notified the "General," the latter sent troops who captured the culprits; then he had them publicly whipped, after which he ordered them to leave the country and not to return under pain of death. Otherwise, the padre added, everything went on as usual. The American officers had treated him and others with all respect and every mark of consideration, and promised to do so in the future. As for the Taos Indians, he said, knowing them to be good Christians, he had asked them to repair the schoolhouse for use as a church, where he now said Mass on certain Sundays – and trusting that the bishop would approve of this. He closed by saying that, early in the preceding year, a newspaper (in Santa Fe) had attacked "our Religion and its priests," and that he had answered the unjust charges and would continue to do the same in the future.[22]

Thus ended the War of the Taoseños, but, as with the termination of the War of the Chimayoses ten years before, it was not the end of Padre Martínez' troubles in connection with the latest one, just as it had not been after the first uprising. Once again, went the political rumors, he had been the secret instigator of one and then of the other. These false accusations persisted even into the current century, and we have a good example in Twitchell, fair man that he was in every way, stating that the house of Padre Martínez was generally regarded as the headquarters of the insurrection. "His power over his parishioners was absolute and his hatred of the Americans and American institutions was recognized by all."(!) Ample proof for this, he wrote, were opinions expressed by such men as Governor Bent, Colonel St. Vrain and Colonel Kit Carson! Moreover, Pascual Martínez had once commanded a company under Governor Armijo in Mexican times, and hence persons still living held that he had participated in the rebellion at the instigation of his brother the priest![23]

Such is the logic of politics, which Twitchell failed to question, and of a certain type of individuals, like the editors of that newspaper mentioned by Martínez, whose bigotry was no less ethnic than religious.

All of the preceding accounts more than suffice to show that it was not in Padre Martínez to see the new American regime overturned, much less in such a savage manner which had no hope of success to start with. If certain matters had to be righted, and undesireable individuals removed from office, it had to be rather in the halls of debate, and for this he foresaw native young men following his lead in the civil assemblies. As he was telling his students around this time, as worded by Sánchez from the recollections of some of them, and perhaps his own:

> Muchachos, you came to this college to study with the purpose of being ordained priests; in this regard I have done my utmost so that you might attain the desired end. But, since there has been a change in government, it becomes necessary to have a change in ideas. The nature of the American government goes in complete harmony with the toleration of cults and a complete separation of Church and State. From this you can logically conclude that the clergy's razor has lost its edge.

Then, when a pupil asked him what the form of the American government was, and he answered that it was republican, he also added, "You might say that by way of comparison the American government is a burro, but on this burro ride the barristers and not the clergy."[24]

This discourse is obviously sauced with Sánchez' own anti-clerical notions, as were Valdez' often, but the meat and the way of serving it are those of Padre Martínez. What he meant regarding the clergy's power was not so much a picture of past conditions in New Mexico as that more general one of Mexico while under monarchical Spain, and to a certain extent after that. His last quip reveals his own view of democracy as he had experienced it – the common people free to rule themselves but still an imperfect system so long as there was no enlightened leadership. He had been seeing this going on in Mexico where petty chiefs tended to become as dictatorial as the aristocrats of monarchy had been. As for ignorant leadership, he must have had in mind the public uprisings of 1837, and not too long ago the one of 1847. Hence a republican form of government was indeed a stumbling ass which had to be led and ridden by dedicated well-informed men – and here he naturally was thinking of himself. It was the old Hidalgo dream becoming ever more Jeffersonian. Therefore, the lads should seriously pursue the study of law and government rather than theology as future leaders of their people.

It followed that he had to provide them with a prime example. Having been elected from his district to the very first provisional Territorial Assembly, he met in Santa Fe with twelve of his native and English-language peers on October 10-14, 1848, and these in their turn chose him their president! Under his guidance they formulated a petition to Washington for the speedy organization of a purely civil government, meanwhile accepting Kearny's military code with necessary alterations. It was a long list of proposals calling for federal action in every branch of public endeavor, much like the practices pursued today in every state. But among them were two protestations about something which greatly bothered the members at this particular time, concerning current rumors – and the wish of certain Anglo-American residents – about the annexation of New Mexico to Texas and the introduction of black slavery.[25] Here one can see how much Padre Martínez was violently opposed to both ideas, and both of them having to do with the *tejanos*.

After this, says Valdez, the governor issued a short edict which was consonant with Padre Martínez' thinking. It stated that every citizen was free to recur to the religious minister of his choice; as for the matter of rendering church dues or fees, this was no longer obligatory but had to be purely voluntary. Hence, said he, Padre Martínez decided not to demand the church fees which had been customary all along, leaving his parishioners to give what they pleased.[26] What the governor had in mind, even if he had stated it rather ambiguously, was good American doctrine, which granted every American citizen the right to choose his own religion as well as his particular church with its minister. But Padre Martínez, and Valdez after him, misconstrued this as having to do with the *internal* regulations of any given church body, whether Catholic or Protestant, once the individual had made his free choice. This same misconception lay at the bottom of most serious disputes in which the Padre of Taos would become involved in years to come. In short, he unwittingly was having the new government interfering with the practice of religion against its own principles, so blind could he become once he clamped his mind on what can be called a fixed idea.

In fact, in this very same yar of 1848, he had stuck his nose into an internal church problem which was none of his business, and evidently because it also gave him the chance to get at Vicar Juan Felipe Ortiz. The matter has also to do with the same gross misconception among some of the native officials, who erroneously thought that they could meddle in internal church affairs under the American system, as had their predecessors in far back Spanish church-state times, and more recently during the short Mexican regime. Twitchell relays a couple of examples. Donaciano Vigil, who had followed the murdered Bent as governor, for some reason or other suspended Vicar Ortiz from his church post – Twitchell prefacing this with the unwarranted statement that Vicar Ortiz was regarded as an enemy of American institutions. Then, down in the parish of Belén, the local native magistrate had kicked out the lawful pastor and had replaced him with a priest who, as we shall see, was under Bishop Zubiría's suspension.[27]

This second example brings us to the affair in which Padre Martínez had nothing to say, but did. Young Padre Nicolás Valencia, one of his former students according to Valdez, was a devious character as we learn from other sources. After having been suspended by his bishop on February 25 for gravest disobedience, he had stayed on at Belén with the support of the local *alcalde*, who drove out Padre José Antonio Otero whom the bishop had placed there as pastor. It is a long involved story which has nothing to do with Padre Martínez otherwise. A year later, Valencia would be joined by a vagrant and still more devious ex-friar from Mexico City, Benigno Cárdenas by name, in creating a most scandalous schism with the aid of the native magistrates of Belén and Tomé who were backed by Justice Antonio José Otero, one of the three territorial judges appointed by Kearny. The odd personalities and crazy antics of Valencia and Cárdenas will be the subjects of studies to be published in the near future. But now to Padre Martínez' indirect interference.

Vicar Ortiz, as fully authorized by Bishop Zubiría, had been doing his best to solve the Belén problem, but this had not set well with Donaciano Vigil in his accidental position of temporary governor. As Valdez has it, Vigil consulted Padre Martínez, and the latter then answered him with all the legalistic pedantry which he always delighted in, and which Valdez quotes at full length as if it were to his master's credit. Vicar Ortiz had been all wrong in his procedures, the Taos padre said in concluding his arguments, just has he had been in a previous case involving young Padre Tomás Abeyta as pastor of Isleta. (Abeyta was another former Martínez student whom Vicar Ortiz had shipped off to the bishop for similar acts of insubordination.) Furthermore, wrote Martínez, not only had the Church's canon law been violated, but all the censures imposed on Valencia were invalid because the issuance of such censures had been abolished by the American government![28]

Actually, the first censures had bene imposed by Bishop Zubiría himself, but here again we see Padre Martínez, who should have known better, misapplying the American doctrine of religious freedom to the internal affairs of a given church. But, as said at the start, while trying to excuse two protegés of his who were clearly in the wrong, he was underhandedly getting at his legitimate church superior whose high position he had always resented. However, these Valencia troubles in Belén were minor when compared with the ones caused by both Valencia and Cárdenas in the following year of 1849, and this was no doubt the main reason for a third pastoral visitation of New Mexico by Bishop Zubiría in 1850. We know that the Belén-Tomé schism took a great deal of the Bishop's attention during his stay, and so he might have refrained from questioning Padre Martínez about his lesser capers.

On the contrary, according to Valdez, the good prelate had nothing but praise for Padre Martínez and his work, referring to the visitation entries in the Taos parish registers. In these we do find the bishop's secretary, as of September 6, 1850, repeating the same commendations which his clerk predecessor had written during the second visitation of 1845. He also found a surplus in the parish funds, a savings by Martínez prior to the governor's supposed edict about church fees, after which he had not collected any. So as not to contravene the governor's order, the secretary wrote, the customary fees would no longer be obligatory – and here one has to conclude that Martínez had given the bishop his own misconception of the decree. In spite of this, wrote the secretary, while burial fees were to be left to the consciences of the bereaved, the financial needs of the parish would have to be met with a scale of prices according to the grave sites selected. Here he went into details about their locations within the church and in the cemetery.[29]

At this time, as mentioned long before, the bishop declared the Guadalupe church of Don Fernando a full-fledged parish headquarters, a status which was nothing but proper for the pastor's own title of *cura propio*. Here again, in the Read translation, Martínez is quoted in connection with the "Vicariate of Taos," as if he now considered himself in rivalry with Vicar Ortiz in Santa Fe. The Taos padre here wrote that he was paying the sacristan's salary out of his own pocket, and that the other expenses had to be borne by the parishioners; he said that the sacristan had told him that the town magistrate had refused to furnish him with hands to repair the rectory roof, at the same time excusing some of his parishioners from paying him their dues because they had promised to build the church towers and keep the structure in repair.[30] Evidently, his vaunted church-state principle could be bent according to his whim or the call of the moment.

We might finally ask at this juncture if Bishop Zubiría had talked with Padre Martínez during his visit, if not about the differences between him and Vicar Ortiz, about the "deformed" *santos* which had not been removed from the churches and chapels, or about the "butcherlike" Penitentes which had kept on proliferating in the north country. We know that Padre Trujillo of Santa Cruz, just five years before, had warned Padre Gallegos at San Juan about their activities within his parish, referring him to Bishop Zubiría's condemnation of them in 1833.[31] Evidently Trujillo had not dared to remind his former teacher of this same decree, as when the latter had come to say Masses for them in Chimayó. Nothing of this appears in the Martínez papers available to us through Valdez, who by now has more of his own lengthy comments colored as before by his own opinions. Nor, from what we know about him by now, would Padre Martínez have preserved or recorded anything that was not laudatory where he himself was concerned. Or else Bishop Zubiría had preferred to say nothing to him and the other padres about the abuses which he had outlined in his 1833 pastoral, and which had never been remedied.

For, from what we gather from his very much briefer than usual pastoral letter – and written from El Paso del Norte on December 3 while enroute back home – he seems to have given up all hopes about any forthcoming reforms so sadly needed in the region.[32] The only thing that he did, like a tired man burdened by advancing age as well as his heavy responsibilities and difficult travels, was to refer the New Mexico clergy to his long and detailed pastoral of 1833. Once again he advised them to study the document and put its decrees into effect – but as though with the feeling that none of this would be done. It is for this reason that he might have refrained from bringing up these matters with the individual priests, especially when his attention had been distracted almost completely by that serious schism at Belén and Tomé, and for the solution of which he had found it necessary to negotiate with the civil authorities under a new government which was foreign to him.[33]

On the political scene, during September of 1849, Padre Martínez had been one of the nineteen delegates chosen to prepare a full territorial plan of government; again he had been elected president of this body without any opposition. Then, in June of 1850, he stood foremost in having New Mexico's First Territorial Constitution adopted.[34] As a result, he finally saw his beloved homeland become a full-fledged Territory of the United States with the inauguration of Governor James C. Calhoun on March 3, 1851. Among the members of the first Territorial Legislature, we find the supposedly rebel and anti-United States native padres: Martínez himself heading the five in the Council from the counties of Taos and Rio Arriba; Vicar Ortiz and Padre Leyva in the group representing those of Santa Fe and San Miguel; and Padre Gallegos in the one from the counties of Bernalillo and Santa Ana.[35]

At this period, says Valdez, Governor Calhoun had written to Padre Martínez "as a learned and intelligent citizen of broad experience in regard to what is needed in this country." Better laws were needed, wrote Calhoun, as well as the best men to bring them about, and therefore he requested him to work toward this end with a Mr. George Gould (of Taos). He ended by offering the padre his own house as his headquarters during his stay in the Capital. On July 14 the Legislature assembled in full session, and once again Padre Martínez was elected its president, He was a most active member, Valdez continues, during 1852-1853 when many good laws were enacted and passed through his staunch support.[36] Here ends what we have of the Valdez assorted collection of pieces which have been designated as "Notes."

There is also an item around this time which serves to illustrate the padre's attitude where both religion and education were concerned. A Baptist minister named H.W. Read had gone up to Taos during May to confer with the leading citizens, mostly americanos but including Padre Martínez, about establishing an academy there for both sexes. All were for it, but not before the padre had asked Mr. Read if it was to be a Protestant school. Then he gave his assent after the minister explained, whether truthfully or not, that it would be like the public schools in the eastern states. However, he declined to allow him to preach in his church on the score that this was against ecclesiastical discipline.[37]

When one looks back to the Taos rebellion of 1847 and everything which followed up to this point, one begins to wonder why, in spite of the facts to the contrary, subsequent writers could so blandly assert that Padre Martínez had been rabidly anti-American and against all American institutions. Or why, likewise with reference to the Santa Cruz revolt of ten years before, he was said to have wielded absolute power over the common people. It all went back to the deliberately malicious lies and libels peculiar to politics, and no less to the combined ethnic and religious bigotry of certain ones among the newcomers – like those first newspaper editors who still looked down on their fellow citizens of Hispanic or Mexican descent, and most especially their clergy, as low-down Catholic Mexicans.

By now this same type of liar and scandalmonger had already begun composing the scenario for the last act in the life of the Padre of Taos. But this time it had for its backdrop an altogether new dispensation covering the ecclesiastical field in the main, but not without asides into the political wings on either end of the stage.

PART TWO / A New Testament

A Friendly French Bishop / 13

Like the wars of the Chimayoses and the Taoseños of 1837 and 1847 ending in the same month almost ten years apart, each one during radically different civil regimes, there were exactly five years between the occupation of New Mexico by the United States in 1846 and a similar great change which took place in her church government in 1851. This would as deeply affect the life-drama of the Padre of Taos, but with a much more poignant outcome for its being the closing third act of a play which the Muse of History had seemingly intended to be a classic tragedy from the start. It was like a New Testament appended to the Old, and in some respects with their variances in perspective.

As in the first two acts, which can be captioned the Mexican and the American, Padre Martínez would once again strut onto the stage with no less verve and self-confidence than he had done all along, and here in a final act which might as well be called the French one for reasons which will become progressively evident.

It was on August 9, 1851, five years almost to the day after General Kearny had astounded the populace of Santa Fe with his marching columns of blue-clad troops on the 18th of the same month, that two Frenchmen named Lamy and Machebeuf entered the ancient royal villa in a similar blaze of military fanfare. But this was not an armed conquest of any sort. Some three weeks before, Vicar Don Juan Felipe Ortiz had received a most surprising notice from Padre José Antonio Otero of Socorro, in which this priest enclosed or else fully quoted a message of July 1 from El Paso del Norte. It was from "Don Juan Lamy" announcing his impending arrival in their homeland as her bishop in his capacity of Vicar Apostolic of New Mexico. Vicar Ortiz had promptly sent out circulars to all his priests on July 14 counseling them to receive their new prelate with all the honors and respect due his exalted office.[1] Not only that. He got all of his Santa Fe parishioners, the civil *americano* as well as native authorities, and even the commander of the military post, to begin preparations for a grand reception, the likes of which Santa Fe had never seen before. He not only had his own house refurbished as the bishop's residence-to-be, but had rushed a full hundred miles south to greet his new superior in Christ, promptly returning to oversee the final preparations.

And a most triumphant reception it turned out to be for Bishop Jean Baptiste Lamy, as well as an occasion of the greatest rejoicing for all the common folk besides their leaders, as the new bishop and his companions were escorted by them from three miles out of town to the parish church of San Francisco and his new residence – all amid the squeaking of fancy official carriages (including the governor's own on which he was invited to ride), the stamping of the marching soldiers' boots and the blare of the military band, not to speak of the booming of cannon salutes. We have all this from the most enthusiastic descriptions by Bishop Lamy himself and by his aide and vicar, Joseph P. Machebeuf, as well as from another by a native spectator of the event, Don Demétrio Pérez – who happened to be the son of that Mexican governor murdered far back in 1837.[2]

None of the other native padres of the distant outside parishes had come to the affair. They were represented by the chief host, Vicar Ortiz, and his assistant Padre José de Jesús Luján. The evident reason for it is that they could not have been apprised of the precise time of the bishop's arrival. Padre Martínez up in Taos, however, could have had his own reasons even if he had known the precise day, as we shall see. But, had he been there, his intrusive presence would most certainly have made a deep enough impression for Lamy and Machebeuf to remember him among the lavish praises which they had for Vicar Ortiz. This observation is made here because one writer after another to our day has contended that, no sooner was the grand reception over than Vicar Ortiz and all of the native clergy began questioning Lamy's authority to the point of defiance. At first they got this from a very general statement made fifty years later by Archbishop Salpointe, when he wrote that the native priests and people were suspicious of all strangers, and hence Bishop Lamy had soon left for Durango to consult with his predecessor.[3] It was an innocent observation by a good man who was neither a historian nor a master of English, and we know by now that the people had long become accustomed to strangers. Others much later on backed it up with a gross lie which Machebeuf told the Roman Curia five years after he arrived, as will be shown later on.

Nothing could be farther from the truth, as a careful study of all the documentation shows. According to some of the same superficial writers, Padre Martínez of Taos was the one most disturbed by the new turn of events, by merely referring to a letter which he wrote to Bishop Zubiría on August 28. But this letter has nothing of the kind. It concerned itself mainly with financial matters following the change in church administration. While apologizing to the Durango bishop for the meager tithes collected in October of the previous year, due to a severe drought and a plague of grasshoppers all over New Mexico and especially in the Taos district, Padre Martínez went on to say that certain obligations connected with the support of the Durango seminary no longer held, some of them having to do with personal debts of his in this regard; therefore, new dispositions had to be arranged with regard to the parishes of New Mexico since the region had just been created into a separate bishopric under Don Juan Lamy. While grieved by this separation of his homeland from the diocese of Durango, he wrote, he acknowledged with resignation that it all had come about by that authority (the Pope) who thought it best. He said nothing else about the new bishop, whom he duly accepted for the reasons given. But, in his habitual political frame of mind, he unreasonably concluded that all this had been brought about by certain *vecinos* and *americanos* who had allegedly held a meeting for this purpose.[4]

Much less did Padre Martínez ever bear any envy or resentment against Bishop Lamy solely for being his legitimate prelate, not only at this time but to his dying day even after they came to lock horns much later. He soon had to learn that it was the American hierarchy in the eastern states which, after pin-pointing Santa Fe on the map as the historical capital of the only well-populated area in the newly acquired American Southwest, had petitioned the Holy See to establish a vicariate apostolic there. Pope Pius IX had acquiesced by "bulls" of July 19 and 23, 1850, appointing as first bishop a French missionary who had been laboring for past years in the diocese of Cincinnati in Ohio.[5] As Padre Martínez might have put it, *Roma locuta causa finita*. However, had there ever been the least notion in his mind that his New Mexico was to have her own bishopric during his lifetime, we can be sure that he would have set his sights on it. Only then, one can almost say with certainty, would he have been disappointed and resentful, and especially if the appointee had been Vicar Ortiz. In fact, he most likely was very much pleased now by the fact that the latter's long vicarial authority had come to an end.

All this is because he had never heard that, as far back as 1634, a Franciscan *custodio*, whose name was Fray Alonso Benavides, had proposed a diocese for New Mexico. Both the Spanish Court and the Roman Curia had ignored the proposal because the Spanish population was so small at the time, while the Indians were still in what was called their heathendom. As matters stood, the Franciscan custos in mission lands enjoyed the authority of a bishop anyway, besides the episcopal privilege of administering Confirmation and conferring the minor orders leading to the priesthood. (The second one was never used, although lying accusations were made in this regard.) These extraordinary powers had been conferred upon the major Franciscan superiors in mission areas by papal decrees, called as a body the *Omnímoda*, for mission lands far away from any episcopal See. But the bishops of New Spain, like Mexico City and Guadalajara, had always senselessly fought such *custodios* who were not consecrated bishops like themselves, and the mission programs had suffered thereby.[6]

It was only in more modern times that the authorities in Rome had hit upon the idea of provisional mission dioceses which they called "vicariates apostolic," and which were headed by real bishops directly responsible to a new mission bureau of the Vatican called the Propaganda Fide. Nor did Padre Martínez, coming back to his present attitude in these matters, know that even as late as 1812, when he was a nineteen-year-old bridegroom, New Mexico's delegate to the Spanish Cortes had made a proposal like the one of Padre Benavides long before, only to be ignored for whatever reason.[7] Hence the creation of a provisional bishopric in his homeland had come as a complete surprise indeed.

Going back to Bishop Lamy himself and his aide Vicar Machebeuf, we find just as surprising a change in their own attitude following the euphoria of their grand civic and military reception which had been prepared for them by the now ex-Vicar Ortiz. While the latter had been left in his post as pastor of Santa Fe, with Padre Luján continuing as his assistant, both Lamy and Machebeuf now began writing abroad about the gravest suspicions they were having with regard to the native clergy. These, they said, were not only decrepit with age but careless and lazy from lifelong habit; worse yet, wrote Machebeuf, they were all horrible lechers who dreaded a reform of their sexual morals besides![8] But how could they have found this out so recently, when they had not been out of Santa Fe as yet, nor had they met most of the native padres so far? This again brings us to a most necessary digression, one which has to do with the two Frenchmen's characters and background, as well as with certain dormant suspicions they had brought along, and which were now being stirred up anew by their American contacts in the Capital.

Both men, as we learn from the least of their admiring biographers to the much more prominent, came from very pious peasant families in southern France where the Catholic atmosphere had become quite puritanical, or "jansenistic" as Catholic historians put it. Lamy himself had always been a quiet dignified person, and handsome in a way, but subject to spells of depression in times of stress. Machebeuf, on the other hand, was a runt of a fellow who since boyhood had suffered certain "chasms and delusions." (In religious circles it was a spiritual malady called "scrupulosity," an irrational fear of already being damned which ultimately had a sexual basis.) Otherwise he was a determined little fighter.[9] But, as we shall see, with that ingrained spiritual *malaise* which was both attracted to and repelled by anything of a sexual nature, especially in connection with priests. From all that he wrote, one also finds that he loved to exaggerate like a gossipy hen, and was not averse to deliberate lying when it suited his sexual preoccupation best.[10]

Ever since their seminary days, Lamy and Machebeuf had become the most intimate of friends (an *amicitia particularis* or *amitié particuliere* frowned upon in the ascetical manuals), Lamy having come to lean upon his tougher little friend in weaker moments, especially when they left their native land together as recently ordained priests to labor in Ohio. And so it was inevitable that when Lamy was made the bishop of a faraway New Mexico in the western wilderness, Machebeuf had to come with him as his right-arm man.[11] The famed Willa Cather in her classic novel, *Death Comes for the Archbishop*, made this intimate friendship her theme, as something most wonderful to behold. So does another notable author, Paul Horgan, in his more biographical *Lamy of Santa Fe*, in which the characterizations just made are definitely more cavalier. Hence the psycho-religious comments in parentheses. But, as we shall be seeing all the way, this very "particular friendship" would be at the bottom of the many troubles which were to arise in the relationship of both Frenchmen with the native clergy of New Mexico.

This brings us to those suspicions which had suddenly come to life. From the similar phrasing in the letters of both Frenchmen, one can tell that they had been discussing this matter between themselves far into the night. And as one learns from their previous letters and sundry biographers, it all had started down in Texas. For reasons of his own, Bishop Lamy, who was followed sometime later by Machebeuf, had set out from Ohio toward his vicariate by way of New Orleans and Galveston. Here the Galveston Vicariate was also headed by a French bishop, Jean-Marie Odin by name, who began filling their heads with all kinds of evil things concerning the native people and clergy of a New Mexico which he had never seen.[12] Some such stories had been rampant ever since the two defeats suffered by the Texan invaders of New Mexico a decade before; others had been filtering down through American travellers and merchants whose anti-Catholic and anti-Mexican bigotry stands out clearly in the journals which some of them wrote. However, after Lamy and Machebeuf with their small party had reached El Paso del Norte to the north, and then on their last lap up to Santa Fe, the two French clergymen had been sent into repeated rhapsodies by the enthusiastic welcome which the priests and people tendered them along the way. Only once did Bishop Lamy make a passing remark of suspicion in one of his letters, "from what I have heard and the little I have seen here." [13] The little that he had seen must have been the female servants and their children in the padres' houses, enough to arouse bad thoughts in Machebeuf and elicit comments from him – and thus stir up in Lamy's mind what Odin had poured into his ear.

At this point, one cannot help but think of Padre Martínez in Taos, and consequently conclude that Lamy and Machebeuf were right in their suspicions. But this would be following their logic. One man's failings cannot be extended to his peers merely on the score of race and circumstance and much less without positive proof.

Finally, when Bishop Lamy and his party reached Santa Fe, they were totally overwhelmed by their grand reception as we have seen. Speaking of his party, there is ample evidence to show that the bishop and his vicar had not made their long and tedious trek from San Antonio all alone, with only a pair of lay youths, as all the biographers have written with so much awe. There were two other priests with them whom Machebeuf referred to once in passing as a Pole and a Spaniard but did not name – and very likely another French one. [14] The names of the first two were Alexander Grzelachowski, whom we shall meet again, and Antonio Severo Borrajo, who did not stay; the possible third priest was Jean François Pinard, who appears in Santa Fe with them in that same month of August. [15] Nor had the trip been that arduous, even when one considers the hardships of travel in those days, for they had come from San Antonio to El Paso del Norte in a large military caravan, and with the comforts and privileges of "officers' rank" which the American general down there had endowed them with. [16] These facts are brought up here if only to show that the two much admired Frenchmen, when leaving the impression of a hard and lonely journey in their letters, were not averse to doing the same in other matters. This will be seen as we go along.

But, once in Santa Fe, and after the din of the great reception had died down, Lamy and Machebeuf began hearing the same Odin gossip which had lain dormant all this while. This had to come from certain ones among the English-speaking residents of Santa Fe whom they had befriended following the reception, individuals of the very same type who for years had been maligning Vicar Ortiz, Padre Martínez, and their fellow clergymen in general, as we already saw a good while back. Hence this is not mere supposition, and it is further clinched by a casual remark which Bishop Lamy made when describing his successfully carried out first Pontifical Mass on August 15, the feast of the Assumption. The ceremonial music, he wrote, had been greatly enhanced by means of a little organ which he had purchased the day before from a (friendly) Protestant minister! [17] Here one wonders what this gentleman told him. This, by the way, is a passage which all of the worshipful biographers have deliberately passed over in the Frenchmen's correspondence, along with the one about Vicar Ortiz having taken the pains to go a hundred miles out to greet his new prelate, and another one about the unnamed Polish and Spanish priests who had come along in the French party.

Evidently, Padre Martínez had not come down to Santa Fe to meet Bishop Lamy during the first weeks following the 9th of August. It was quite consistent with his proud nature to have himself contacted first, and perhaps he was recalling General Kearny's own spontaneous gesture of five years before. Or if he did decide to come down and meet his new prelate after all, it was too late – upon his learning that Lamy and ex-Vicar Ortiz had left for Durango sometime in September. Their purpose, he might have guessed, was to confer with the former Mexican bishop about diocesan matters which he himself had mentioned to Zubiría in his letter of the 28th. But here again, all the previous writers have flatly maintained that Lamy was already at odds with Ortiz and the native clergy, who were contumaciously questioning his credentials, and that this had been the sole reason for his undertaking a long tedious journey to Durango.

But the actual fact is that Lamy had long set his mind on including within his New Mexico Vicariate the El Paso settlements of Socorro, Ysleta and San Elizario – and the American army post of Fort Franklin nearby – along a pleasant stretch of the Rio Grande valley which, by a previous change of the river's bed, had been left on the bank taken over by Texas. Bishop Odin of Galveston had dumped these places on Lamy when they met, heedless of the fact that the Holy See reserved to itself the division or alienation of any diocesan territory. In Santa Fe, ex-Vicar Ortiz must have told Lamy that his own previous jurisdiction as vicar for Durango had embraced the New Mexico settlements only, and not those of that separate southern area, and hence their trip. For it was most certainly not because Ortiz had challenged Lamy's authority as the same writers have maintained, but just the opposite. In a letter to the French prelate of New Orleans, Lamy had made no such complaint about Ortiz, merely adding a brief postscript that he was soon leaving for Durango "with the old *vicaire*, 500 leagues of travel, a great part desert and dangerous."[18] Not even a hint about any dispute between them. And Machebeuf himself, who would have most avidly made capital of any such dissension, stated simply that Lamy had just left for Durango because "the interests of the diocese have obliged him to undertake the journey to see the old Bishop who had been in charge." As for Ortiz, he wrote, "the old Mexican vicar general [sic] has also left." But nothing more.[19] Five years later, when in Rome, even when falsely accusing Ortiz of other things, Machebeuf wrote that Ortiz had "offered to accompany him [Lamy] as far as Durango to confer with Mgr. de Zubiria about [the territorial extent of] his jurisdiction." There is another Machebeuf passage in the same vein, but with nothing about any contumacy on the part of Ortiz and the other native clergy.[20]

In Durango, both Lamy and Ortiz were the simultaneous guests of Bishop Zubiría, who graciously hosted the former as a fellow successor of the Apostles and the latter as a dear old friend and his former vicar. But in a long official decree that he wrote at the end of the visit, Zubiría politely but firmly refused to cede the Texas places in question to Lamy, and simply because he could not do so without papal authority; at the same time he counseled Ortiz to get all the New Mexico priests and people to render their respectful obeissance to their new lawful bishop.[21] However, Bishop Lamy, for all his better personal qualities, and apparently as crassly ignorant as Odin was of standard Roman procedures with regard to territorial jurisdiction, returned from Durango in a huff.

It is here that one wonders if Padre Martínez himself went down to Durango, if only out of curiosity, and so secretly that neither Lamy nor Ortiz ever learned about it. There is a gap in his Taos ministrations from November 17, 1851 to January 14, 1852, when the parish duties were performed by Padre Vicente Saturnino Montaño.[22] Had he indeed done so, Bishop Zubiría would have given him the same advice he gave Ortiz. Or else, Martínez had not left Taos at all, perhaps having been ill during this time. What is more important to note at this time is that Lamy and Ortiz did not return from Durango as enemies, and that their good relationship continued through the many months ahead. In Santa Fe, meanwhile, Machebeuf and Ortiz' assistant Padre Luján had been having their minor tiffs, and this was because the French vicar had gotten on his high horse as soon as the bishop had left. He continued to act the same way whenever Lamy was absent from the vicariate. As for Luján, he must have felt Machebeuf's open aversion for the native padres, and had acted accordingly when his own immediate master, Ortiz, was away.[23]

Bishop Lamy was still steaming from his disappointment in Durango when he got back to Santa Fe on January 10, 1852, and his *cher amí* Machebeuf must have made his temper boil still more, not only by what he told him about Luján's open disrespect, but about an old padre called Leyva at San Miguel del Vado far out on the river Pecos. Incidentally, while lingering among the officers and soldiers at Fort Franklin on his way back, Lamy had accepted the services of that Mexican scamp, Padre Benigno Cárdenas, who had there insinuated himself into his good graces. But he promptly dropped him like a poisonous champignon after reaching Socorro in the north, when Padre Otero told him that Cárdenas had not only created a scandalous schism at Tomé two years before, but had been preaching heresy as well.[24] As it looks, this must have been a humiliating experience for Lamy with regard to his judgment about men, thereby spilling more coals on the embers of his original disappointment. Nor would this be his last such error, as we shall see when we once again come upon Cárdenas' erstwhile partner in crime, Padre Nicolás Valencia.

And now Machebeuf told him the scandalous news concerning that old pastor of San Miguel. It was that old assemblyman and politician, Padre José Francisco Leyva, who had badly injured himself sometime in November when falling off his horse while drunk, and who knows under what other shameful circumstances. Hence Machebeuf had sent Father Grzelachowski to replace him – that Polish priest who had come with them and whom Lamy had already placed as pastor at San Felipe Pueblo and its Hispanic missions.[25] Lamy immediately set out fuming for San Miguel, where he severely berated the pain-stricken old Leyva and suspended him from all his priestly functions. Back in Santa Fe, he was still angered to extremes when he wrote all the details to his former Cincinnati bishop, declaring that he was ready to bear down on the rest of the alcoholic and unchaste native padres as soon as he "caught them in the very act."[26] By now he was fully convinced, it seems, about all the bad things which Odin had told him down in Galveston, and the gossip that he had begun hearing in Santa Fe since his arrival. But it also looks as though there was a more immediate source which greatly contributed to his growing irritation.

In the letter just cited, Lamy had stated that he had all this "from good authority," as if some knowledgeable person had recently furnished him with new and most definite information. Now, at this very time, he had accepted the services of Padre Nicolás Valencia, as the parish records show, and whom he sent down to San Felipe to replace the Polish priest, who was now at San Miguel. Valencia was still under the suspension which Bishop Zubiría had imposed on him for his crimes at Belén and Tomé in his association with the heretical Benigno Cárdenas, but perhaps Lamy was unaware of it all at this time. Yet all this points to the fact that Valencia, during Lamy's absence, had struck a close friendship with Vicar Machebeuf, who now had recommended him to Lamy as a fine priest. Valencia himself, besides what we already know about his former schismatic capers, was actually a limp-wrist fop who had been catering to the American forces from the day they had arrived, and afterward to the new civil authorities whom he had gotten to help him and Cárdenas with their schism. It was for this reason that Bishop Zubiría during his last visitation had blamed his aberrations on his taking advantage of the "civil change" in government.[27]

Hence it is not impossible, but altogether likely, that Valencia had been filling Machebeuf with what he liked to hear, with the juiciest gossip about the other faithful padres by the time Lamy returned from Durango. Machebeuf in his turn had brought this up as proof and confirmation of what they had been suspecting all this while.

Bishop Lamy, however, was a fair-minded man at base as well as most charitable; that is, when he was beyond the influence of his bosom friend, as all the evidence shows. His mood suddenly changed shortly thereafter when he went up to inspect the nearby large parish of Santa Cruz north of Santa Fe, as well as its pastor.[28] He must have found Padre Juan de Jesús Trujillo to be a pious and zealous middle-aged man, and so much to his liking that he decided to take him along as his companion to a council in Baltimore a few weeks later; in his letters he always had a good word for him.[29] What Machebeuf thought about it we can only guess. Then early in March Lamy went further up to the next big parish, Taos, and once again he was both surprised and pleased by what he encountered there.

From what we learn later, Padre Martínez must have impressed Bishop Lamy with his convivial manner as a host, and no less with his conversation which, from what we already know so well, tended toward theology and canon law. If he had intended to impress the bishop, he succeeded. Nor did Martínez, already fifty-four, appear the least decrepit as Lamy must have expected; rather, both the man's vigorous presence and the many parish activities he saw made the bishop realize that he had come upon an extraordinary personality. As a result, Martínez not only got his new bishop to found his very first parish at Arroyo Hondo on March 24, but to appoint his assistant, the Padre Abeyta referred to long before, as its first pastor.[30] It also looks as though he persuaded Lamy that old Padre Leyva of San Miguel was not the depraved character which he had been led to believe, for, as the San Miguel records show, he promptly re-instated the poor man in his parish.

But what really amazed Bishop Lamy was something else which, as we will learn all along, was very dear to his heart. Presumably after boasting to the bishop about all the native priests whom he had trained for the Durango seminary in the past, Martínez now told him that he still had four young men studying under him with the priesthood in mind. Lamy must have then charged him with the continuation of their training, with the hope of ordaining them as soon as possible. This can be gathered from later communications on the subject.[31] This hallmark of a genuine bishop, the desire to build up a good body of young native clergy was something he possessed far ahead of his time, for even as late as the third decade of this century, Pope Pius XI had to remind the missionary bishops all over the world of this prime obligation which had been largely neglected. In this, besides his overall zeal, Lamy resembled his Mexican predecessor, who had collaborated with Padre Martínez toward this end. Subsequently the new bishop had the consummate pleasure and satisfaction of ordaining three of those young men, Padres José Sambrán Tafoya, Miguel Vigil and Ramón Medina, all of whom remained faithful to him to the end. At this period he likewise ordained the much younger half-brother of the old vicar, Padre José Eulogio Ortiz of Santa Fe, who likewise never disappointed his ordaining prelate.[32]

In short, Padre Martínez and Bishop Lamy, despite what all the former writers have parroted from each other, had immediately become fast and mutually respected friends, although their friendship was to be stretched not quite to the breaking point within the next twelvemonth, and not directly through any personal reasons on either side. Or, if both men were to blame, it was on Martínez' part because of his habitual harping on canon law as the savant which he had always held himself to be, and on Lamy's because of his amitié particuliere with Machebeuf.

Grey Eminence of Taos / 14

On April 1, 1852, Bishop Lamy left for Baltimore with Padre Trujillo as his priestly companion, and he would not be back until late in September. In this same month, Padre Rafael Ortiz, who had been ailing during the past two years, quietly passed away among his Indians of Santo Domingo, and Vicar Machebeuf promptly hied himself thither to make himself the pastor, but choosing to reside in the nearby village of Peña Blanca rather than among the Indians. In doing so he had abandoned his quasi-parish at the old *Castrense*, or military chapel in Santa Fe, which Lamy had founded the year before as an "American parish" where sermons in English could be heard.[1]

Machebeuf had a sister back in France who was a nun, and in a letter to her of May 31, he told her and her fellow sisters how much he had fallen in love with the picturesque valley of Peña Blanca. But why had he left Santa Fe, he asked? He told her that he had absolutely nothing to do in the Capital when in the meantime so many parishes lay abandoned and totally deprived of what he termed "religious sermons." He went on to say that through the neglect of the sacraments and the general pervading ignorance the grossest immorality had set in among the people, and to such an extent that any priest among them, and who was determined to remain faithful to his sacred calling, had to place himself under "the protection of Mary, *la Reine du Clergé*," as well as in the prayers of pious and fervent souls – meaning his sister and her fellow nuns. Only the establishment of Christian schools for both sexes, but especially for girls, could remedy the terrible situation, and also provide "*le bon exemple*" which was so rare in New Mexico.[2]

This letter alone, but also backed up by others in similar vein which Machebeuf kept writing, amply illustrates that innate morbid "scrupulosity" mentioned previously, a sick preoccupation with sexual matters which in its headlong blind fanaticism took a grim delight in sniffing out immorality everywhere he turned, and most especially with regard to the relationships between male and female. This is why, as one also gathers from the tone of his letters to the convent, he worshipped those religious women, since they were unsullied by men and, better still, because they had not contaminated men themselves. Hence the uninhibited ways of Spanish village life among young and old in Peña Blanca, so different from the outwardly puritanical if not necessarily more moral life in the French towns of his youth, had now brought that same fanaticism to a critical point. For, as we shall be seeing soon, it even caused him to reveal the secrets of the confessional in the sermons which he impassionately delivered in the town. This indiscretion would soon be at the bottom of Bishop Lamy's greatest worries as well as his coming contentions with the native clergy during the five years following, and with Padre Martínez up in Taos playing a most singular rôle – not as one of the accused, but as a sort of self-assigned *éminence grise* or *amicus curiae*.

Machebeuf's titillating impressions at Peña Blanca naturally had to arouse in him the old Odin and subsequent Santa Fe gossip he had heard about the native padres. With the bishop still far away, he donned the mantle of his friend's authority, and sometime in midsummer he once again abandoned his parish by going up to Taos in search of clerical scandals. Evidently he found none there against Padres Martínez and Abeyta, as he would against others, for he never made any charges of immorality against either one. In Padre Martínez' case, his old paternity secret was still a perfectly kept one. From Taos Machebeuf crossed over the sierra to Santa Gertrudis de Mora, where he did find what he was looking for, but not among the "Mexican padres." Father Grzelachowski, whom Lamy had sent there provisionally after re-instating old Padre Leyva at San Miguel, happened to have an attractive female for his h ˙ sekeeper, and someone in Mora – probably a French-Canadian who tried a similar trick later on – told the French vicar that she was a woman of ill repute. Without further ado, he suspended the Polish priest, whom the natives fondly referred to as Don Alejandro or Padre Polaco. Incidentally, we have all the details from a formal investigation which Padre Martínez made afterward, not out of any personal spite, but as the guardian he assumed himself to be of the correct procedures prescribed by canon law.[3]

Having returned for a brief stay at Peña Blanca, Machebeuf then went up to Santa Clara, having heard from his gossipy friends in Santa Fe – or else from his foppish friend Padre Valencia whom he had now placed in Santo Domingo – that the pastor there was a drunkard living with a married woman. As he had done at Mora, he immediately suspended the Santa Clara pastor, whose name was Ramón Salazar, taking over the parish funds besides. (Mora was not a constituted parish, hence there were no funds to sequester.) Here again, the first information of this act comes to us from a letter which Padre Martínez wrote months later to Bishop Lamy, and still playing the part of a grey eminence at his lofty perch in Taos.[4]

Finally, Bishop Lamy returned from Baltimore and Kentucky on September 26, bringing along the first Sisters of Loretto. He also had with him a French seminarian from New York named Carlos Brun, whom he would ordain at Christmas and who will appear again. Ex-Vicar Ortiz, still the pastor of Santa Fe, once again got all of his people to greet their prelate with a grand procession and other ceremonials at the church, once more giving the lie to those who have maintained that he and the bishop had become bitter enemies long before this.[5]

But days before this took place, Machebeuf had rushed as far north as the Cimarron river to meet his dear friend, not so much out of their cherished amitié as to inform him that the pastor of Albuquerque, Padre José Manuel Gallegos, was soon leaving on a mercantile trip to Durango – and that now was the propitious time to grab the parish from him.[6] For, from what we learn elsewhere, Machebeuf already had his eye on Albuquerque as the parish best suited for a vicar general. As we also gather from his subsequent accusations against Gallegos, he must have also told the bishop that Gallegos had been living with a whore who was both his housekeeper and his partner in business, and so Lamy authorized him to go down to Albuquerque, suspend Gallegos, and take over the parish for himself. But he did not do so immediately as the admiring biographers have written with so much glee, depending on Machebeuf's own lies about the episode. He waited for two whole weeks, until Gallegos was far enough away enroute to Durango; then he sneaked down there, quietly dismissed Padre Luján whom Gallegos had gotten to take his place during his absence, and assumed the parish – meanwhile giving the parishioners the impression, as one gathers from his first entry in the registers, that he was merely filling in until Gallegos returned. Again, the first information we have comes from that letter of Padre Martínez already cited.[8]

Once more, sometime in November, and leaving his Albuquerque parish unattended as he had done twice before in Santa Fe and Peña Blanca, Machebeuf went back up to Taos on what he called a mission preaching tour. Or was it to ferret out things against Martínez and Abeyta which he had missed finding during his summer trip? He found nothing, but, after he had gotten himself involved with some marital problems in one of the outlying villages, he again found himself accused of having violated the seal of confession during his preaching.[9] Well before he learned about this new impasse, probably at the end of this second Taos excursion, he stopped at Abiquiú early in December in order to suspend its pastor, another Salazar priest whose first name was Antonio de Jesús. The excuse was the usual charges of drunkenness and adultery, and here he likewise appropriated the parish funds. As with the former suspensions, the first information we have appears in that same letter which Padre Martínez, as a solemn *amicus curiae*, wrote to Bishop Lamy shortly after the new year began.[10]

But how could Bishop Lamy, the zealous and fair-minded man we have come to know, have condoned all these summary suspensions by Machebeuf, the first two at Mora and Santa Clara without his knowledge while he was away, and the second two with his evident approval? There were no preliminary investigations at all, as one would expect from any good superior when the circumstances were so serious. Was the hold which Machebeuf had over him that strong, his arguments that compelling, that he completely lost all sense of justice and good judgment? And how about Padre Valencia whom Machebeuf had befriended? There is no other way to explain it, except to say that their "particular friendship," whether either one realized it or not, was something less than an admirable one – and with no imputation at all on our part with regard to their own personal morals. History is replete with such examples even down to our times, as when a high statesman, while most upright in every other regard, gets easily hoodwinked by those whom he cherishes as his dearest friends and then stands by them no matter how serious their misdeeds.

Little did either of these two friends know that their pigeons of injustice, so hastily released, would be coming home to roost soon after the next year came around.

Thus the year 1852 came to its close, with Bishop Lamy ordaining that Brun individual at Christmastide, when he also assigned him to ex-Vicar Ortiz as his assistant in Santa Fe; he thereby replaced Padre Luján who, perhaps because of his connection with the Gallegos incident, was out of favor for the moment. In the meantime, Lamy had also been preparing a lengthy Christmas Pastoral Letter, which he issued under date of the Lord's Nativity to be read at all Masses on the following Sunday throughout his vicariate. Except for one last directive, which will be pointed out, it was a very practical and sensible set of regulations and counsels for his far-scattered flock. It had not a single word about what had taken place during the year, much less any reference to the native clergy with regard to their conduct and morals.

Nonetheless, its entire contents must be detailed here because every previous writer on the subject has maintained, and obviously without having examined the pastoral letter, that the native padres rebelled against Bishop Lamy because it attacked their evil morals! What is worse, this gross misconception can be blamed directly on the bishop and his vicar, for soon both Lamy and Machebeuf began using the letter as a red herring before the Roman Curia and the American hierarchy to draw their attention away from that one most serious accusation brought up against Machebeuf – the one about his having violated the sacrosanct seal of the confessional.

The now famous, or infamous, "Christmas Pastoral" of 1852 can be reduced to the following points: 1) Because of the educational and other pressing needs of the vicariate, *finances would be centralized in the bishop*; this in not so many words, but according to the tenor of the preamble, and something which Lamy had every right to do. 2) Despite this, there would be *a reduction of parish fees.* (This reduction was not so drastic, as Machebeuf made it look later on when lying in Rome, that the native padres would object to it, and which they never did.) 3) People requesting a service or *ceremonies with pomp should come to an agreement with their pastor,* who would then charge them *according to his prudence and judgment* (nothing changed from former custom); regarding *patronal feasts and sung Masses,* the same custom should be observed *as before,* except that the priest should not demand the fees before the service was performed; this also held for other fees. (The French priests soon found out that this did not work, and returned to the former custom.) 4) The priests should say Mass once a month on a weekday in chapels one league away from the parish church, and which had over thirty families in the neighborhood.

Finally, and here the native padres would have objected, but never did for a long time, Lamy made this observation: The faithful, after seeing how collections were being so well spent by the bishop, should contribute generously and not try to excuse themselves, even though the civil law did not oblige them; but there was Church law binding them in conscience. All well and good, but here Lamy went on to say: "We have the great solace that during the past year the greater part of the faithful has complied with this obligation, and we are confident that the few who have refused...will not oblige us to employ the severity they deserve...*otherwise we will be forced, though with much heavy sadness, to deny them the Sacraments and consider them as not belonging to the Catholic Church."*[12] Any good Catholic today, priest or layman – the Pope himself – would strongly object to such a statement. If the native padres had stood up to the bishop because of this, they would have had good reason to do so. But they overlooked it, as we shall soon see in the first letter of Padre Martínez.

The second part of the Christmas Pastoral concerned itself with laudable paternal admonitions toward an upright Christian life. It was not addressed to the clergy as such, but to all the faithful under Lamy's care. He warned them in all charity to avoid such scandalous occasions of sin as divorces, dances, and gambling, and ended with a quotation from I Corinthians 6:9-10: *Be not deceived, neither fornicators, nor adulterers, nor thieves, nor drunkards, nor railers, nor extortioners, shall possess the kingdom of God.* [13] If the later detractors of the native clergy in general took this biblical citation as directed at them personally, which it most certainly was not, one could then ask with the same unfair reasoning why Bishop Lamy happened to leave out "*nor the effeminates, nor sodomites*" between the words "adulterers" and "thieves." This would be entirely reprehensible, to say the least. But to the francophile biographers, it seems, everything was fair in love when it came to their French heroes – and in war when it came to the so-call Mexican opposition.

On the 5th of January 1853, as we learn from subsequent letters of his on January 24 and April 2, Padre Martínez drafted a respectful but just as blunt a communication to Bishop Lamy, and signed by some other padres. Besides the date, the copy on hand lacks the signatures of the padres who endorsed it. These were most likely Padres Abeyta of Arroyo Hondo, Lucero of Picuris, and perhaps Luján, whom the bishop had already pardoned and made pastor of Santa Clara. From the tenor of the letter's references to them, the two suspended Salazar priests were not among the co-signers. As for ex-Vicar Ortiz in Santa Fe, one can suppose that he had not gone up to Taos because of the early date and the winter weather, if Martínez had even thought of inviting him. Padre Gallegos of Albuquerque was still in Durango.

Unfortunately, the document itself is so long, the legal phrasing so involved in page-long sentences, that a full quotation of them would turn away the reader as it must have vastly annoyed Bishop Lamy, over and above by what it said. The first folio-long page is a direct attack on "Don Preyecto Machiuf" for his having acted as vicar with *quasi-episcopal authority*; his sermons everywhere he went had the payment of tithes as their sole theme; he threatened those who did not pay in full with the refusal of the sacraments even at the hour of death; if a pastor did impart the sacraments in such cases, the rites would have no effect because the bishop would have removed his faculties (automatically), and the persons dying in such a state would be denied Christian burial. These false assertions, the accusers said, were contrary to "the benignity of the Church" according to what the Council of Trent decreed in its Chapter on Penance. Next they criticized Machebeuf "with regard to the clergy of New Mexico, whom he seems to look upon with an eye of rancour," as proven by his conduct toward them while the bishop was away in Baltimore the previous year, as well as after he returned to the Territory. From here on the rest of the letter has to be quoted, since it furnishes the first accounts of Machebeuf's rampage of suspensions and appropriations of funds – as well as the first accusations concerning Machebeuf's violation of the confessional secret.

In the month of August he suspended from his office, and perhaps also from his ecclesiastical benefice, the priest Don Ramon Salazar, placed by your Excellency in the parish of Santa Clara; he suspended him on suspicions of incontinency, without there having preceded the steps set forth in the sacred canons and curial authors...and it even looks as though your Excellency tolerated such conduct of his; nevertheless, this does not justify the Señor Machebeuf's violence in that case, in which he appears as an unjust despoiler; wherefore, while we attribute to your Excellency all the respect which is due, you are after all a subject under Canon Law, and in no way above it. The Señor Machebeuf took Salazar's parish into his charge and also the neighboring curacy of Santa Cruz de la Cañada, confided entirely or in part by its *cura propio* Don Juan de Jesus Trujillo who was accompanying your Excellency in the aforesaid trip to the Council; but the Señor Machebeuf appropriated the obventions of both parishes, and at least the whole of Salazar's and whose act of such fraudulent usurpation is not far from having been the real reason for the suspension imposed on him, and which he [*Salazar*] suffered either through ignorance of the law as did Señor Machebeuf, or from fear of his vexations, while ignorant of other unjust suspicions which were current; but what is certain and without the shadow of a doubt is that he [*Machebeuf*] did appropriate the obventions...

Your Excellency, not much different from the above case regarding the suspension of the priest Don Ramon Salazar is the suspension which the Señor Machebeuf practiced against the *cura propio* of Abiquiú, Don Antonio de Jesus Salazar, in the month of December of the preceding year...it is certain and sufficiently known that said clergyman has had many faults in connection with the administration of his parish and a "distraction" from the excess of inebriating liquors; but there is still the right for a case to be instituted and the judgment to be passed according to justice; if such was the case, and [*Machebeuf*] did it by mandate of your Excellency, there is nothing left to say about the matter; but it does greatly matter to those who [*here*] protest with regard to a more recent case which he is said to have carried out in the Parish of Albuquerque.

It is said, and it appears with all moral certitude, that the Señor Machebeuf publicly suspended from office and ecclesiastical benefice the *cura propio* of Albuquerque, Don Jose Manuel Gallegos, on Sunday the 12th [*overwritten 5th*] of the preceding month and year, and with said Parish church *interdicted* whereby no priest could celebrate Mass in it under penalty of being suspended and the church violated, since it was reserved to himself [*Machebeuf*] and he alone was authorized to do so; moreover, that in the same Parish church he denounced the same Gallegos, publicly accusing him of immoral conduct in his private life as scandalous and open. Is it not clear, your Excellency, that such conduct presents the Señor Machebeuf as a reprehensible detractor, with scandal so outstanding that the injured party can with very strong right demand a suit against him for injuries of such magnitude? Those who protest judge that it is all patent for the high scrutiny of |the courts|.

The aforesaid Gallegos is absent and away from his curacy for a just cause, and he went to Durango in September of last year on pending matters of his of great importance before his Excellency Bishop Zubiria; but he left the administration of his parish provided for with the priest Don Jose de Jesus Lujan; but, when about to depart, he heard that your Excellency had arrived in Santa Fe, having returned from your trip to the council; since it was impossible for him to present himself because he was ready to depart, and in respectable entourage which could not be detained any longer, he gave your Excellency a submissive and hastily sent notice, advising you how his parish was being cared for, and begging of you, as those who protest understand it, the approval which he [*already*] had; for previous to said notice the aforesaid Don Jose de Jesus Lujan went down there to take care of the said administration of that parish, even though, by disposition of your Excellency, things were done otherwise...

It is also said, your Excellency, that the Señor Machebeuf, by agreement with some to gain further lucre, celebrates Masses in private homes, failing thereby in the reverence due the respectable and awesome Sacrifice of the Mass, and thus when only the bishops may do it...Moreover, we add to the consideration of your Excellency, with regard to the conduct of the Señor Machebeuf in his clerical actions, which is probably and perhaps certain, that he is a revealer of the seal of sacramental confession because, after having heard the confession of one or various persons, he has spoken about their faults, at least in genere, which they had confessed, or that they had been in the state of mortal sin. This horrifies one, and many persons on hearing about such conduct, say that they will never make their confession to him; several other things are omitted, your Excellency, judging that what has been told suffices. [14]

To here the Martínez letter of January 5, 1853. From all of it one can see that it was not an attack on Bishop Lamy, nor about his Christmas Pastoral. What stands out in all the verbiage is that Padre Martínez was indulging in his vaunted superior capacity as an expert in canon law. His defense of the injured padres looks more like an exercise in jurisprudence than any earnest plea for the defense and acquittal of his clients. This will become more and more apparent later on. While trying to impress his bishop with his expertise, he nevertheless was deriving great pleasure from his needling of Machebeuf for his crass ignorance of canonical procedure. Was he thereby trying to replace him as Lamy's righthand man? Whatever, he was indeed trying to institute formal church proceedings against the unpopular French vicar, and with himself closely associated with Bishop Lamy as the judge while he himself, as an amicus curiae, basked in the reflected dignity of his prelate. He had never heard of that grey-robed Capuchin friar in France, Pére Joseph, who had been behind Cardinal Richelieu's political decisions, and hence had come to be known as the éminence grise – the grey cardinal for more than one reason.

Padre Martínez was aspiring to be just that, just as he had always tried to advise Bishop Zubiría, who in his turn had done little else but let Martínez feel his own imporance. While it is true that this letter had followed hard upon the Christmas Pastoral of December 24, 1852, it is most evident after a comparison of the two that there was no connection at all. For not the least reference was made to it – the one and only subject of discussion was Vicar Machebeuf. Nor was the pastoral to be brought up later by Martínez or the other native padres, and, to repeat, it was not Bishop Lamy's authority which was before the jury, only the erratic and fanatical conduct of his friend Machebeuf.

The Seal of Confession / 15

This Martínez letter of January 5th placed Bishop Lamy in a most painful dilemma. The jurisdictional and monetary charges brought against Machebeuf did not bother him in the least; these he could allay one way or the other as the chief man in authority that he was. It was altogether different with that final one about the seal of confession, which did oblige him to institute a formal investigation. At the same time he could not get himself to believe that his *intime amí* had gotten himself into such a most serious predicament, the worst that could happen to any priest. For Rome could overlook any other crime, such as the most scandalous one of concubinage or any acts of grand theft on the part of a clergyman – once the culprit had done sufficient penance for his sins. But a violation of the confessional secret was something else. It entailed a summons before the Roman Curia, and then perpetual defrockment and consignment to some strict monastery for life.

Machebeuf happened to be away at this time, out in the Las Vegas countryside, and so Bishop Lamy could not have an immediate good explanation from him as he fondly hoped. His grave worry was such that he promptly answered Martínez on January 7, as we learn from subsequent communications on this particular subject. In this letter, Lamy demanded positive proofs, not about any of the many other charges against Machebeuf's repeated abuses of authority, but only about that single issue – his alleged violation of the sacrosanct confessional seal. [1] Padre Martínez did not reply immediately, but in the meantime the poor bishop was suffering other inconveniences. A burglary had taken place in his house during this very week, when a considerable amount of money had been stolen; and so the newspaper editor advised him and all other clergymen (the Protestant ones included) not to keep monies in their residences. [2]

However, what brought Bishop Lamy's alarm to a higher pitch was another barrage against Machebeuf from an altogether different direction. Sometime prior to mid-January, there came an unsigned complaint from the Hispanic parishioners of Santo Domingo and Cochiti south of Santa Fe. Since the death of Padre Rafael Ortiz, they said, they had not had a resident priest, although the "French vicar" who had made himself the pastor did stop in occasionally. They had seen folks die without the consolations of religion because the vicar was always running off to Taos, Mora, San Miguel, Albuquerque and Socorro. *Es tan ambulante*, he's such a rover, they put it. But whenever he had visited them, all he preached on was the Church's fifth commandment about paying their tithes; if he turned to other subjects, it was to reveal the secrets of the confessional! [3]

This new attack on the very same ticklish matter brought the poor bishop's deepening apprehension to a raging wrath, especially when he learned, very likely from Padre Valencia of Santo Domingo, that the actual writer of the complaint was a presumptuous layman by the name of Francisco Tomás C. de Baca. He was the civil magistrate of Peña Blanca, and who for many years had been a leading politician at the Capital during Mexican times as he now was in the American Territorial government. He was also a brother-in-law of ex-Vicar Ortiz, and an elder brother of young Padre José de Jesús C. de Baca, the pastor of Tomé who a couple of years before had been driven out of his parish through the machinations of Valencia and Cárdenas. Four years later, in Rome, Machebeuf would name his *beau-frère* Ortiz and his *prêtre frère* C. de Baca as the secret connivers behind Don Francisco Tomás.[4]

The latter actually did not need their help as the educated barrister that he was, and who had his very own axe to grind as will soon become evident. Nor was their any conniving between himself and Padre Martínez up in Taos, since there is no reference to each other's allegations in their respective correspondence with the bishop. Even so, this was no consolation to Bishop Lamy. Upon learning that Don Francisco Tomás was in Santa Fe at the time, he promptly wrote him a curt note on January 14. In it he demanded "judicial proofs" for what he considered a "most malicious calumny" against a priest's character. Consequently, he said, it was his duty to punish any person making such grave accusations, obviously referring to the confessional business. Señor C. de Baca, still in Santa Fe, answered with his own short note on the 16th. He denied that the people's petition had been a direct attack on Vicar Machebeuf. All they wanted, he said, was a resident pastor. Throwing back at the bishop the latter's expressions of malicious calumny and his threats of punishment, he now intimated the possibility of a lawsuit. On January 18, Lamy replied with a half-dozen lines, this time directly on that matter of the confessional. He wanted to know when and where the violation had taken place, who the injured party was, what had been disclosed, the very name of the person whose sins had been revealed.[5]

Evidently, to Lamy at this time, all the accusations which his friend Machebeuf had made against five padres, including the Polish one, had not been malicious calumnies. Meanwhile, he had re-instated most of the ones whom Machebeuf had suspended, very likely because his vicar's wild charges had not stuck, or else because, wherever there was some guilt, there had followed promises of amendment. But this one most serious charge now being repeated in another place against his dear friend was beginning to look as though it might have some substance, and so the divinely annointed David was becoming increasingly worried and wrathful when such things touched on the person of his beloved Jonathan.

Up in Taos, Padre Martínez had been mulling over Bishop Lamy's January 7th demands for legally stated proofs, and making some investigations on his own, when he decided to reply in a second letter of January 24. Its details are alluded to in a letter which Machebeuf wrote to Martínez on February 3, and they are cited again by Martínez in a letter which he wrote to Lamy on the 24th of this same month of February. Padre Martínez' January 24th missive evidently contained, as just said, the specific proofs which Lamy had demanded on January 7th. By the end of January, Machebeuf had finally stopped in Santa Fe after one of his "missionary trips," when his dear friend presented him with the Martínez letters, and most likely those of C. de Baca. There must have followed the loudest protestations of innocence, which Lamy was most avid to accept. Still, this was not enough to allay the fears and alarm which the two friends now felt. Machebeuf himself knew that he was in most serious trouble, for on February 3 and in a conciliatory manner that was not his, he penned a long letter to Padre Martínez.

"Most respectful Sir," he began, "on my return from Las Vegas, and while still enroute, I learned that you along with other clergymen had made a protestation to his Lordship against me, full of the gravest accusations." Here he told Martínez that upon his arrival in Santa Fe, Lamy had shown him his first letter, saying that Martínez had promised to furnish proofs by Friday of the same week but had not done so. As he had to visit the Rio Abajo during the next two weeks, Machebeuf went on, he had given his accusers plenty of time to produce their proofs. Upon his return to Santa Fe, he had found the second Martínez letter (of January 24) which repeated the same charges. Now he went into all the details which Martínez had outlined in this letter, about his preaching and other activities in the Taos villages some months before, contending that the things he had mentioned in his sermons had not come from the confessional, but from his open dealings with certain couples whose marriages he had rectified. Here, he said, he had not needed any knowledge by way of sacramental confession "to invite the people to thank God for the conversion of a lost soul, and to join their rejoicing to that of the angels in heaven – these were my words."[6] As for the other charges, he ended by saying, "I do not want to say a single word...regarding the suspension of some padres...his Lordship will inform you: I have to obey his orders. Without anything more to say, I am always your affectionate servant and squire."[7]

Then, what must have been the joyful surprise of the two friends, when, after three weeks of anxious waiting, Bishop Lamy received the following reply from Padre Martínez, dated February 24:

> On the 20th of this current month, I received a letter dated on the 3rd of the same which the Señor Vicario Jose Machebeuf addressed to me in answer to the communication which, at the beginning of the preceding month of January [*January 5*], I presented to your Lordship with the signature of other associates, and to the letter which in confidence I sent your Lordship from here in Taos, dated on the 24th of the same January. Señor Machebeuf says in said letter that your Lordship communicated to him said script and letter, and in consequence he gives us a reply which in substances comes to follow the judicial processes of a lawsuit; and in producing this duplicate [*of January 24*] on the matter contained in the first writing [*of January 5*], I submit said letter as coming before, and request your Lordship to kindly append them to the first communication where it belongs, and be kind enough to pass it on to Señor Machebeuf in order to renew the presentation; and in such a case the cause can be accepted as proof, provided your Lordship considers this sufficient at this time. Señor Machebeuf relates in his letter that your Lordship had told him that the proofs should have been there since a certain Friday in January; and so he judges on it, not knowing the intention of the plaintiffs orally disclosed by me to your Lordship, that they should precede the formalities which are now being set forth, and whereby the question will have its required [*juridical*] aspect.[8]

This first part of the Martínez reply, besides providing another sample of his pet legalese, shows that Martínez was still aiming at a formal ecclesiastical court trial. What is more important, it reveals that he had amicably conferred with

Lamy in person as a friend of the court, Lamy evidently acting outwardly for his benefit as a neutral judge so as not to excite the "friendly prosecutor" any more than was necessary. Poor Lamy must have been reading the preceding section with growing impatience and ennui when his heart gave a leap at what came next. For Martínez, himself willing to make concessions in order to win on other scores while also assuring himself of the bishop's good will, went on to say:

> I remain satisfied with what Señor Machebeuf answers [emphasis his, and referring to the confessional problem], and from it I observe the motive of his good faith while functioning here [in the Taos villages], while we also criticize him in our communication which remains pending [regarding the other charges], and I see that the resolve he keeps to go on with his preaching, and the motives which animate him, were in his soul the basis of religious zeal [his emphasis] when alluding to the parties referred to...whose conversion he had been requested to bring about...and who with the rest should rejoice with the angels in heaven. 9

This paragraph Machebeuf promptly clutched to himself as a drowning man desperately takes hold of a floating branch. He still had it with him four years later when he was in Rome, during the worst state of panic in his life. As for the rest of the letter, Martínez brought up further charges with regard to a certain marriage which Machebeuf had performed, still under the impression that a church trial was forthcoming, and ending it with his usual respectful regard for the bishop.

But if Padre Martínez had generously and so graciously absolved Vicar Machebeuf from all guilt with regard to his having breached the confessional seal, Don Francisco Tomás C. de Baca at Peña Blanca had not given up. He replied to Bishop Lamy's challenge of January 18 with a second barrage of legal verbiage and involved forensics on the 28th. Here he was evidently having his fun besides, as if demonstrating to the French foreigner that not all of the New Mexico natives were ignorant and illiterate clouts. 10 We already know that Machebeuf had written Martínez about his urgent two-week trip to the Rio Abajo; one of his stops had been in Peña Blanca, when he furnished its magistrate with further ammunition for his guns. Now, in a second letter to Bishop Lamy on February 2, Don Francisco Tomás accused Machebeuf of acting unlawfully by bringing Padre Valencia to administer the parish of Santo Domingo. He then went on to say that on Sunday, January 20, Machebeuf had preached at the Indian mission against the people of Peña Blanca, when the vicar stated that "they wanted to threaten me with protests to the bishop; he and I were reared together, were ordained together, went on mission together to the United States; he knows me for many years, and the bishop does nothing without consulting me first." 11 Here Jonathan had found a chance to taunt the Philistines with his close friendship with Champion David.

Now Señor C. de Baca left off playing with legal twists by coming down straight to particulars. On February 1, he wrote, while in the village of Cubero across the river, Machebeuf had tried to persuade a man to have the Cochiti and Peña Blanca people formulate a popular petition in his own favor; then Valencia would be allowed to function in both places also. Here the magistrate argued, not anxious to have Valencia's services, that the vicar should have been removed as pastor from the beginning. This is when he brought up three specific instances of Machebeuf's breaches of the seal of confession:

First, on May 25, 1852, Machebeuf began a novena of Masses in the Trinity chapel, and all of which C. de Baca had paid for; on the third day he heard the confessions of an adult man and a youth, and then during his sermon he mentioned having heard the confession of a boy of ten who did not know his catechism nor how to make his confession, *but that at that early age he already knew how to commit very grave sins in his parents home!* All those present knew to whom he was referring. – *Second,* on the fifth day, the local prefect (Señor Baca himself) had gone to confession along with many women and children; in his sermon the vicar remarked how much pleased he was that so many had gone to confession, *among them a leading citizen who had not gone for eight years!* "Your Lordship will judge if this was not a revelation." – *Third,* on the following day a certain man, who in the past had lived sinfully with his sister-in-law, went to confession; after publicly refusing him holy communion, Machebeuf called him to the sacristy where, *in the presence of the writer and others,* he berated him for it and forbade him to contract a marriage he had been contemplating. [12]

Now, said C. de Baca, the proofs he produced were "as clear as the light of noon." He had only decided to produce them at this time so that his Lordship could see that, originally, all that the people had requested was a resident pastor. He himself had held no previous animosities against Machebeuf, but now the latter had gone so far as to prohibit Masses in Peña Blanca and Cochiti. These privations, said he, were due to the wide ecclesiastical authority with which his Lordship had invested the vicar, and if his Lordship did not remedy the situation, it would have to be considered as an act of autocratic vengeance on his part. [13] Here the magistrate was still writing with tongue in cheek, while he was wrong in claiming at the end that church authority, like the civil one, rested in the people.

On February 22, Bishop Lamy replied by first saying that Vicar Machebeuf would justify himself, within a few days, against these and other such false accusations. Now borrowing from C de Baca's own sarcasm, he chided him for not having sent him any judicial proofs since their correspondence had started. He would welcome more letters from him, but not written in the elaborate style of a judge censuring his own ways of administration, or by intimating that if such accusations had been made against any other (native) clergyman, the bishop would have deprived him of his priestly functions. The priests he had suspended, Lamy continued, while still skirting around the confession issue, had all incurred censures by reason of grave faults which were known all over the Territory. He regretted very much that a gentleman of honor and good education like C. de Baca should become so confused as to criticize his administration. Then he ended by saying that the latter must have written all these things under the pressure of some "private preoccupation." [14]

Here the bishop himself was being sarcastic, but it looks more like a conciliatory effort to get Machebeuf off the hook, since he completely ignored those specific abuses of the confessional which C. de Baca had brought up. But the latter promptly replied on March 1 with heightened sarcasm and a more florid style, saying that he could use no other language to support something which was a common cause and not a private feud. Hence his letters were not the result of any personal worries or insecurity. Still, he hoped that the entire problem could be resolved by allowing the priest now in charge (who was not Valencia) to extend his ministrations to all the towns of the Santo Domingo parish. Otherwise, said he, the people would begin faltering in their faith, and so forth, and the towns which he himself represented as magistrate would refuse to pay their tithes in the future.[15]

This is the end of this particular correspondence at this period. What stands out in all of it, and to the growing discomfiture of Bishop Lamy and his friend, is Machebeuf's alleged violations of the sacred seal of confession. If C. de Baca was truthful as well as correct in the three instances he gave, Machebeuf was certainly guilty – at least *in genere* as Padre Martínez had once put it – of such serious violations. Or else, presuming that the magistrate of Peña Blanca had exaggerated somewhat, the vicar had come "dangerously close" to violating the sacred seal – and this the Roman Curia considered very serious also. What will become increasingly apparent from now on is that the bishop and his vicar had become more deeply aware of the latter's *faux pas* and its possible consequences, and these entirely dependent on the Roman auditors' collective mood should the matter ever get to the Holy Office.

Thus ended those first two exciting months of 1853, but not the troubles which had been initiated by the first letter of Padre Martínez to Bishop Lamy. He had absolved Machebeuf in the meantime of all guilt with regard to the seal of confession, as far as his own parish of Taos was concerned. But he was still determined to continue prosecuting the French vicar on his other abuses of canon law, and yet without having to alienate what he presumed to be the bishop's good will toward himself.

Still The Amicus Curiae / 16

A t the very end of February or the 1st of March, 1853, Padre José Manuel Gallegos returned to Albuquerque from Durango, after a six-months' absence, to find that he had been deprived of his parish and suspended besides in *absentia*. It had been his very first absence from Albuquerque, as his signatures in the sacramental books clearly show, since he had assumed the parish in 1845.[1] Hence this had not been one of several habitual mercantile excursions as Machebeuf frequently wrote in his letters to his sister, and later in his Roman *Defense* of 1856.

In the meantime, ever since his coming to Albuquerque in mid-October of 1852, Machebeuf had been absenting himself so often from the parish that the people loudly criticized him for it, so much so that he was then forced to compound his authority by getting new faculties from Bishop Lamy to suspend Gallegos – as if he were the cause of his present troubles. He did so on December 5 with all the histrionics which Padre Martínez described. We also have the Machebeuf letters in which he glorified his own heroicity with all kinds of exaggerations peppered with lies, the source which the admiring biographers have used without as much as doubting their complete veracity.[2] These details, and everything that Lamy and Machebeuf wrote about the native padres, will be left for another book.

But the real nub of it all is contained in the correspondence which the probate judge of Albuquerque, Don Ambrosio Armijo, started with Bishop Lamy at this time. Padre Gallegos, immediately reacting to the situation, had gotten Armijo and all the heads of families in the district to begin a counter-attack, not against the bishop's person or his authority, but, as with Martínez at Taos and C. de Baca in Peña Blanca, against the very same kinds of abuses which his dear friend had now been committing in Albuquerque. The Armijo-Lamy correspondence is quite as lengthy as those others, but the main points have to be brought out here if only because the francophile biographers have merely skimmed over these letters and dwelt exclusively on Machebeuf's hysterical versions. Under dates of March 3 and 15, 1853, Armijo sent his first protest to Lamy, appended with 950 signatures of heads of families, and making the following allegations:

On September 24 of last year, Gallegos had announced to them that he had some important affairs to discuss with Bishop Zubiría, besides some private matters. (On September 21, he had written the following in the parish register: "In virtue of absenting myself from the parish with previous notice to the competent authorities, I have consigned this book to my *coadjutor*, along with the church properties...[signed] José Manuel Gallegos, José de Jesús Luján, *coadjutor*.")[3] – 2) Gallegos had officially notified Bishop Lamy (while he was back east, but what happened to this letter?), and he had gotten *permission from his vicar*, leaving Padre Luján to take his place. (If Gallegos was lying here and in the parish register, Machebeuf's credence is no better, and he might have played such a trick by giving Gallegos oral permission.) – 3) But, to their sorrow, Padre Luján was removed a short time later, leaving them without spiritual care and at the mercy of Machebeuf's hurried and infrequent visits. (The parish entries bear this out.) – 4) In his tiresome sermons, the vicar leaned on the payment of tithes, threatening to deny absolution to those who did not comply; he began his sermons with the gospel but ended with the private lives of some, *even by revealing things from the confessional!* – 5) Let Machebeuf say if anyone had stood up to protest when he defamed their pastor (on December 5), when Padre Gallegos was 600 leagues away. – 6) It is fifteen days (a fortnight in Spanish) since Padre Gallegos returned; when they begged him to minister to them, he told them that he was *abiding by the suspension imposed on him;* hence they begged his Lordship to have their pastor back and to suspend Vicar Machebeuf instead![4]

No doubt, Padre Gallegos had a hand in this. And once again Bishop Lamy was being challenged, not, as far as he cared, about Machebeuf's absences and money madness, but about that painful thing of the confessional. With C. de Baca's accusations still sticking in his craw, and now these just as brazen ones by another presumptuous layman, he must have blanched with fury. For he promptly answered Armijo on March 17, at first rather calmly in requesting that his reply be read to all of the 950 signators, but with rising gorge when he came to the attacks on Machebeuf's person. Here he continued:

> The rehabilitation of Padre Gallegos will be difficult enough, at least for the time being, because he did not obey my orders during my absence [?]...As to the suspension which, according to the judgment of the undersigners, the Señor Machebeuf has deserved, I will tell them that this is my business, and when they shall have given proofs...I shall see what I must do. At the same time I will give them a counsel in all charity, and this is to submit themselves to ecclesiastical authority, because otherwise they place themselves in danger of falling into very great difficulties.[5]

Not a single word here about the secret of confession, but Armijo took up this matter again three weeks later. Shortly after this, the poor harried bishop began writing abroad about his troubles – not the chief one – only about the alleged rebellion of the native priests against *his own person and authority,* which was a lie. Writing to the superior of the Jesuits, asking him to send him some of his priests, he said that he had only four good ones (Machebeuf, Pinard, Brun, Trujillo – not Grzelachowski and Martínez?). The small number of the Mexican ones remaining, he said, were only an embarrassment.[6] This was because ex-Vicar Ortiz in Santa Fe had resigned his parish, not because of the fight which was going on against Machebeuf, but simply because his unalienable parish of a *cura propio* had been divided. Up to this time Ortiz had steered clear of everything, and ever since he had gotten that young French Brun as his assistant to replace Luján, he had let him have all the baptisms, as the Santa Fe records show, reserving to himself the more lucrative weddings until past the middle of February.[7] Nor had he complained long before when Lamy formed the "English-speaking parish" at the *Castrense* chapel, back in that September before he and Lamy set out for Durango. But this breaking up of his historic and indivisible "Mexican parish" had cut him to the quick.

Machebeuf was to state later in Rome that it was Ortiz who had been the *first* to rebel against Bishop Lamy immediately after the latter's arrival, causing the rest of the native clergy to follow in his steps![9]

At the very same time, before the close of this month of March, two others of the native padres had suddenly left the vicariate to offer their services to their old bishop of Durango. These were Padres José Antonio Otero and José de Jesús C. de Baca, both zealous younger men from two of the most prominent families in the Rio Abajo. Padre Otero, the very first pastor to get Lamy's message about his impending arrival, and the one who had fêted his party at Socorro in that happy July of 1851, had previously suffered the persecutions of the infamous Nicolás Valencia at Belén, the latter abetted by his first cousin and almost namesake, Antonio José Otero, whom General Kearny had made a territorial justice. This Judge Otero was still a favorite with the *americanos*, while Valencia was a pet of the new bishop and his vicar. Hence he had become disgusted with the new American order, both on the civil and the ecclesiastical level.[10]

His friend and classmate, Padre C. de Baca, had undergone the very same humiliations at Tomé across the river from Belén, when that villain Benigno Cárdenas in consort with Valencia had caused that terrible schism a little more than two years ago.[11] What is more, he must have heard from his elder brother of Peña Blanca that Machebeuf had placed Valencia for a time at Santo Domingo, to which his beloved birthplace of Peña Blanca belonged. Then there were those scandals, which he and Otero had come to believe to be true, about the disclosures of the confessional secrets by the French vicar, first at Peña Blanca and now in Albuquerque. And so both he and Otero abandoned their parishes of Socorro and Tomé, and went south toward the end of March. Machebeuf would later lie to the Roman Curia that C. de Baca had abandoned his parish weeks ahead, Otero following later, and that their reasons for leaving had been their opposition to the Christmas Pastoral![12]

By this time, Padre Martínez up in Taos was ready to act once more. On April 2, 1853, during Easter week, he had descended from his juridical aerie to the Capital, after having called some of the native padres to a supposedly very secret meeting. According to Bishop Lamy in two different letters abroad, as we shall soon see, there were five or six of them, or six or seven. But from the three other signatures in the letter which Martínez drafted at this time, there were only four: Vicar Ortiz of Santa Fe, then Martínez of Taos, Luján of Santa Clara, and a younger padre from as far south as Belén, named Rafael Chávez. However, from the letter's contents, one can presume that there was a fifth one who did not sign it, Gallegos of Albuquerque. Being the only one under the bishop's suspension, he refrained from signing; besides, as we just saw in the Armijo correspondence and as we shall see in another much more serious protest, he preferred to have others make his complaints for him.

Now we let this Easter letter speak for itself, again because it is Padre Martínez' own composition as the seasoned pastor, teacher, publisher and jurisprudent that he was so proud to be. His grey eminence was back on the job.

> Most Reverend Lord Bishop of Agathonica [*Lamy's titular diocese as a non-Ordinary bishop*] and Vicar Apostolic of New Mexico, Don Juan Lamy: The undersigned pastors, in due form and as best defined by law, declare before your Reverence that on the 5th of January of the current year [*1853*] we submitted to you a written complaint denouncing your Vicar Don Preyecto Machebeuf for unruly behavior which he practices in the churches of New Mexico, now vexing the clergy, now exercizing jurisdiction and taking possession of obventions with the infraction of Canon Law. Your Reverence, in a letter dated on the 7th of the same month of January, demands juridical proofs on one point in the denunciation – *suspected* [*emphasis his*] of having revealed the secret of sacramental confession, there being no mention of the other particulars brought up in said written protestation concerning matters of great importance.
>
> However, on seeing that your Reverence has not wished to place a trial in motion according to the norms provided by law, but rather has taken steps of such a nature that they look like excesses – for example, your having divided the parish of Santa Fe without observing the canonical dispositions, furthermore also having appropriated said parish to be administered by you through one of your household whom you have as assistant, and who was ordained a priest in this present year [*Brun, ordained at Christmastide 1852*] – also in keeping under suspension the lawful pastor of Albuquerque, Don Jose Manuel Gallegos, without observing the law, with other like misconducts which one fears will result in harm to the spiritual ministry; and also how it is patent with regard to your aforesaid Vicar Machebeuf, who is your fellow seminarian, associate, and member of your household – wherefore, observing toward your Reverence all the respect due through your Episcopal dignity, not in any offensive spirit but solely as touches upon our right and that of the public good, we have gathered together to serve notice to your Reverence through this present letter with everything it contains and pertaining to the undersigned; and therefore legally notified, that you be pleased to desist from proceeding with your decision; for we intend to appeal said matter with the cases it touches upon to higher authority...

This last sentence is so badly copied as to be almost illegible, a final note stating that the original is in Lamy's possession. It says something about the fear of New Mexico being left without spiritual ministrations as a result of the priests' illegal suspensions, and that future adverse decisions will be considered null and void. Written in Santa Fe, April 2 of the year 18(53), it ends with the copied signatures of the four clergymen previously mentioned.[13]

The Lamy biographers have always contended that this very first threat aimed at Bishop Lamy himself, along with the one of appealing the whole matter to Rome, constituted the final break between Padre Martínez and Bishop Lamy. We shall see that this was not so, especially when we come to the Martínez letter to be quoted in full at the end of this chapter. But even here in this Easter letter one can see Martínez playing both sides. As far as he was personally concerned, the chief and only important theme of this complaint, as in all his previous letters, was Machebeuf's prosecution in due legal form. But did he actually mean it now? What was briefly said, as though in passing, about the Santa Fe parish, was a mere sop thrown at Ortiz in exchange for his signature – with a smaller one tossed at Luján, who had been replaced by Brun. The same may be said about Gallegos' case, who decided not to sign. In this same spirit, Martínez graciously allowed

Ortiz to sign first, although his old vicarial standing was long over.

It would not be at all surprising if Martínez did not talk it over with Lamy just before or right after this letter was written, since in a former letter he had mentioned oral conferences between the two. He was now enjoying his self-assumed rôle as friend of the court while Lamy, with reservations about ever bringing his friend Machebeuf to trial, silently went along. He went along with Martínez, not necessarily because he still liked the fellow or else feared his political clout, but to forestall any such trial in which more evidence about the violations of the confessional seal might be produced. Note also that Martínez, when referring once more to Machebeuf's violations in this regard, underlined the word "suspected."

By this time Lamy had heard that Padre Gallegos was planning to return to Durango, and bearing copies of all the previous complaints against Machebeuf in order to forward them to Rome through Bishop Zubiría's office. Martínez could well have advised Lamy about this, and that Ortiz had prepared his own personal complaint against the bishop himself concerning his Santa Fe parish, and which he intended to direct to the Vatican along with the Peña Blanca and Albuquerque accusations. For it is now that Lamy desperately began seeking aid elsewhere on this very score.

On April 10, only a week after the padres' Easter meeting, he wrote to Bishop Purcell in Cincinnati, and starting out with a deliberate obfuscation of the facts: "Now that I have commenced to reform some abuses, and to lay down few rules for the clergymen [!], I have met with great deal of opposition, having been obliged to suspend four Mexican priests for their faults." Nothing here about the actual contents of the Easter letter, which did not mention those former suspensions and as if the New Mexico padres were complaining about the innocuous regulations in the Christmas Pastoral. These latter had not even been touched upon in all the previous letters from Taos, Peña Blanca and Albuquerque. "They have submitted," Lamy went on, "but have said that I did not observe the rules prescribed by canon law in inflicting these censures." The padres here referred to were evidently Leyva, Luján and the two Salazars. "The fact is that if I would comply with all the formalities they want, I would never stop abuses." These were a thing of the past, since Martínez, even in his first letter of January 5, had not pressed their cases any further. "Five or six Mexican clergymen had a meeting to oppose my authority [*on April 2, but nothing about what they said of Machebeuf*], and they have determined to bring their claims to higher authority [*Rome*]; because they say, they are supported by the rules of the Church in their rights [*the old European rules which neither Lamy nor the other American bishops were observing*] which I cannot change as I please." [14]

Next, Lamy dismissed the case of ex-Vicar Ortiz and his Santa Fe pastorship with one sentence, and finally found himself obliged to bring up Machebeuf's chief problem, and his own, but as one who happened to be an incidental innocent victim in the whole affair – and without laying any blame whatsoever on Padre Martínez, who was after all the main actor in Machebeuf's prosecution. "They have accused Mr. Machebeuf of several things," he went on, "amongst others of having revealed confession, but they could bring no proofs." [15] No doubt he was thinking of Padre

Martínez' written absolution on this score, to be used as a clinching argument should any formal defense become necessary. True, Martínez in this last Easter letter had mentioned this matter as suspected, but there still were those more definite and menacing "proofs" from Peña Blanca which were "left pending," while others might be forthcoming from Albuquerque. The ones from Peña Blanca could get to Rome through Ortiz and Gallegos, either by means of the Durango chancery or the Apostolic Delegate's office in Mexico City.

Hence Lamy here had to excoriate, besides the natives padres in general, certain laymen (C. de Baca and Armijo) who, he said, led the most scandalous lives. Then he continued: "Some of the clergymen [not Martínez] who look upon Mr. Machebeuf with jealousy, on account of his zeal and good qualities, have taken up the pretended accusation and they would try their best to injure him; but the most evident proof that he was not guilty of the like is that in the same place where the accusations originated, and also in the neighborhood, he was kept in the confessional day and night for weeks.[!]"[16] Machebeuf himself made a similar exaggeration in one of his letters,[17] hence his close friend must have been lending an eager ear to this rot, something that can bring a smile on the face of the busiest Catholic preachers of missions.

This was another sophism to be employed hereafter, and tucked inside the larger red herring of the Christmas Pastoral. Lamy then closed this letter by begging Purcell to intercede with his friends in Rome in case these "unfortunate priests" should get their plea to the Roman Curia, and as a back-up, he said, to what he already had written to Rome himself. Here, as will be noted, Padre Martínez is not alluded to at all, nor in a similar letter which Lamy wrote to Bishop Zubiría in Durango five days later, on April 15. In fact, Martínez himself could have advised this course of action. Here Lamy likewise told the Mexican bishop that the native clergy's opposition was due to the reduction of the parish fees "in my last pastoral [the red herring again] and to my suspension of different priests for many scandals [a dead issue by now]." He also brought up the Ortiz case in Santa Fe, and the fact that six or seven priests (to Purcell, five or six) had met there to mock his authority by means of a letter which four of them had signed. He then mentioned that Gallegos and two or more other padres were leaving for Durango in this very same month without as much as obtaining his permission.[18]

One of these others was Ortiz, bearing only his own complaint with regard to his Santa Fe parish. Two others, Otero and C. de Baca, were already on their way, and without any such portfolios. Then the carrier of the incriminating evidence against Machebeuf had to be Gallegos who, as we shall learn later, possessed copies of all the charges that had been made against the French vicar. Lamy also wrote a similar letter to the prelate of New Orleans, using the Christmas Pastoral as the reason for the native priests' opposition, and stating that two of them had already left with the purpose of carrying their complaints to Rome as they had said (Ortiz and Gallegos); two others (Otero and C. de Baca) had already resigned, but there were others who continued to give him plenty of trouble.[19] There is no evidence at all that the remaining dozen padres, excluding Martínez, were causing him any trouble at this time. As for the latter, he had been becoming more of a gadfly, but he had also been kind enough to absolve Machebeuf in that most important matter.

Referring back to Lamy's letter to Zubiría, one can detect his desperation and his main purpose for writing it, for he ended by warning him that, should his former subjects succeed in getting their papers to Rome, he already had several bishops and three archbishops interceding *in his own behalf* (nothing about Machebeuf as their intended victim), besides a famous Jesuit missionary named DeSmet who happened to be in Rome.[20] From now on Lamy kept writing in identical vein to all the helpful contacts he could make back east and in Europe, but these three letters discussed suffice to show how much he was worried about his *intime amí*, as well as the tack which he and Machebeuf had agreed upon and taken in order to keep the latter from the clutches of the Holy Office.

But now back to Padre Martínez. As said before, he is no longer heard from, or about, in this particular affair. From now on, old ex-Vicar Ortiz is Lamy's main target, as is Gallegos Machebeuf's exclusive own, along with the anonymous native padres in general, and it all has more to do with church real estate than any strictly religious problems. Instead, on the very day that Lamy was writing to Bishop Zubiría, Padre Martínez was noting down in the Arroyo Hondo books that he was gladly carrying out an instruction from Bishop Lamy concerning the registration of burials; and that as of June 4 he was taking over this parish temporarily under his good bishop's express orders.[21] Hence, everything must have been going evenly between himself and the bishop, especially with regard to the seminarians whom he continued preparing for ordination. Then, to cap it all, as the year 1853 drew toward its end, he wrote a most revealing letter to Lamy, something which further clinches the many assumptions which have been made all along since the start of his career.

Sometime in September, Bishop Lamy had received most welcome news. Through the efforts of the American hierarchy, and as a result of his desperate cries for help in overcoming those who were undermining his authority – as he always contended – New Mexico's Vicariate had been elevated to the status of a full-fledged diocese, the Diocese of Santa Fe. This made him a full "Ordinary," whereby he would be fully empowered as Archbishop Kenrick wrote to Rome, to apply "the ecclesiastical rod" on all those wicked priests of New Mexico. Padre Martínez up in Taos was also affected by this turn of events, and in a manner which might be startling to some. Yet it turns out to be a confirmation of certain judgments which have been made all along. On December 17, 1853, he sent Bishop Lamy the following letter with an inclosure.

> Most Illustrious Lord Don Juan Lamy, most Worthy Bishop of New Mexico. My most Illustrious Prelate of my highest respect and esteem: I report to you about Padre Abeyta who is residing in the parish house of Dolores [*Arroyo Hondo*] and, according to what I observe, is conducting himself well in his duties. It also occurs to me to tell your Most Illustrious Lordship that the enclosed tablet of six written folios contains the *apologia* which, through Don Ramon Trujillo, I

had sent word that I would do; in it your Most Illustrious Lordship will be informed of the Chapters of accusation that the Señor Don Juan Felipe Ortiz is carrying for the Pontificate [in Rome] – and, since it might not be received, or if it is, so that your Most Illustrious Lordship may have its contents before your eyes and may prepare your answer beforehand, I have checked on it for said purpose; and, while it covers the extensiveness for which I tried a fuller resumé of it, it sets forth the causes for complaint which appear to me the most obvious, although your Most Illustrious Lordship might prepare them with a better and stronger argument; nevertheless, I deem that this might somehow be of service to your Most Illustrious Lordship in this matter.

I, in having made the said Apology available, under the conviction that the steps taken by your Most Illustrious Lordship with regard to the administration of these churches of New Mexico, formerly as Vicar Apostolic and now as Ordinary Bishop, are for the sole purpose of achieving the best ends toward God's honor and glory, either through yourself or through your Vicar General, the Señor Don Jose Preyecto Machebeuf – and with such knowledge may you deign to receive with good grace my services regarding said Apology as obligated by my intention. I wish your Most Illustrious Lordship the best of health and the most prosperous felicity as your affectionate, assured servant and squire, who affectionately kisses your hand. Antonio Jose Martinez. [22]

The letter speaks for itself. Nor had any previous communication of his to Lamy been as fawning as this one. It is not only a shameless piece of sycophancy, but the lowest form of betrayal. Poor naïve ex-Vicar Ortiz must have left a copy of his personal appeal to Rome with Martínez, probably at that Easter meeting of April 2, and now Martínez had betrayed that trust. It was no less a betrayal, while all during this time having acted as their champion, of all of his fellow native padres. In comparison, one could almost overlook his most grave breaches of celibacy many years back.

And yet, at the very same time, one might be able to excuse it as the beginning of a serious breakdown in the personality of Padre Martínez, as this will become gradually but steadily more evident in the few years ahead. His Hidalgo dream was now dead, due to the quirks of history and no less his own character and his unrelenting ways. But still it was not in his nature to retire from the stage. He had not effected Vicar Machebeuf's downfall, as he was pleased to see that of his former innocent nemesis, Don Juan Felipe Ortiz, who had first lost his vicarial standing and now had been shorn of his cherished parish. He had now given up his prosecution of the French vicar, evidently hoping that he could still salvage some of his old dream under the Frenchmen's favor, and so keep himself in the limelight of this radically new and unexpected scene. At least he could continue playing the part of a grey eminence. Besides, it was time that he returned, with the blessing of the new regime, to the public forum as a molder of public opinion once more. As we shall soon see, it was the beginning of madness.

F or Bishop Lamy, the year 1854 began most auspiciously with his happy ordination of Padre José Eulogio Ortiz on January 5, which was followed eleven months later by those of the three students prepared by Padre Martínez.[1] He also had been preparing for a trip to France and Rome, meanwhile issuing a brief "Circular to the Clergy" on January 14 which contained seven regulations; the first four were good practical points on parish administration, but the next two still prohibited the sacraments and Christian burial to those who refused to pay their full tithes, and now tripling the sacramental fees for the members of the recalcitrants' households. But still, as with the 1852 Christmas Pastoral which it resembled in parvo, nothing at all about the native clergy's greed or sexual morals.[2] Nor did any objections come from any of the native padres left, much less from Padre Martínez. Rather, he approved of it most heartily.

But Bishop Lamy's greatest joy by far came during June when he was visiting the Holy City and his friends in the Vatican. No packets of incriminating evidence against Machebeuf had reached Rome from ex-Vicar Ortiz or Padre Gallegos. Bishop Zubiría in Durango, as the stickler to law that he was, had not forwarded them, since he could not interfere in the internal affairs of another diocese. Nor had the Apostolic Delegate in Mexico City, since the United States was out of his jurisdiction.[3] And so the worries about Machebeuf's violations of the seal of confession were now over for good, or so Lamy and Machebeuf thought.

As for Padre Martínez up in Taos, we learn that he was having his own troubles of an altogether different nature. Carlos Beaubien reported that an Apache brave had been captured by one of the padre's herders while making off with some of his livestock.[4] Then on October 14, Padre Martínez wrote obsequiously to Vicar Machebeuf, in charge of the diocese while the bishop was in Europe, giving him a detailed report of the tithes collected, or not collected, by Padres Abeyta and Lucero at Arroyo Hondo; he had advised them, he wrote, that either Lamy or Machebeuf were the sole arbiters in this matter, not Martínez himself. He also humbly begged Machebeuf for instructions on the matter, closing with the most affectionate regards and kissing the vicar's hand.[5] These were standard Spanish expressions, true, but in these contexts they smack of that obsequiousness so evident in his previous long letter to Lamy.

In November the bishop returned from Europe with young Padre Eulogio Ortiz whom he had taken along, and also with another Espagnol by the name of Dámaso Taladrid; this latter was a vagrant priest from Spain whom he had picked up in Rome, and who would soon become an unexpected nemesis for Padre Martínez. There were also four other priests and three seminarians whom he had recruited in France. All of them arrived in Santa Fe on November 18.[6] What Padre Martínez thought of this sudden augmentation in the foreign diocesan clergy, one cannot tell. Or, might he have been thinking even at this late period that the young brood of native padres compensating for it could somehow be manipulated by him for his own ends? Nor does he appear in any extant source until the following year. A signed note by him, dated May 28, 1855, and written by someone else with a very poor hand, has to do with the purchase of land next to the oratory of Talpa by some person "not of the Christian profession," and as to how the proper respect due the said chapel was to be safeguarded.[7]

Incidentally, while Bishop Lamy and his French vicar had been writing abroad about the evil morals of the native clergy almost since the day of their arrival, an interesting development had taken place during the year following Lamy's introduction of the four new French priests in November 1854. One of them was surnamed Martin – Lamy called him "Jean Martin," but obviously he muddled his first name as he did that of Etienne Avel, misnaming the latter as "Antoine." Fifty years later Salpointe referred to the former as "C. Martin."[8] Anyway, the only contemporary French priest named Martin, referred to elsewhere as having died sometime later at Ysleta del Paso, was designated either as "N. Martin" or "Francisco Martin."[9] Vicar Machebeuf had personally placed this "Mr. Martin" at Isleta in New Mexico in that same November month.[10] Sometime after this, Bishop Lamy received a most serious complaint against his morals from a prominent lady of the Isleta parish, Doña Dolores Perea, who referred to him as "Padre Martinez."[11] At first reading, one would naturally think that she meant the Padre of Taos, but, as one can see, it could only refer to that first French Father Martin of 1854. And, of course, neither Lamy nor Machebeuf ever mentioned him again.

Meanwhile, ex-Vicar Ortiz had returned from a two-year sojourn in Durango, when he began having his piteous troubles with Bishop Lamy once more. For by this time the distraught old man had lost all sense of reality – still hoping that Bishop Lamy would restore him to his Santa Fe parish on the score that he was the cura propio.[12] But not a word on this episode from Padre Martínez, naturally. One cannot doubt that Martínez and Lamy talked about it during the week of August 12 when the bishop was visiting the parishes of Taos and Arroyo Hondo; all we know is that Lamy inscribed his hearty approval of Martínez' orderly entries in one of the parish books.[13] Then, on November 29, Martínez wrote another fawning letter to the "Lord of my highest respects and esteem," its lengthy contents reduceable to the following points.

1) He had published the bishop's Circular on November 12 in his parish church of Our Lady of Guadalupe, and on Sunday the 25th at Ranchos de Taos; next Sunday he would read it in the Indian pueblo church; all the people had received with greatest joy the news about the newly proclaimed dogma of the Immaculate Conception, which they planned to celebrate with all solemnity on the day which the bishop would designate. – 2) The second part of the Circular, dealing with persons who did not pay their tithes – this, he now said, the people were ready to comply with as they had done with the Circular or Pastoral of last year (January 14, 1854). – 3) With regard to marriages during Advent and Lent, and the publishing of banns, he humbly asked the bishop if his orders of the previous year still held. – 4) Seminarian Tafoya, who was studying under him until the end of December, wished to continue his studies in Santa Fe, and would the bishop sell

him a theological book from his own library. – 5) Finally, Martínez went into many details about the tithes which had recently been collected in Taos, and which he was graciously remitting to the bishop.[14]

Toward the end of this same year of 1855, Padre Martínez began writing letters to the Santa Fe *Gazette* which elicited sharp responses as one would expect. Since he was no longer active in the Legislature, and his own press was silent, he now sought another channel for molding public opinion as he had done long before Lamy came, or at least to keep himself in the limelight. This "writing to the paper" was something which became a growing habit, and progressively more of an obsession, as he came to be contradicted by lay correspondents of every persuasion on the public scene. It would end with his own criticism of Bishop Lamy's policies after he had reached a critical point in his last years.

On December 1, 1855, he wrote a letter to the editor on special laws he had long ago proposed concerning marriages in a republic, and signing it with the pen-name "José Santistéban." (Lest we think this a sneaky subterfuge on his part, it was a Hispanic or Mexican practice of the times which we will find illustrated anon; that it also had psychological implications will also become progressively more evident.) This issue of the *Gazette* is not extant, but, according to what a Protestant minister named Samuel Gorman wrote to the paper four months later, his "friend Santisteban" had contended in his letter of December 1 that marriage was a civil contract. Now the good preacher took a whole column of biblical citations to prove that it also was a moral and a religious one (which Padre Martínez had implied but not stated), and hence it was wrong for priests and ministers of any faith to so obfuscate matrimonial matters among their flocks. Martínez must have then written a second such letter which we do not have, for on February 25, 1856, Mr. Gorman had written in from Laguna criticizing another Santistéban letter which proposed a civil law to regulate church fees. Now there were two columns of biblical and other quotations by Gorman contradicting the proposal.[15]

Incidentally, the Santa Fe archdiocesan archives had a copy of the *Gazette* for April 2, 1856, which carried a long Santistéban letter dated April 16, but it has long disappeared as have other items, simply because the chancellors or secretaries allowed unescorted individuals to rummage through the files, or else lent such items out. Coming back to Padre Martínez and the *Gazette*, he was correct in stating that marriage was also a civil contract, while giving Mr. Gorman an opening to pick a fight. But he was wrong, as he had been in the days of Bishop Zubiría when, directly contrary to his own views on the separation of church and state, he had expected the state to interfere in purely internal church affairs.

This has brought us well into the year 1856 – a most critical one for Bishop Lamy and Vicar Machebeuf. This is because the dead issue of the latter's confessional violations had suddenly come to life again. Here we have to go back to the year's very beginning before taking up again Padre Martínez' letters to the *Gazette* in their sequence, and the impasse which they would finally bring about in his relationship with Bishop Lamy.

Padre José Manuel Gallegos, who had given up all hopes of ever being re-instated by Bishop Lamy, had plunged into politics, and with such *savoire-faire* that he had been elected as territorial deputy to the national Congress more than once. The election campaigns had been most bitter ones, and dirty besides, still more so because the editors of the *Gazette* and his other foes had injected the religious issue. Here they had berated Gallegos as an immoral defrocked priest who was solely interested in enriching himself through his political and mercantile ven-tures. At the same time they held up Bishop Lamy as the heroic injured party who had been suffering so many injustices from some of the native clergy, among whom Gallegos was the worst. It was a ploy to get the Catholic vote, but it had miserably failed up to this time, especially in the newspaper's county of Santa Fe.

Bishop Lamy always disclaimed any political activity on his part, and one can believe him. But it is interesting to note that the newspaper editors and other writers used the Christmas Pastoral of 1852 as the reason for the native clergy's opposition to Lamy, as well as certain false accusations which Machebeuf had been making against Gallegos. In short, a person can talk with one's friends without raising a finger otherwise in a controversy. The details of these election fights are much too numerous to have more than a single reference here, since they do not affect Padre Martínez, but they will be treated in another book.[16]

Now Gallegos determined to get even, convinced that both the bishop and his vicar had been working underhandedly against him. During the late summer campaign of 1855, or shortly afterward when he had won the election, Gallegos drafted a very long complaint against Bishop Lamy, and addressed to none other than the Pope himself. To this he appended the copies which he had of the 1853 Martínez–C. de Baca–Armijo correspondence against Machebeuf, the one which he had not been able to put through to Rome by way of Bishop Zubiría's chancery three years before. As the big *político* that he now was in Washington, and head of his party in New Mexico, he got the members of the New Mexico Territorial Legislature, who were all his partisans, to draw up a formal document and affix their signatures to it. The resulting declaration, a big broadside in imposing large secretarial script, was then issued as of January 1, 1856. Now, below the signatures of all the protesting solons, we also find that of the territorial secretary, W.W.H. Davis.[17] He was the bitterly anti-native author of *El Gringo*, and who, as we also learn from his book, was a close acquaintance of Bishop Lamy at this time.[18] Hence it was from him that Lamy could have gotten word of the thing some days or weeks later.

This "Legislators' Letter to the Pope" was a direct attack on Bishop Lamy's alleged abuses of power, but so bumbling in the nature and presentation of its charges that the details do not merit space here. In general they reflect Padre Gallegos' own ignorance of church law and its procedures as well as the actual facts referred to, something which Padre Martínez would have handled in an en-tirely different manner. For this reason, Bishop Lamy should have had no serious reason to worry as to its contents, except for one thing. The imposing but vacuous document stated that, enclosed with it, went all the correspondence of 1853 which we have been treating thus far, all of it directed at his friend Machebeuf and not at his own authority as he had always contended – and with those most damaging charges about Machebeuf's breaches of the seal of confession. Here the documents in question were enumerated and described as follows:

Papers No. 1 and No. 2, *two writings from five clergymen against Vicar Machebeuf for the gravest abuses* (the Martínez letters of January 5 and April 2, the latter including Gallegos himself besides the four signers). Paper No. 3, *a petition from Santa Ana County* (the controversy between Lamy and C. de Baca of Peña Blanca). Paper No. 4, *some testimonials confirming the above* (C. de Baca's accusations). Paper No. 5, *another petition from the Albuquerque parish* (the Lamy-Armijo correspondence). Paper No. 6, *Lamy's Circular exacting tithes under gravest penalties* (the 1854 Circular to the Clergy and not the 1852 Christmas Pastoral). Paper No. 7, *a petition from the faithful of the Santa Fe parish* (not extant, and most probably ex-Vicar Ortiz' "Apology" on the loss of his parish).[19] We know that the Christmas Pastoral was not included because Machebeuf in Rome had to make a very false summation of it, and making it look as though it had been directed at the native clergy themselves.

As just said, Bishop Lamy had no real cause for worry about the Legislature's florid document's effect on the Roman Curia. The Vatican was always being deluged with complaints of this sort from all over the world, and, unless they dealt with what looked like hardfast cases of heresy or simony, or any violation or near-violation of the sacramental seal of confession, the officials there shelved any such general denunciations. Much less was Rome impressed by complaints coming from civil governments which had no *entente* with the Church, particularly from a minor assembly like New Mexico's in a faraway lost continent of uncouth pioneers and Indians. In this regard Padre Gallegos himself was suffering from a grand delusion, as when he also wrote a letter to the Pope from Washington on April 14, repeating the charges against Lamy in brief – as if the Holy Father would be impressed by a suspended priest simply because he happened to be a solon in the parliament of what was then considered a Protestant nation far across the sea.[20]

As for the unexpected resurrection of the confessional charges against Machebeuf, as contained in the enclosed "Papers," the reaction of Bishop Lamy and his vicar must have been immediate after having learned about it days or weeks later after the first of January. This is no empty surmise, for it is most evident in the decision they made of one or the other going to Rome. Machebeuf insisted on going himself (he left Santa Fe in March), purportedly on diocesan business in France and to defend his bishop against the Legislature's charges.[21] Once in Rome in late June, he must have been summoned to appear before the officials of the Propaganda Fide – *interpellato*, as this strictly juridical term in the final Italian verdict suggests. One can almost see him in wildest panic at a table on which the legislators' imposing broadside was spread out before him, along with the numbered "Papers" which accompanied it. He was in such a frightful dither that what he wrote in French as contestation covers page after page of hurried scribblings, mostly unpunctuated or else replete with dashes.

First he dismissed, in what he labeled *Remarques*, the legislators' charges against Lamy, simply by running down the native people of New Mexico as "a people ignorant and vicious," and in particular their elected representatives as crassly ignorant and unlettered politicians who were under the dire influence of the more wicked native clergy – especially ex-Vicar Ortiz before whom they *trembled!* (Underlining his, and the opposite picture of a meek fellow whom nobody feared.) Another section he entitled *Notice sur Jose Manuel Gallegos*, in which he summarized all the lies about him which he had previously written to his nun sister. (Here, for example, he denigrated his housekeeper as a prostitute, when in fact she was the widow of a prominent Mexican Commandant of 1833 who in her charity had reared a number of orphaned children; in this same vein he made Padre Luján the impossible paramour of Doña Gertrudis Barceló, simply because he wept at her funeral, and this is another story to be told elsewhere.)[23] The largest section, which he captioned his own *Defense*, he reserved for all the native priests whom he had suspended, besides others against whom he held a special grudge. His most vicious calumniations of each one can only be explained by his most evident panic. Other investigations, which will be published, prove the innocence of all these men at the time Machebeuf wrote, except in the case of Padre Ramón Salazar who could well have furnished him with a basis for such malicious exaggerations[24] As for Padre Martínez of Taos, Machebeuf had this to say about him:

> Mr. *Antonio Jose Martinez*, Pastor of Taos, is a priest of the same age as Mr. J.P[*hilippe*] Ortiz, of more than 60 years. He is certainly the best educated of all the priests of New Mexico; he himself had conducted a preparatory school in his house whereby the young priests which we found in the territory received *the little instruction* which they had. We have been able to prove nothing as of now about the accusations made against [*his*] way of living, but it is *certain* that *public opinion* [*the American bigots and his political foes*] condemns him – – – he is of a character so *false*, so *underhanded*, so *fawning* that while bent on working hard to destroy the authority of Mgr. Lamy he *appears exteriorly* to be his best friend; *duplicity* is therefore the dominant trait in him, but even when he has tried in plenty of occasions to destroy the people's confidence in Mgr. Lamy and his vicar general, the truth obliges me to say that he has never personally failed him in respect.
>
> Concerning one of the accusations which have been directed against the Vicar General of Mgr. Lamy as well as against his Excellency, he himself [*Lamy*] charged P. Martinez to prove the accusations; after several demands he cited several vague instances which evidently showed the bad faith of those who falsified them. To this he answered him [*requesting*] an exposition of the facts, and Mr. Martinez wrote anew to say that he *was satisfied* that he had found nothing about the revealing of confession as they had accused him of – (see herewith adjoined the 2 letters, the one of the vicar general and the one of Mr. Martinez)...[25]

The two letters referred to were their respective ones of February 3 and February 24, 1853. Then Machebeuf went on for fifteen more lines in defending that allegedly unauthorized marriage performed by him at San Juan, the one which Martínez had brought up in his February 24, letter. Here he said that Martínez had retracted by saying that he was "*entirely satisfied*" as to is validity, something which Martínez did not do. All this too, said Machebeuf, demonstrated once more his "*duplicity*" along with his "*bad faith*." Here all underlinings are his, as are those in the main section quoted above.

Had the panic-filled French vicar only known about Padre Martínez' clandestine and by now grown-up *bâtard* brood in Taos! What a story he would have had to tell the Roman Curia!

When Machebeuf finally laid down his pen, the Italian curial *segretário* in charge, as he is referred to, must have gathered up the folio-sized sheaves of atrocious French scribblings, along with the Legislature's broadside and the batch of the 1853 accusations clearly written in Spanish. Whether hours or days later, during which time Machebeuf must have suffered the torments of hell, the verdict was returned. It was written in a little more than two narrow columns of miniscule Italian script, entitled: *Reclami dedotti al S. Padre contro Mons. Lamy Vescovo di S. Fé e contro il suo Vicario Machebeuf.*

And what must have been Vicar Machebeuf's relief and elation when he read it! The *Signore* Machebeuf, it said, *interpellato* while visiting Rome on the feast of St. Peter, had satisfactorily answered all the charges against himself and his bishop. The "disorders of the American clergy in the provinces once belonging to Spain" had come about through their opposition to "the pastoral of Bishop Lamy issued in 1852." Some of these priests, besides, found ready followers among "a people ignorant and vicious." The prime mover had been "a certain Gallegos priest and pastor of Albuquerque who found himself in a scandalous union with a *donna di mala vita.*" Finally, the clinching proof for the falsity of the accusations with regard to the sacramental seal of confession was the declaration of the "Priest Martinez who is purely one of the adversaries of the Bishop" – and therefore most believable! With this quoted phrase the verdict ended.[26] *Roma locuta, causa finita.*

Voilà! The red herring of the Christmas Pastoral had worked! But no less had the vicious calumnies against the Hispanic people of New Mexico and their civil representatives, and in particular against the several native padres who had been selected as special targets. As for Padre Martínez far away in his little mud village of Taos up by the Sangre de Cristo peaks, little did he know that one small paragraph of his, in his letter of February 24, 1853, had been used atop one of the early Christian martyrs' blood-drenched Seven Hills of the Eternal City to get Machebeuf off the Fisherman's hook! It was a greater stroke by far than being published at greater length by the editor of a yellow sheet in a little adobe town named "Holy Faith."

Lamy Versus Martínez / 18

P adre Martínez must have soon learned about the Legislature's Letter to the Pope of January 1, 1856, for among the signers of it were his own brother Pascual Martínez and his foster-son Santiago Valdez. But this does not necessarily mean that he approved of it, and both Pascual and Santiaguito might have gotten a good dressing down when they brought him the news. For that upstart Gallegos had by now stolen his political thunder, a resentment which later becomes clearer. Besides, this was at the very time when he was still courting Bishop Lamy's favor. On January 3, 4 and 7 he had triumphantly sent Lamy his certifications on some of his seminarians, one of them the young Ramón Medina who was slated to be ordained on February 16.[1] But what is also most significant at this time, Martínez had reached his 63rd birthday on January 17, when he must have taken serious stock of his life and past achievements, as well as his failures and disappointments, while realizing how so many undreamt-of political and ecclesiastical developments had shot down his Hidalgo dream.

It does look like a long-delayed climacteric. For he began feeling very sick and helpless, as he wrote to Bishop Lamy on January 28, when he sent him a fine chalice as a gift, while remarking that he might be retiring soon.[2] To make matters worse, there were those sarcastic contradictions by Samuel Gorman in the Santa Fe *Gazette*, taking potshots at his vaunted political and religious wisdom, and all brought about by his own sapiential essay on December 1 of the year just ended. This we gather from the extant Gorman ripostes in April, which were soon followed by a much more vitriolic attack on Martínez, more or less on the same topics, by that old arch-enemy of his, the Spaniard Manuel Álvarez. The latter now called him "The Pseudo-Santistéban" – although he himself used the pseudonym "Recluta."[3]

As if these newspaper blows were not enough, the Utes and northern Apaches had continued raiding the Taos pasturelands, to such an extent that a meeting of 139 stockowners was held in Taos on April 21 for the purpose of protesting to the President what they deemed an ill-advised treaty which Governor Merriwether had concluded with those Indian tribes. Padre Martínez and his clan must have been hard hit, for he himself was there to get Judge Carlos Beaubien to preside over the meeting. Then he proposed a committee of six to draft the protest, and among those selected were his three brothers, Pascual, José María and Santiago, while the memorial itself was finally adopted on the motion of Santiago Valdez.[4] Evidently the Padre of Taos still felt quite ailing and depressed even at this later date, for on the following day, April 22, he wrote as follows to Bishop Lamy:

> *Señor de mis mas distinguidos afectos é estimación:* As I said to you in my letter [*of January*] of this year concerning certain ills that plague me, I now tell your Illustrious Lordship that if there were some priest whom you could send to serve this parish, I, in the hope of conserving my health, would like to be relieved of the one I have, for I find myself burdened a-plenty, perhaps for not being able to discharge the parish duties perfectly. But if it were possible, and your Illustrious Lordship found it convenient that Padre Ramon Medina would

finish the [scholastic] year by coming here, he would acquire practice and direction under my supervision and within a short time he could remain and ably continue [the pastorship], I myself then tendering my resignation. I propose this to your Illustrious Lordship regarding Medina in this fashion, because the populace here is so seriously dead-set against priests who are not natives of the land...since they judge them to be *Americanos.* I try to dissuade them, providing them with explanations and chiding them for their temerity, but it is after all their general disposition. With Carlos Beaubien I send you 16 dollars which I believe belong to you.[5]

It stands out clearly that Padre Martínez was not resigning his parish then and there – but now began that famous or notorious contest between Bishop Lamy and the Padre of Taos which the biographers have made so much of while taking the bishop's part. In his reply of May 5th, Lamy gently but trickily served the first ball, although the acrimonious matches between the two would come a good while later. In answer to his letter of April 22, Lamy wrote, unctuously repeating what Martínez had said concerning his health and his scruples about not administering the parish perfectly, that he was most happy to comply:

Now, so that the parishioners will not have to wait, I send not Don Ramon Medina because he is quite behind [in his post-ordination studies] – but Padre Don Damaso Taladrid who is well instructed in the sacerdotal ministry for having had other parishes under his care. In this way you shall be left free and unburdened of every worry so as to be able to rest, so much the more in the advanced age in which you find yourself.[6]

Unwittingly, the once so sly Padre Martínez, while planning to unburden himself of heavy parochial administration and still remain in charge of Taos by getting a native former disciple whom he could manipulate, had left himself open to what the bishop had long been waiting for. Lamy no longer needed his training of candidates for the priesthood, having already started a Latin school in Santa Fe and placed two lads in a French seminary.[7] He could not forget that the proud padre had once tried to prosecute his *cher ami,* although later he had relented and had become most cordial toward the vicar; he himself had gone along at the time, thereby successfully deferring a trial by letting the arrogant fellow believe that he was his valued sage adviser. All that was over. Now he could get rid of Martínez by shooting him down with his own petard.

Since Martínez had said that his people were loathe to have one of his French or other alien priests, he would send them one who by racial background spoke their language, not realizing that while the people might accept a priest from Spain, Martínez had despised European Spaniards (except for his long-dead friar friends) as a Mexican super-patriot, and most especially one such in Santa Fe named Manuel Álvarez. From what happened afterward, and from what one gathers from the pages of the *Gazette,* Padre Taladrid and his compatriot Álvarez had become fast friends while he had made himself Lamy's close adviser. Here was Álvarez' big chance to get back at his old critic and foe through Taladrid. As for the latter's parish experience, it was practically nil if it is true, as the old French priests used to say, that he had been nothing else than a Carlist revolutionary chaplain who had fled to Italy where Lamy found him.

To make matters worse, the substance of Martínez' letter to Lamy had not remained a private matter, for the Taos padre had grandiously announced his retirement in the *Gazette*, which carried a much longer letter to his Taos parishioners in this regard. Dated May 4 at Taos, before he got Lamy's reply of the 5th, it is reminiscent in spirit of his apologetical *Relación* of 1838, and also a strong indication that he had returned to live in the past. The points he now made are as follows:

In 1826 he had started out in Taos as a temporary pastor, and in 1840 (1842) as *cura propio* because of his fine showing at the *concurso* in Durango. – 2) He had never insisted on collecting the full tithes and fees prescribed by the Durango diocese; but in the disorders of 1837 (the Gonzales revolt) which began at Santa Cruz in August and spread to Taos in September, he had been obliged by force of arms to furnish the Taos insurgents with a protest against the *arancel* prescribing them, the one which had been abrogated at the time by the Mexican civil laws (a different story than the one told by Valdez). This, he said, was what had motivated the *Relación de mi Carrera (de Méritos)* which he printed, and copies of which were still extant. (Rather, it had been motivated by the political attacks of Manuel Armijo and his gang.) – 3) He had always been open with the people and had never exacted a full payment of (Zubiría's) diocesan fees and tithes – nor even the current ones (Lamy's) which demanded the minimum for the priests' sustenance, and this was because of the unwillingness of so many people who wanted their services without paying for them. (For exactly two centuries now, the New Mexicans had been niggardly in supporting their padres, a long story to be told elsewhere, but this is the first time he criticized them for it; at the sáme time he considered Lamy's requirements fair and just!)

4) Now he was resigning, he continued, and he apologized for any faults as a pastor, while ready to meet his Creator by publicly professing his Catholic Faith. His reasons for resigning were: *a)* his advanced age and physical disability, which must have been noticed in his preaching; *b)* a Pastoral and a Circular of Lamy forbidding the sacraments and Christian burial to those who did not pay their full tithes, etc., and penalizing the priests who did not carry out those orders. (This is the very first time that Martínez, nor had the other native padres done so, brought up the Christmas Pastoral of 1852, and this from its having been bandied about during the Gallegos election campaigns; the Circular referred to was the one to the clergy of 1854, and which Gallegos had used for the very first time in the Legislature's Letter to the Pope.) *c)* The third reason for his resigning was the refusal of the faithful to help in the repair of churches and cemeteries according to Lamy's orders which had been read on Sunday, April 13 (again a reproof to his *paisanos* and another approval of Lamy's recent regulations). – 5) Finally, on April 22, he had written to Bishop Lamy requesting a priest to take charge of Taos – "although I did not then resign, I told him that I would when the replacement arrived [*another strange contradiction*). So far he has not replied. But I suppose that in time he will send someone capable [Medina]. Taos, May 4, 1856."[8]

In this very same issue of the *Gazette* there appeared a letter of his directed to the editor himself, wherein he mentioned that on May 8 he had turned over the parish to Padre Taladrid (as he also noted down in the baptismal book on the same date). Taladrid, he said, had come with official letters of appointment. Now, he continued, he wanted all the people of New Mexico to know the three reasons for his resignation, and in which his Superior had concurred, and therefore that it was not a *removal* for any other cause. The *Gazette* editor then added his own brief comment, wherein he praised Padre Martínez as one of the few priests who had worked hard in behalf of his people and for the education of youth. He had his faults, he ended by saying, but who hasn't?[9]

Although Padre Martínez had received the Spaniard Taladrid in good faith, as we have seen, soon they began quarreling as one would have expected. On May 14, less than a week after he arrived in Taos, Taladrid wrote to the bishop about his troubles with the Taos fold concerning parish fees, since they had been wrongly trained by Martínez. The latter, he said, was now claiming that he had not really resigned his parish, but had simply asked for an assistant.[10] On May 21, Taladrid wrote much the same in greater detail, and with some unkind words about Padres Abeyta and Lucero.[11] On June 7, writing once more to Lamy from Ranchos de Taos, Taladrid hinted that Martínez was planning to build a private oratory, and that some *vecinos* might try to deceive the bishop in requesting his permission for its use; he mentioned Father (Pedro) Munnecom at Mora, and certain Apache raids; lastly he counseled Lamy to be chary of giving ex-Vicar Ortiz permission to leave New Mexico.[12] The reason for the private oratory, as we shall soon see, is that Taladrid was making it difficult for Martínez to say Mass in the parish church.

Another Taladrid letter followed on June 28, accompanied by some papers relating to some mission chapels; here the Spaniard told Lamy that Martínez was sick in bed, and that rumors persisted about the oratory he was going to build. Father (Etienne) Avel was ill in Mora, and to whom should this parish be entrusted, to the priests Pedro (Munnecom, a Hollander) or Abeyta.[13] In a subsequent letter of July 14, Taladrid relayed further troubles with Martínez after treating about the oratory of El Llano, the altars at Taos, and so forth; here he also mentioned the recent death of his countryman, Manuel Álvarez. Padre Montaño had arrived in Taos, he said, and Padre Lucero was as bad as Martínez.[14] In a second July letter of the 23rd, Taladrid brought up a debt which Bishop Lamy owed his late friend Álvarez (having to do with Taladrid's appointment to Taos?), and he said that Padre Martínez was now working on an article for the *Gazette* which dealt with the abolishment of tithes; Padres Montaño and Lucero were now more often with him.[15]

Although we have no other correspondence of this sort about the Taos situation until October of 1856, we know from letters of this Fall period that the intervening months since July had not been peaceful ones. By now it had become an unrelenting struggle between the conniving Spaniard, which was partly due to his bellicose nature if not also an inbred scorn for the "colonials," and the still Mexican-conscious Martínez who likewise never ran away from a quarrel. But still the latter failed to realize that the bishop was working against him. In his invariably polite and respectful way of addressing his prelate, he wrote Lamy a long complaint on October 1, in which he treated the following points.

First, Taladrid was trying to take charge of the Penitentes at Ranchos de Taos – or the "Tertiaries of St. Francis of Assisi" and "Order of Penance" as Martínez put it – but he could not cede this authority to Taladrid since he had received this strictly personal privilege from the second-last Franciscan Custos of New Mexico, and with Bishop Zubiría's approval(?).[16] In a subsequent letter of October 23, Taladrid wrote Lamy that he had composed a set of rules for the *Hermanos Mayores de la Hermandad*, a strictly Penitente term used by the brethren themselves which again shows how Martínez and the *hermanos* had for long confused this society with the true Third Order which no longer existed in New Mexico.[17] (Incidentally, Bishop Lamy would soon be doing the same in his own ignorance of Franciscanism.) Secondly, Martínez said that he had surrendered the parish (on May 8) with the best of good will (in spite of Lamy's trick), but, because the people had not taken to his methods, the Spaniard suspected him of being behind it. However, he added, he had smoothed things out by getting them to accept him. In spite of this, Taladrid did just the opposite by talking against him behind his back, even going so far as to instruct the sacristan not to prepare anything in church whenever Martínez wanted to say Mass. In fact, Taladrid had been acting this way ever since May, when he had told Martínez, while grasping both of his hands, "that he knew how to deal blows and fight!" Since then, too, Taladrid had been making the people believe that there had been a serious rift between Martínez and the bishop – all of it contrary to what Lamy himself knew and to what Martínez himself had published in the *Gazette*.[18]

By now poor Martínez was beyond realizing that, in spite of his having backed the bishop's more recent regulations and having chided his own people for their failings in this regard, he had also taken potshots at the 1852 Christmas Pastoral and the Clergy Circular of 1854. Now he went on to say that it was Taladrid's instructions to the sacristan which had prompted him to build an oratory on his property, with a cemetery-like wall around it, and why he had begun saying Mass away from the parish church. What is more, Taladrid displayed an open hate for some of his brothers and for a certain nephew of his (Santiago Valdez or Vicente Ferrer Romero?), whom he had called a heretic; the latter had threatened to sue, but the affair had ended in a compromise. "From what has been said, and from what he has done to me, I feel myself obliged to press my views further than I had intended, but always by way of justice and the acknowledgement I owe your Lordship as my legitimate superior, and for the good of the religion which we profess. Wishing you the best of health, your most affectionate servant kisses your hand."[19]

Padre Martínez has been accused of duplicity particularly at this time, long after Machebeuf had furnished his detractors with this term. But, as anyone can see thus far, he had not the least intention of fighting his bishop. It was the bishop himself who had laid the foundation for the padre's present state of perturbation by placing Taladrid under the saddle blanket of his psyche. For the nonce, the Spanish priest was acting as his whipping boy, just as Machebeuf proudly boasted of himself as the one whom his bosom friend had commissioned to "flog the cats" – *fouetter les chats.*[20]

What certainly looks like Taladrid's deliberate intent, even if Bishop Lamy had no such base end in mind, was to harrass the sickly and disturbed old man until he broke down completely. For this turned out to be the final straw which broke whatever ruptures inside a person's psyche under such circumstances. In the case of Padre Martínez, as the accepted observation goes, there was a very thin membrane between genius and madness. As if groping about for anything that might relieve the pressures straining inside his poor head and chest, he – José Santistéban, that is – turned once more to the Santa Fe newspaper.

O nly four days later, on October 5, 1856, after he had confided his latest troubles to Bishop Lamy, and writing as José Santistéban, Padre Martínez sent a long letter to the *Gazette*, evidently the one Taladrid had said he was composing. It was a reply to Samuel Gorman and other such "literary" contestants or adversaries whom he did not name. .The letter, or article rather, consisted of four full columns of his counter-arguments and other ramblings replete with citations from standard ecclesiastical sources. His main points were the avaricious accumulation of Mass stipends by certain (foreign) priests, and the sad plight of the native padres who had been under suspension; the right of the Legislature to write to the Pope; the fact that the editor had his real name on file; certain unjust regulations in the Christmas Pastoral of 1852 and the Circulars of 1853 and 1854; and, finally, that his printed letters had been meant for the instruction of the ordinary Catholic faithful, and not with his current critics in mind.[1]

Right away one can see a startling difference between the preceding most respectful letter to Bishop Lamy of October 1 and his newspaper article. Here he not only backs up the Legislature's Letter to the Pope condemning the bishop, but he goes deeper in his attacks on the now famed Christmas Pastoral and two others of Lamy's regulatory Circulars. It also bears repeating that up until now, none of the New Mexico padres, nor Martínez as "Martínez," had ever said anything about or against the Christmas Pastoral. But it had been tossed to and fro so often in the *Gazette*'s court, during the past three years since Padre Gallegos began running for Congress, that it had become a political football which even Padre Martínez – as José Santistéban – now took for granted as a genuine old issue. Lamy and Machebeuf, as we have seen, had done their work well in this regard. But for Padre Martínez this was a complete turnabout within the short space of four days, one which his critics have attributed to that duplicity which Machebeuf and his bigoted friends always liked to bring up.

However, the Taos padre in his right senses knew that Bishop Lamy would read this printed article shortly after he had read the personal letter he had received from him. Consequently, he was laying himself open to charges of duplicity, something which a sane Martínez would now allow. The only explanation, as can also be gathered from further developments, is that a latent schizophrenia had finally and almost of a sudden reached its climax. The Martínez personality had been splitting down the middle, and one side of it was hardly aware of what the other side was doing. One of the persons was José Santistéban writing to the *Gazette*, the other was Antonio José Martínez, *pbro.*, addressing himself to his bishop. Nor could it be anything like paranoia, since his being persecuted by Taladrid was as real as had been the attacks of many a former foe during his long active career. As for the Christmas Pastoral and related Circulars now coming into play within the Santistéban consciousness, it again bears repeating that it was because Lamy and Machebeuf, at least indirectly through their bigoted acquaintances, had injected them into the political columns of the *Gazette*. And it was with the *Gazette* alone that José Santistéban associated himself and his jumbled theories.

Bishop Lamy, unable to diagnose the old padre's malady, just as he had failed to recognize (or acknowledge, which is just as necessary) the pitfalls of his own *amitié particuliere* with Machebeuf, promptly suspended Martínez on October 24 or 27, 1856.[2] At last, the smartest and most powerful of the obstreperous Mexican clergy had taken up arms specifically against his Christmas Pastoral. This must have pleased him no end, since it confirmed a lie which he himself had come to believe to be true. Padre Martínez on his part, perhaps vaguely aware of what he had just done, stewed alone in his psychotic torments.

Writing to Lamy on October 23, Padre Taladrid observed that "our wise man of the north" was a person "much disturbed," little realizing how well he put it. He said that Martínez was not only celebrating Mass in his own private chapel, but had been reciting the prayers for the dead at wakes, and this with the purpose of depriving the parish (and Taladrid) of the accompanying fees. One example he gave was that of a deceased female neighbor of his who had died, a woman by the name of Luz Trujillo.[3] Actually, Taladrid himself conducted her funeral on October 8, 1856, giving her age as fifty and as having been the third wife of a Julián Sandoval.[4] Her full name, which is not an uncommon one in the Taos records, immediately conjures up Teodora Romero's mother. Whatever, Taladrid wrote in this connection, "I try to use all possible prudence, but this class of sparrows I attribute to something else."[5] Was he referring to some rumor he had heard about but could not pin down, about a suspicious relationship between Padre Martínez and the old lady?

In this same letter, Taladrid had also mentioned the recovery of some chalices which either Padre Martínez or Padre Lucero had sequestered, referring to a Padre (Antoine) Juillard, one of the French priests who had come from France with Taladrid and others, and who had been sent to Arroyo Hondo. (For some unknown reason, Lamy had already suspended Padre Lucero on September 15, who on October 8 wrote to the bishop from Arroyo Hondo, saying that he had been surprised by the suspension and humbly begged to be rehabilitated. Had this censure of Lucero been meant as a warning to Martínez?)[6] Sometime before this, Taladrid continued, he had been away from Taos, and upon his return had learned that Martínez partisans were accusing him of engaging in illicit trade – something entirely false as he now assured the bishop. He ended by referring to those rules he had drawn up for the Penitentes, trusting that Lamy would approve of them, besides asking him to advise him how to deal with a man "who has nothing of a human being but the shape."[7] From this last remark one might infer that poor Martínez' face did have the look of a madman, at least when confronting the Spaniard.

Almost at the same time, on October 24, Bishop Lamy had written a letter to Padre Martínez, who referred to it later on, and most likely having to do with what the Taos padre had published in the *Gazette* thus far. Then he wrote him a second one, dated October 27, the one in which he announced his suspension of Martínez, although he might have also done so in the one of the 24th. This we

> I received and have on hand your letters dated on [the 24th and] the 27th, in which you express a *suspension* against me because of certain writings which you intimate I *should recant*, and which I placed in *La Gaceta de Santa Fe* – and which you call *scandalous*. As to the contents of said letters, I say that I give and am ready to give complete acknowledgement as to my lawful superior, in everything that he may dictate or dispose according to the Canon Law which rules us; but, when acting beyond it he seeks to impose penalties arbitrarily, I protest the nullity of such procedures for thus I am backed by canon law, by virtue of which I do not consider myself suspended, nor am I so.[8]

Here Martínez went into paragraphs of ecclesiastical legalisms, all logically put according to his own premises, but which for the most part no longer held in the peculiar set-up of the hierarchy of the United States. He dealt mostly with his newspaper articles, something which he said was his republican right and privilege, and then with his saying Mass in his private oratory. (This he could not do without episcopal permission, and here he was being illogical.) As for other church matters, "especially the question of tithes for which your Lordship exacts their total amounts under penalties," such regulations overburdened mostly "the people among whom I was born." This, he said, had been his lifelong concern. Here he went into monetary calculations as the fees and tithes were being exacted by Lamy and which, Martínez held, made all the funds collected by the territorial legislature for education and other expenses seem puny in comparison. Next he erroneously argued that since there was no state religion, the collection of church tithes was not obligatory, comparing the trafficking by his priests in this matter with rank simony. He then ended by saying that he would retract if Lamy recalled certain regulations in his Circular of January 14, 1854, like the one tripling the fees for the households of those who did not pay their tithes in full. This was his humble petition, said he, while still convinced that he was not bound by any suspension.[9]

Here it is interesting to note that the very first marriage which Padre Martínez entered in his private record book on November 26, 1856, was that of Pedro de Vincula (St. Peter in Chains) Sánchez, the son of Cristóbal Sánchez and Guadalupe García, and Refugio Martínez, the daughter of his brother José María Martínez and Carmen Sánchez.[10] We know that the groom had been baptized as "Pedro Antonio" at Tomé on February 27, 1831, and this was the Pedro Sánchez who many years later published his *Memorias* of the padre. The marriage witnesses were Santiago Valdez and his wife Agustina Valdez, and this man was none other than the author of the *Biografía* of Padre Martínez. The next day after this wedding, on November 27, the Taos padre wrote to Lamy again. It was another long letter reviewing the causes and incidents which had led to his unjust suspension, and also his continuing troubles with Taladrid and what he thought of him. He furthermore complained that the old silverplate of the church had been replaced with sacred vessels made of base metals, ending up with the problem of the Penitentes and Taladrid's interference in this sphere.[11]

All in all, whatever his rebellious views now being so boldly expressed, Padre Martínez was not questioning or denying Bishop Lamy's authority as the lawful

Bishop of Santa Fe, as he never would, and much less trying to destroy it as Machebeuf always accused him of. But by this time the old question of fees and tithes, which had always been somewhat of a fixation with him even in Mexican times under the Durango diocese, and now so radically penalized by Lamy's drastic regulations, had become a pathological *idée fixe*, one which now began dominating both sides of his personality. Taladrid caused the idea to become further fixed by publishing, under the pseudonym "Religioso Observante," eight columns in two issues of the *Gazette* mocking the arguments of José Santistéban, who, he revealed as though it had been a great secret, was none other than the Padre of Taos. Here he called him a Voltaire and a Rousseau, as if he were an avowed enemy of the Church like those two famous Frenchmen, also disclosing that the pseudonymous "Recluta" who not too long ago had attacked Martínez in the press was the late Manuel Álvarez. Finally, he grossly calumniated the mentally disturbed padre by saying that Martínez himself oppressed the poor people by selling them grain at inflated prices, and that he appropriated the parish collections along with his brother Pascual and his "beloved Santiaguito Valdez."[12] To say the least, these were the boldest of lies.

In his turn, the newspaper editor evened things up by disclosing that Taladrid, who so piously criticized Martínez for writing under a pseudonym, was the person who had been signing himself "Religioso Observante."[13] Finally, the event-crammed year 1856 ended with one more letter from Martínez to Lamy, dated December 17. It had to do with his having read, "with belated meditation," his own article in the *Gazette* which had elicited Lamy's letter of October 24. He now confessed that in another article of October 8, some things had been said against his Lordship, but this was because of a previous article written by the "Recluta" (Manuel Álvarez) which had gone beyond the limits of moderation. The photo copy of this December 17th letter is mostly illegible, but one gathers from scattered snatches that, when referring to another letter of his of December 9, Martínez was expressing his respect for the bishop as his lawful prelate, while at the same time holding fast to his fixed idea. He then added in a postscript that certain bad feelings between himself and Taladrid had been ironed out, and that they had forgiven one another's injuries.[14] Had the poor man arrived at a lucid interval, or had he cagily decided to call for a truce during the battle, a rest period during the game?

Some "mad geniuses" are so gifted that they can bring a split personality back together again, and thus continue pursuing a monomania with all the apparent marks of rationality. This seems to have become the case with Padre Martínez in his broken-hearted *sentimiento*. The dream of his youth had been that of a Padre Hidalgo of his beloved New Mexico, bent on relieving the common people from what was to them, in his opinion, a heavy burden of taxation from every side. For this, Padre Hidalgo had been condemned as a traitor to the state, defrocked by his Church, and then executed by the Spanish forces who quartered his corpse and hung up the parts all over Chihuahua. On the same score, Padre Martínez might have felt that he himself had been condemned by his political peers, both during

Mexican and American times, and he was now being executed inch by inch through the machinations of a priest from Spain. What was most painful of all, he now stood divested of his priestly faculties by his own prelate. Now he stood alone, armed only with the lance of his *idea fija*, and oblivious of the fact that he was tilting at windmills. In this he was being a quixotic Castilian to the core, even when he had always gloried in the fact of being a down-to-earth Mexican.

As for Bishop Lamy, he looked upon Martínez as a stubborn old fool with wickedness thrown in. The best course would be to ignore him, since he was so wrecked physically that he could not last for long. This was when the year 1857 began, but Martínez fooled him by continuing acting with surprising spurts of vigor for ten more years. Whatever we know about this final period comes from further correspondence by Martínez and others, from some tracts which some of his clan printed in Taos, and from the private ministerial records that he kept.

From the opposite side there are only hints of his continuing intransigence, followed by much later statements about his final excommunication by Bishop Lamy and the so-called schism which the Frenchmen said that he started in Taos. Writing to Bishop Purcell on March 3, 1857, Lamy told him that Gallegos and the old Ortiz were still causing him trouble, "and worse than these two together, the old padre Martinez of Taos whom I was obliged to suspend last October." Their tactic, he said, was to deprive him of the tithes and firstfruits which the people had been accustomed to give, following it up with this lie: "The three clergymen mentioned above have got a handsome fortune from the church, and they know very well that if we were deprived of the temporary means, we could not stand for long."[15] The actual truth is that these three men enjoyed the fruits of their patrimonies as the eldest sons of well-to-do families, and they had expanded their holdings by means other than squeezing their parishioners. Most of the other native padres were not that lucky by birth, and the niggardly ways of their flocks had left them relatively poor. As for Padre Martínez, as we have seen, he had shared his patrimony and the good use he made of it with the needy.

Since the new year began, it seems, Padre Martínez had continued writing to Bishop Lamy, and was deeply hurt by not getting any further replies. On April 13 he wrote the bishop a very long letter which can be reduced to the following points. First, he had not received any replies to his letters of November and December of the preceding year, nor to one at the beginning of this March when he complained that Taladrid had injured him with oral and written detractions, and even during his sermons – and lately in the bishop's name! Secondly, Lamy had kept silent after that letter of October 24 whereby he had been suspended; here he went into the reasons that led up to it, repeating at great length the very same legalisms to show that the suspension had been null and void. Thirdly, he went further back to his letter of April 22, 1856, when he had asked for a priest to relieve him, and to the much later one of November 27 which explained why he had not resigned because of Taladrid's ill-conduct toward him, and who got worse every day by also proving himself to be a libertine, a drunkard and a gambler. In fact, he said, Taladrid had also boasted that he was the one behind the false charges made against the native clergy by Don Antonio Miguel Otero in Congress, a speech which was printed on May 10, 1856, and copies of which had been sent back to New Mexico.[16]

This Miguel A. Otero, a much younger brother of that Kearny-appointed Justice Antonio José Otero who had sanctioned Valencia and Cárdenas in their schism back in 1849-1850, had unseated Gallegos by means of the speech which Martínez now mentioned. Trained in both Catholic and Protestant schools back east, he had a good command of English, but the speech he gave against the native clergy was not original at all, merely a compilation of the standard lies contained in American publications of the times. Bishop Lamy was most elated by this turn of events, and wrote how much he admired this young man who at last had told the truth. The details of this episode, as well as many others, will be left for the book mentioned a good while back.

But we are not finished with Padre Martínez' letter, tedious as the detailed review of all these communications has been. Martínez now went on to say that the bishop ought to know that by church law his own status as *cura propio* was as unviolable as Lamy's own as bishop, neither of which could be lost except by resignation; here he was not interested in parish emoluments, he said, but only in getting a good priest to succeed him – once again plunging into many intricacies of old church law that no longer held, at least in this country. Furthermore, instead of Lamy answering him in writing concerning some points in his letter of November 12, he had to hear about it from some layman. Repeating that he was free from suspension, he went into a discussion on the matter of free expression in the press, and now he demanded three things of the bishop: To recall the Circular of January 14, 1854 as prejudicial to the spiritual welfare of the faithful; to declare his letter of November 12 as unjust, and finally to recognize him as the irremovable pastor of Taos, and to remove Taladrid by sending him a good priest who could ultimately succeed him. Or did the bishop wish to treat him as he had done the other defenseless clergy?[17]

Here he briefly mentioned the removal and suspensions of Gallegos and ex-Vicar Ortiz – about whose plight he had cared less at the time, except for using them as cases in point when he was playing the part of a grey eminence. He followed next with some matrimonial cases, as when both Lamy and Machebeuf had sanctioned the marriages of certain couples he now named, and who had previously been married to different partners – again something he had not brought up when he had thought himself to be the bishop's sage adviser. Then he concluded by recurring once more to the unjust penalties imposed on those who did not pay their tithes in *toto*.[18] What these most tedious repititions mainly show is that the poor fellow was far gone in his madness as he kept on jabbing at impassive windmills. But, alas, he was no gentle Don Quixote.

Meanwhile, Vicar Machebeuf had returned from Europe in February, and very happy, we can suppose, with that Roman verdict which had set his spirit free. Sometime after this Bishop Lamy must have summoned him from Albuquerque, when he asked him to go up to Taos and reason with Padre Martínez. After all, it was Martínez who had absolved his friend three years before on that confessional matter, and he might listen to him again. This we gather from a letter of May 2, 1857 which Martínez wrote to Machebeuf, referring to a personal interview which they had on the night of April 15. Here, after going through the same old routine of Lamy's unjust treatment of himself, Martínez referred to noisy riots which had taken place in Taos, and the possible use of armed force against himself and his own people – for as long as the exacting of money was commensurate with "Catholic Faith," as Taladrid had intimated in his famous libel in the No. 42 issue of the *Gazette*. "I so explain myself," Martínez now told Machebeuf, "so that you may understand me, and not come to molest me in my house." [19]

Evidently, the vicar had stirred up some of the people, among them some of the French-Canadians and *americanos*, and perhaps had given Martínez an ultimatum on that night visit of April 15. But all he wanted now, Martínez concluded, was only to help those folks who recurred to him as their legal pastor, and as one bound by the Catholic religion which he professed. He knew his duties in conscience as backed up by Canon Law and the liberal government of the United States, confident that all the machinations designed to vex him would never succeed. [20] Here he was telling the truth, for he had no intention to start a schism as Valencia and Cárdenas had done. Sooner or later, he thought, Bishop Lamy would see the error of his ways, just as the civil government had absolved him of guilt after those two crucial crises of 1837 and 1847. As we can see, this was the thinking of a mind which had parted ways with reality.

Schism and Excommunication? / 20

I In one way, Bishop Lamy did come to realize that he had made a grave mistake. A month later, in late May or early June of 1857, he sent young Padre José Eulogio Ortiz of San Juan to replace Taladrid in Taos, and the latter turned over the parish books to him on June 5.[1] Since Padre Martínez had originally requested the native young priest Medina, the appointment of this other young native padre in whom he placed the fullest trust would now help the bishop save face, and at the same time restore peace in the Taos valley. But belated wisdom in this case could not undo the damages caused by a previous foolhardy act, for little did Lamy realize that Martínez had taken a psychopathic path from which there was no return.

At first the old man welcomed the new replacement, but under the condition that he was still the real pastor, he himself firmly convinced that his status as *cura propio* continued despite his earlier resignation, whether conditional or not, and that the latest suspension by the bishop did not count. In his derangement, he must have thought that the removal of Taladrid implied a restoration of things as they had been before the inimical Spaniard came. For, writing to the young Ortiz on June 22, only two weeks after the latter's arrival, he quoted a letter which he was writing to his bishop, and in which he told Lamy that he and all the parishioners of Taos had accepted Ortiz *for the administration of the sacraments,* hence rather as an assistant and not a full pastor. He said that on June 16 Ortiz had asked him certain questions concerning the revalidation of marriages which Martínez had performed since the beginning of November the previous year (like the one of Pedro Sánchez), claiming that these were legal because he was still the *cura propio,* even though he had to suffer the humiliation of being merely an assistant (to Taladrid). This, he now told Ortiz, was his answer to the bishop and to him as well; while he repeated Ortiz' status as administrator, he had recently conducted the funeral rites for a poor man whose brothers had guarded his oratory from being burned (probably when Machebeuf came to Taos in April).[2]

On July 23, young Ortiz wrote to Lamy that he had missed seeing him in Santa Fe after the latter's return from El Vado, but had spoken with Vicar Machebeuf (before July 15) concerning new troubles he was having with Martínez. Now the bishop would learn more from the copies he was remitting of the letter which Martínez had written to him and from his own reply. Here Ortiz, and without realizing it as with Taladrid before him, laid a finger on the poor padre's dementia by remarking that in his "crazy" letter Martínez had designated himself four times as the pastor of Taos, and once as the assistant pastor. "*Pobre Martínez desgraciado!* He desperately wanted to visit me: he first sent word if I would receive an excommunicate, and my answer to his messenger was that, if he was already condemned, I also had the faculties from the lawful head of the New Mexican Church to receive the condemned." The old padre did come to see him, wrote Ortiz, and he conversed with him for about an hour, the old man answering with "Amens" to the topics under discussion as the young priest laid them out before him. Finally, Martínez told Ortiz that his differences with Taladrid had been out of pure caprice on his part; now, under more favorable circumstances, he was acknowledging Ortiz as the pastor of Taos, and henceforth he would no longer exercise any parish ministrations.[3]

What certainly looks like double talk here was more the wiles of a deranged mind, as we saw before in a truce he had made with Taladrid. For, as Ortiz went on to say, it was all directly contrary to his former letter and his consequent behavior. Then Ortiz assured the bishop that "Padre Martínez is getting ever weaker and from now on will not meet with the successes he had intended to have."[4] Padre Martínez, of course, was thinking just the opposite in his delusion, as he had written to Machebeuf in April.

It will be noticed here that Padre Martínez had used the word "excommunicate" with reference to himself, but in such a sarcastic way that it is obvious that he was using the term loosely, as a synonym for "suspended." Nor does it come up in a letter which he wrote to Lamy on October 21, and which dealt with these three topics. First, Ortiz had written to Martínez on September 23, requesting a conference on the 26th, which they both had. Since then Ortiz had been administering the parish in peace because the disturbances caused by Taladrid were now over. Secondly, Martínez had told Ortiz that he would write to the bishop in the month of October, but illness had prevented him until now; meanwhile, everything was all right, and the Taos community was satisfied. Thirdly, he now went back to that article of his in the *Gazette* (here his monomania surfacing anew), which he said had merely repeated another writing of his which had been published in Mexico far back in 1826, as by a free citizen, and for which the Durango diocese had never taken the writer to task. Why, he asked, could he not do the same under a more liberal form of government?[5]

But three weeks later matters had come to a head between him and young Padre Ortiz. The old fellow wrote the latter a very long missive on November 12 which, aside from a resurgent spirit of animosity against Ortiz, was no more than a recurrence of his *idée fixe*. Reaching back to a letter which Ortiz had written him on September 21, parts of which he regarded as threats, Martínez recalled that both he and Ortiz had made an agreement whereby the latter would administer the parish as a whole, while at the same time the old man reserved to himself the services requested by his own *familiares, parientes y amigos*. He argued that he had kept his part of the agreement (which Ortiz certainly could not and would not make), even sending some of these adherents of his to Ortiz for his services; but Ortiz had then gone beyond the bishop's list of fees by charging them extra. He had also gone to the homes of the Martínez brothers and other persons, telling them that they would be denied the sacraments if they did not pay their full tithes to him; hence this business of demanding pay beforehand smacked of simony.[6]

From here on Martínez (at one with Santistéban) went into the old song about church collections under monarchic and republican governments, saying that in the United States the old Spanish *patronato* now resided in the faithful, who nevertheless should contribute to the support of the clergy through their free-will offerings. Here he also criticized the pertinent points in the Christmas Pastoral of 1852. Next he brought up that 1849 decree by a territorial governor which had allowed people a free choice of ministers for marriage ceremonies, and then went further back to Bishop Zubiría's decision of September 6, 1850 (written in the Taos books), which stated that people unable to pay anything should not be denied the sacraments. All this, he said, he had passed on to Bishop Lamy on November 13, (1856) – and this is why Lamy had suspended him on October 27, and without any previous canonical warning![7]

In the same vein he now lashed out against young Padre Ortiz. Contrary to that agreement between them of September 26, Ortiz had spoken evil about him in his absence, and had taken back what they had agreed upon in his letter of October 24. In this one Ortiz had claimed that he was simply following his bishop's instructions, which Martínez now supposed had to do mainly with tithing, a subject which he himself had already treated in published articles, and which had not pleased Lamy. For, he added, he himself and Vicar Machebeuf had talked about it (on April 15). Furthermore, he said, this is what Ortiz himself had preached about in Taos on November 1, and at Ranchos de Taos on the 25th of October, asserting that tithing was not merely a church obligation but a divine one as well. A divine decree it certainly was not, Martínez maintained, and here he dived again into his hoary arguments to illustrate the differences between himself and the bishop. He ended by advising Ortiz to keep their agreement of September 23, and assuring him that he himself would continue ministering to his own few followers amid the confusion.[8]

Ortiz then replied at full length with a strong letter on November 12, rightly disclaiming any pact he had ever made with Martínez, while re-asserting his own fidelity to the bishop's regulations, and answering paragraph by paragraph all the legalistic assertions which Martínez had made.[9] It was a good piece of exposition, but, in his inexperience, young Ortiz did not know that he was wasting his time arguing with a demented man, and one whose genius enabled him to pursue a fixed idea with every mark of rationality despite several overt contradictions. All of this was being mistaken for pure stubbornness in an evil and vengeful character. But not a single hint in all this correspondence of any excommunication having taken place.

Nor had the political press in Santa Fe been letting poor Padre Martínez alone, and sundry letters being sent to the *Gazette* make it look as though he was also feuding politically at this particular time. But this was not the case at all. Rather, it was some Taos foes of the Miguel A. Otero "American party" who had been writing to the newspaper under different pseudonyms, or else printing their attacks on the press at Taos, and purposely making it appear as though Martínez was behind it all. For example, in July 1857, one Francisco Gonzales had accused him as the "pseudo-Santistéban" who recently had been writing from Taos under such signatures as "El Joven del Norte" and "Democrata sin Cola."[10] This sounds more like a much younger man – Vicente Ferrer Romero, for example, who was connected with the small press in Taos. Also, if there was anything like a religious schism building up in Taos, it was Romero who was behind it, and not Padre Martínez, from what we learn later.

For Francisco Gonzales himself had to concede that those writers in the north could else be what he called the padre's foot-licking pimps and minions, his *chuchos y alcahuetes*. He himself, Gonzales claimed, had been a Martínez pupil and follower until 1855 when the padre began calumniating him; now he accused his former teacher of having fomented the revolt of 1847 against the American government, claiming to possess a letter from Padre Martínez to a Manuel Cortez whom he at that time had appointed a captain in the "Militia of Mexico." The only things which Gonzales had learned from him, he ended by saying, was to be a revolutionary and to love women.[11] Here he was obviously mouthing the old Anglo-American canards about Martínez and the native padres in general as they were being rehashed at Otero's headquarters for his wardheelers to circulate all over.

The same stripe of dirty politics being printed came from a subsequent letter by a certain "A.C." (Albino Chacón?). He chided Padre Martínez for being against Otero, who was now running on his own for Congress, although, he said, the Taos padre had formerly upheld Otero's own principles; to wit, Martínez had once stood for the Church, and so did Otero and his party who were faithful to Bishop Lamy; Martínez had been against Padre Gallegos when the latter ran for Congress, and so were Otero and his men against a Texan fellow named Baird who has supported Gallegos; Martínez had distrusted the Americans who had been getting high goverenment posts, and so did Baird. With this kind of political logic behind him, the writer went on to claim that he had extracts of three letters which the Taos padre had written to Albino Chacón: One of May 13, 1851, in which he had been against Diego Archuleta running for Congress, and another of September 1, 1853, in which he had also been against Gallegos when he was running for Congress; the third one of August 25, 1854, in which Padre Martínez was against several candidates, Francisco Gonzales being among the others of the American party, he had recommended Santiago Valdez and his own brothers instead.[12]

Whether any of these old accusations have some elements of truth or not, it appears practically certain that Gonzales and Chacón were using the distraught old man as a whipping post in their own political squabbles with those Taos relatives and friends of his who were against Otero's faction and, according to them, likewise against Bishop Lamy – whose name they had been using for their own ends ever since Padre Gallegos had first run for Congress four years before. In this regard, the newspaper editor got in his licks by falsely stating that Miguel E. Pino (a seasoned Santa Fe politician of the Gallegos faction), as well as Padres Martínez and Juan Felipe Ortiz (both of them in their dotage) were the current leaders of the "Mexican party." Furthermore, he stated, resurrecting a ten-year old lie, both of them had been against the American government when it was first introduced! Bishop Lamy and his priests, he went on to say, were wrongly being accused (by the Taos opposition) of working for Otero, but this was not true even if they all did favor Otero! Then the editor contradicted himself by saying that old

Padre Martínez' public career had already come to an end, while calling him the Revolutionary of the North, the Catilina of New Mexico, a religious Quijote, and a schismatic priest with his gospel for the ignorant poor.[13]

As far as the Quijote reference goes, and Padre Martínez' lifelong campaign for the poor and downtrodden, the editor was not far from wrong. As for the lay Protestant's use of the schismatic idea, we can readily guess where it came from – just as had the red herring of the Christmas Pastoral entered into the political jargon four years before. Then that same Francisco Gonzales followed with another attack on Padre Martínez, whose alleged political sallies, he said, were being printed in Taos by an American named Bonsall, *alias culo roto*. But the man actually behind the scene had to be the same old José Santistéban, chief of the *campos santos de honor* (whatever he meant) who claimed to be as legitimate as the Catholic Church itself, and who held that tithing was not obligatory because Bishop Lamy was more of a political partisan than a minister of the gospel.[14] What logic! Now, we know that in all his latest aberrant criticisms of Lamy, Padre Martínez had never accused him of meddling in politics. Nor as José Santistéban either.

As said before, this was all a politicians' game being played by the Otero and anti-Otero factions, some of Padre Martínez' friends and relatives in the latter, and with the once politically active and powerful Padre of Taos being tossed to and fro between them.

During the greater part of 1858 we have nothing to go on about Padre Martínez, except that by this time his rebellious actions, as others saw them, were more frequently being referred to as a "schism." We have just seen this idea being expressed by the editor of the *Gazette*, and it could have only come from the French clergy in Santa Fe. And it was Machebeuf who wrote in May 1859 that in the previous year he had preached a mission in a large northern parish which was divided by a "deplorable schism" caused by two "wretched Mexican priests" (Martínez and Lucero).[15] This term, which both Lamy and Machebeuf continued using, was passed down the generations of writers, and in connection with the Taos situation it bears explaining.

A real schism in the Church (literally the Greek word for "split") is one caused by an individual or group whereby they not only break away from papal authority, but continue recruiting followers and fighting that same supreme authority. The classic example is the Great Schism of early centuries when most of the Eastern Churches seceded from Western Rome through a combination of political motives as well as some doctrinal differences with regard to their precise definitions. We also have a modern example in much smaller scale in a French archbishop, Marcel LeFebvre, who not only spurned the liturgical changes made by Vatican Council II and the Popes who implemented them, but also, besides establishing his own seminary, has travelled throughout Europe and parts of America to preach his separatist views and recruit more followers.

Padre Martínez did no such thing. He never rejected the Pope's supreme authority as Head of the Church, nor Lamy's authority as the Bishop of Santa Fe.

When protesting his suspension, he merely held that Lamy was wrong in doing so, not that he did not have the authority. As far as all the evidence goes, he did not even try to split the Taos parish in half, but simply retreated within his house and oratory where he continued ministering to a limited number of household relatives and friends who chose to adhere to him while he licked his wounds. Among these was his simple disciple, Padre Lucero, long mesmerized by his master's overbearing character and his purported wisdom. That this or the other of his adherents, like Vicente Ferrer Romero as we shall see, did try to form a separate church body is a different thing, and Padre Martínez was blamed for it. What he in his madness still hoped for was that his bishop would eventually see the light, still piteously insisting that he had no other immediate prelate or superior than Bishop Lamy. At the same time his mind kept reverting more and more to the past.

A letter which he wrote to Lamy on March 29, 1858, deals with a previous one he had sent him on October 21, 1857, in which he had complained about Father Eulogio Ortiz and his sermons; these sermons, he said, and those of Padre Abeyta along with those of two others at Arroyo Hondo (French Fathers Juillard and Ussel) were pure attacks on his own person which scandalized the faithful. What was still worse, Ortiz in Taos had addressed the Virgin of Guadalupe in such a blasphemous manner that she punished him by allowing him to commit another sacrilege – by further violating the Marian oratory of a Nicolás Sandoval when he removed its *santos* and was taken to court as a consequence. Still, this letter ended with the writer's recognition of Lamy's authority as his legitimate prelate.[16]

Now, the only explanation for these strange charges against Padre Ortiz is that the latter had been waging a campaign against the native-made *santos*, apparently by Lamy's orders. He might also have read Bishop Zubiría's previous prohibition of them in the parish books. And so recently, during a sermon, he must have derided the "ugliness" of the patronal *bulto* or *retablo* of Our Lady of Guadalupe in the Taos church, and this must have cut Padre Martínez' Mexican sentiments as well as his devotional sensibilities to the quick. Then Ortiz had removed similar images from a man's private chapel, only to be hauled into court for private trespassing and theft. It is quite evident that this young padre, eager to carry out all of his bishop's regulations, had gone too far. These incidents graphically illustrate the clash of cultures which lay at the bottom of the misunderstandings between the old and the new clergy. If Bishop Zubiría had deemed the *santos* "deformed," accustomed as he was to the realistic but well-formed images in the Spanish tradition, how much more did Bishop Lamy and his French clergy who were used to their own pretty and sugary statuary which they were now importing, actually a decadence from the classic Rennaissance. In short, Padre Martínez and his simple country folk were far ahead of their time, since the appreciation of what is now called primitive art was yet to be born.

We have nothing more about the Taos padre for the remainder of 1858, and we can only speculate that he found himself all the more abandoned, even by those new native priests whom he had hoped to have under his influence. The older Abeyta, with whom he had always been on the best of terms until recently, was now preaching against him. Those last three men whom he had trained, including Medina whom he had first asked for, were keeping their distance. This Eulogio Ortiz, the *santos*-destroyer, and who was doing what he pleased with his Taos church and parish, he now considered a sharp thorn in his side. As for Padre Gallegos, who long ago as a young padre had plotted with him against Governor Armijo, he had left the priesthood – something that he would never do – but by this very fact Gallegos was able to make more noise in politics than he had ever done. Then there was the case of Don Juan Felipe Ortiz, once his superior whose position as vicar he had always resented; after losing his Santa Fe parish, that urbanely weak ninny had lacked the courage and the necessary knowledge to fight for his rights effectively, and so he had died of a broken heart. This he himself would never do either.

As the year 1859 began, Bishop Lamy replaced Padre Eulogio Ortiz in Taos with a younger Frenchman named Gabriel Ussel. Ortiz turned over the parish to him sometime in January. Either Ortiz had asked to be changed or, what is more likely, the bishop now thought that Ortiz – after having completely renovated the old church and kept the majority of the faithful from joining the "schism" – had cleared the path for him to install one of his compatriots in one of the diocese's largest parishes. This is an educated guess, because the same thing was taking place everywhere in New Mexico. Father Ussel, who had been assisting at Arroyo Hondo since the year before, and who seems to have been a level-headed person all his life, might have done nothing to further antagonize Padre Martínez.

But this very appointment of a European priest could well have caused an uproar among many parishioners without any help from Padre Martínez. They had liked their Padre Ortiz, going so far as to help him restore the entire church structure while Martínez stewed alone at home. Hence it is quite possible that Martínez now added fuel to the fire; or else, which is more probable, some of the hot-headed members of his clan, Vicente Ferrer Romero in the lead, took the opportunity to cause more trouble. As a result, Bishop Lamy decided upon an extreme measure – a formal excommunication of the old man and his partner Lucero, and through the agency of his seasoned cat's paw or cat-whipper, his ever ready *cher amí* Machebeuf.

Also the more immediate cause for such a drastic action could have been some tracts being printed in Taos. The extant copies begin late in 1859, but the press could have been active well before this. While the definite Martínez essays were harmless in themselves, there were others with a schismatic flavor by Vicente Ferrer Romero comparable to the political ones treated just before, and which were attributed to Padre Martínez himself. But now to the excommunication itself. Father Howlett, in his Life of Machebeuf written about fifty years later, has been the source for the particulars of this unfortunate episode. He stated that after Martínez had resigned his parish, and Taladrid had been sent to replace him, he soon set up an independent church! He said that Bishop Lamy first went up to Taos to confer with Martínez, but old Martínez would not listen and was suspended as a consequence! The same thing happened with Lucero at Arroyo Hondo, and then these two padres joined forces! Bishop Lamy then sent Vicar Machebeuf to pronounce the solemn sentences of excommunication with all kinds of fanfare, after the proper admonitions had been read in the churches of Taos and Arroyo Hondo on three successive Sundays; however, no popular disturbances followed in either town, and this is when both padres started a schism which lasted until the death of Padre Martínez![17]

Here one can see how history is too often made *post factum*, and with no wrong intent on the author's part. We saw this long ago with regard to an innocent passage in Salpointe, also written half a century after the events in question had happened. This is when Howlett also remarked that "Kit Carson, Charles Beaubien, Ceran St. Vrain, and other prominent Catholics" stood at the ready to defend Vicar Machebeuf in case violence arose, and the Frenchmen's admirers have always made much of this passage. Whether this was the stance of those men or not, or whether or not Carson and Beaubien were practicing Catholics, Howlett did not know that Beaubien as a land-grabber had once been Padre Martínez' foe, or that St. Vrain was a *francmason*. Then what Howlett did was to telescope and invert the events and their causes as he set them down.

Now, it is very doubtful that Bishop Lamy had gone up twice to Taos to confer with Martínez and Lucero. It was not his style, especially when he had Machebeuf around to skin the cats. Hence what is more probable, the latter did go up to read the excommunications in the churches of Taos and Arroyo Hondo with just enough fanfare to impress the people if not to scare the two dissident priests back to their senses. We say this because there is nothing, nothing, about any such drastic measures, much less about Machebeuf's histrionics in carrying them out, in the contemporary correspondence of Lamy and his vicar – or in the writings of Padre Martínez himself. All three of them would have made this a clamorous issue. Or was Bishop Lamy chary of mentioning the matter to the American bishops back east or to his friend Cardinal Barnabo in Rome, simply because his action was questionable, if not illegal? And how could Machebeuf have restrained himself from painting this great dramatic triumph of his to his nun sister and others? As for Padre Martínez himself, were his senses so befuddled by now that such an act of excommunication was merely a meaningless extension of his previous suspension?

What we do know for certain is that Bishop Lamy did record the two excommunications which he had imposed, but in a place where no Bishop Purcell or Cardinal Barnabo would see them. These he entered in the Taos burial book on July 1, 1860, and in the Arroyo Hondo baptismal book on July 8. In Taos, Lamy wrote that he had pontificated on that day and confirmed more than five hundred adults and children. Since his last visitation in August 1855, he said, Taos had had several pastors "who due to grave and critical circumstances we had to remove." In the beginning of 1857, he went on, he had to punish Padre Martínez

for his grave and scandalous faults and his writings against the order and discipline of the Church, but unfortunately he paid no heed to the censures; on the contrary, he began to say Mass, administer the Sacraments, and publish still more scandalous things. We then saw ourselves obliged to excommunicate him *servatis servandis* |*all things being equal*| with all the required formalities. Since that time this unhappy priest has done all he can to make a schism both publicly and privately, daring to say Mass, administer the Sacraments, and thus perverting a great number of souls; but in spite of this schism, the greater part of the faithful remains in favor of law and the legitimate authority, as the books of entries prove; the parish church has been well renovated inside and out, especially during the administration of the *Señor Cura* J.E. Ortiz. There are new bells, a new tower, a new altar and new and good vestments both in the parish church and in the several chapels; there are also more of the faithful who frequent the Sacraments; thus, while some lose the Faith because they abandoned good works, others strive to procure the good of souls and the glory of God. [18]

What Lamy wrote at Arroyo Hondo on the following Sunday is more interesting in a way. This parish had been created on May (March?) 16, 1852 (1853), with its missions of Arroyo Seco, San Antonio and Rio Colorado, the last without a chapel at the time; but it now had a large and pretty one, even if unfinished because of the schism. New missions which had been added since then were Costilla, Culebra and Fort Garland. After offering this information, Lamy criticized *"el desgraciado Lucero"* simply because he had left fifty entries in the book unsigned. (Machebeuf had done the same in Albuquerque!) This was nothing to wonder about, he commented, because sometime afterward "this same priest incurred suspension and excommunication and is now carrying out a schism, daring to say Mass" – and so forth as he wrote about Martínez. Then he proceeded to describe the improvements made since his last visitation, and ended by saying that the zeal of the faithful was compensating for the schism caused by Lucero and his "Master Padre Martinez." [19]

From all this it is most obvious that Bishop Lamy had indeed imposed the sentences of excommunication on both Martínez and Lucero, but with misgivings about his powers to do so, *servatis servandis* – hence nothing about it to his friends in the American hierarchy and at the Roman Curia. For he and Machebeuf continued writing to both audiences about their past troubles with the native padres, most of whom were now dead or gone elsewhere, and still dragging in the old red herring of the Christmas pastoral by the tail. But nothing about any excommunications. Since Lamy left no official record of them, we do not know when they actually took place. This could have been in 1858 or 1859, or even as late as the Spring of 1860.

T he tracts mentioned before, as being published on the old Martínez press in Taos, could have been the "writings" which Bishop Lamy mentioned, besides those previous ones in the *Gazette*, which finally forced him to excommunicate the Padre of Taos. This is on the supposition that there had been some printed prior to the examples we have, which begin late in 1859 and end in 1861. We already saw how certain Taos individuals had been making political use of the press two years before, in 1857. According to the extant tracts, in 1859 the press was in the hands of a José Manuel Medina, with Vicente Ferrer Romero as editor of publications; later, Romero appears in full charge. The only examples that we have are thirty-two typewritten pages which someone transcribed very poorly many decades ago.[1]

Some of the tracts appear to have been written by Padre Martínez himself. They are not political in nature, but rather an extension of his old fixed idea on tithing and a mental recession and preoccupation with the past. There are also some bitter criticisms of Bishop Lamy, mostly because of alleged abuses committed by some of his priests. But on the whole, as it will be pointed out as we go along, it seems as though Vicente Ferrer Romero wrote the tracts himself by incorporating and editing some of the padre's writings, whether the latter was aware of the fact or not.

The first three undated pages are addressed to the editor of the *Gazette* in Santa Fe, stating that the writer had sent him some "Notes on Religion" (which are the same Notes printed under date of September 24, 1859, as shown below). Here the writer is no doubt Padre Martínez, as may be seen from the following points he makes: 1) Since the *Gazette* is the only newspaper in the territory, he wishes to defend himself in its columns because his *religious* character had been besmeared in the September 3 issue. – 2) He had visited Santa Fe in August when all kinds of prominent leaders, including the Protestant minister Mr. Gorman, had come to see him, Mr. Gallegos also being present; they had not discussed the establishment of any religious cult or system as an editorial had erroneously conjectured. – 3) The *Gazette*'s only purpose was to get votes for Mr. Otero, and this by mixing politics with religion; as for himself, the Taos padre emphasized, he still considered himself a "Christian, Catholic, Apostolic and Roman," as well as a minister of said Faith until death. – 4) The differences between himself and Bishop Lamy were the result of his repudiation of the 1854 Circular which imposed taxations which were wrong and unjust, and here he went into the details of its 5th and 6th regulations which denied the sacraments and Christian burial to those who did not pay in full.[2]

Although undated, this letter to the editor seems to have been written in 1859, but with reference to events of three years before. Or was Romero printing a letter of 1856? Next we have the tracts themselves, but which were not typewritten later in chronological sequence. They are put in their correct order as follows.

The first one, dated September 24, 1859, is a dissertation on the Seven Sacraments, in which the author claims that Confirmation is "of counsel only," that Extreme Unction is only by Church precept, and that Matrimony is a civil contract which becomes a sacrament administered by both parties when the priest, as the Church's official witness, imparts the nuptial blessing. Then he goes into the subject of church fees. These, he holds, are according to the gospel, but to be offered spontaneously and not by way of a price – and hence Lamy's regulations are nothing but simony. Here he goes into the same monetary speculations which Martínez had previously published in the *Gazette*, and as a final note he refers to the Inquisition as having produced the worst abuses in the name of Religion. Now under a republican form of government, he says, there exists a "Pure Religion" which all kinds of worshippers profess. This blessing of Pure Religion, he adds, suffers nonetheless from the problems inherent in John 5:39 with regard to searching the Scriptures. As for himself, the undersigned Antonio José Martínez y Santistéban protests that he will live and die in the Christian, Catholic, Apostolic and Roman Faith.[3]

Here we can see how the mentally disturbed padre had succeeded in getting back Martínez and Santistéban together again in one personality. The article itself is addressed to his critics in the *Gazette*, not to Bishop Lamy, and there is a sly dig at private biblical interpretation.

The next tract, dated, May 10, 1860, is a shorter dissertation called "A Simple Parallel of Religion and Fanaticism." Here both the theme and the contrasting style point to a different author. Religion, it says, pays worship to Divinity in all its rightful aspects, while Fanaticism is the fruit of a false conscience which enslaves the rational creature through religion; it places a person on the border of disordered passions, whereby that person becomes irresponsible and intolerant.[4] This all sounds like the letter which follows it, as well as two other tracts which will be discussed in their place. For the same issue carries a "Letter to the Editors" (Medina and Romero), dated at El Llano April 12, 1860, as if by an anonymous correspondent who betrays the mentality of a Penitente or a Pentecostal, or both.

The letter is a salute to a Miguel Griñé and a Juan de la Cruz Medina "in the philanthropic union with the mystical brotherhood of *la Sangre de Cristo*," and it dwells on the death and burial of a Rafael Hurtado – "Alleluia!" – who had been buried "in the house of prayer" because the parish priests had refused to do so, for the reason that he had received the last rites from Martínez and Lucero in Taos. This writer now compares the Church of New Mexico with a poor widow married to a foreigner (Lamy), and who weeps for her starving children because the avaricious stepfather is chasing them away through his demands for gold and silver. Therefore, long live the Christian Religion (as typified in Martínez and Lucero) and the (United States) Constitution which has made everybody free in religious matters![5] Although sparked by Padre Martínez' disputes with Bishop Lamy, these are not his sentiments, even in his madness, and the style is most certainly not his. The writer of both the tract and the letter could be the editor himself, Vicente Ferrer Romero, as will become more evident later on.

The third tract, dated June 18, 1860, is an "Allocution on the Sacred Ministry," which starts out as a sober essay on the subject, but soon goes on a wild rampage. What seems to have been an original short essay by Padre Martínez appears more like an editorial expansion by the author of the preceding piece. The writer goes on to criticize priests who have insulted the people from the pulpit for not bringing in enough money, and further deriding them as Protestants, schismatics and excommunicates. (Here the reference is to Martínez' few adherents, and to the terms which the French clergy were applying to them at this time. Unlike Padre Martínez, this writer all this while seems to regard his adherents as a separate cult or sect.) Now he brings up a rumor about a certain priest who had disinterred a child's body until its father paid for the funeral and promised to follow his (Lamy's) party; this means *ipso facto* excommunication for said priest, since only the Pope is above Canon Law and not the bishop. (A lapse of logic somewhere!) In fact, there is also *ipso facto* suspension for bishops who impose censures without due process (as in the case of Martínez and Lucero), also for one who disposes of church properties (silverplate and *santos*) without the required formalities, and who sells church buildings (the *Castrense* chapel in Santa Fe) and gives them over to profane uses while doing nothing to prevent simony.[6]

Long citations of Canon Law follow, but this does not mean that the Taos padre wrote the tract. Some ideas and the latter examples given are the voice of Padre Martínez, but the smell and the wild hairy touch come from someone else's editing or superimpositions.

The next article, dated July 18, 1860, tells of a visitation which Bishop Lamy had recently made of the Taos parish (in this same July when he recorded the excommunication), and one which had very much displeased the people (the writer's own partisans). The bishop, he says, told them that Padre Martínez had sworn to him that he would no longer write on subjects which disturbed the prelate, and this was not true. It was Lamy's hatred for the padre who had never done him any harm, but had merely called his attention to Canon Law, two volumes of which he had given him for the purpose. Hence he had written the bishop on July 9, 1860, telling him that his sermons had shocked the people since the 1st of June, when he preached at Trampas, and then at other places until today (his visitation) when he blamed two clergymen for everything.[7]

Here the writer goes into Padre Martínez' old routine about tithing, contrasting specific details with the former practices of the bishop of Durango. This and the whole tract show that he was using a letter which Martínez wrote to Lamy on the 9th of the month. It goes on to say that Lamy's 1854 Circular had made him request an assistant, and only because he personally did not want to incur the Church's censures by carrying out its unlawful regulations! Then he goes back to his letter to Lamy of November 13, 1856, and to his arguments in subsequent letters, which, he now says, Lamy had assented to through his silence! He is also enclosing his printed tract on the Sacred Ministry. (This is the one of June 18 described before, but if Padre Martínez did write the whole thing himself, José Santistéban had taken over completely for the nonce, or else he had adopted the editorial additions.)

Finally, in this same quoted letter of July 9, he says that he will continue ministering to those who recur to him and, so long as his suspension holds, he will disavow Lamy's authority over his own person, since his crimes now stand out clearly because of his suspension (perhaps meaning excommunication) of himself, his sale of sacred church silverplate, his nullification of the sacramental services performed by himself and Lucero – and the sale of the *Castrense* chapel in Santa Fe which since ancient times had been furnished by the King for the royal militia, and which now was a business establishment operating over the bodies buried therein and in its surrounding cemetery.[8]

By this time one can see that the act of excommunication had changed the former respectful manner of address and the pathetic pleadings of a hurt Padre Martínez to bitter invective. As said before, one can blame José Santistéban for taking over. But then, since this is not the original letter, the blame must fall on Vicente Ferrer Romero and his editing.

The next tract, as of August 10, 1860, carries what the author calls "Reflexions on Church Obligations Due and on Certain Preachments in New Mexico." This one compares the reasons for tithing in the Old and New Testaments, and in the Church during monarchical times, with what should now be observed in republican nations. The church's own commandment on church support is legitimate enough, the writer says, so long as fees are requested for each ministerial service and not as overall tithing. Again he goes into details regarding the offensive regulations in the 1852 Christmas Pastoral and the Clergy Circular of 1854. Now he further claims that the good regulations in them were made to deceive the people, since Lamy had made a secret verbal agreement with his own priests to do just the opposite! As for the preaching of Lamy and others in Taos, they were aimed solely at Padres Martínez and Lucero, what the former had adequately covered on the 18th of June and July. Also, rumor had it that in Rio Colorado the preaching on tithes had been toned down for fear that the people might move away; there the priests in their sermons had said that Martínez was in error when he insisted on spontaneous offerings only.[9]

Furthermore, on Sunday, July 15, 1860, a visiting priest in the Taos church had based his sermon on Matthew 7:15-16, about bewaring of false prophets and wolves in sheep's clothing, obviously applying it to Martínez and Lucero; on the contrary, it was Lamy's men who could be judged by their fruits, as when they (Eulogio Ortiz and others) violated a private oratory in Taos by forcibly removing some *santos* which they still had in their possession. In the same year, these same clergymen had abducted a married woman and had kept her until a sum of money was paid, the reason for this being unclear.[10]

Incidentally, Padre Martínez used a letter of his, dated May 13, 1858, to fortify the cover of his small private baptismal book. This pasted scrap mentions that Padre E. Ortiz and others had helped the priest José de Jesús (Luján?) carry away his niece, a Romero woman who was the wife of a Pablo Martínez. Another such scrap is from a letter of December 28, 1858, which mentions Ortiz as having removed some *santos* from an oratory. A third such scrap is from a letter where Martínez referred to Representative Otero's speech against Padre Gallegos in Washington.[11]

Coming back to this particular tract of July 15, we have the author asking if those were good fruits when another Lamy priest borrowed considerable sums of money in Santa Fe and the Rio Abajo, and then disappeared from New Mexico. Another such priest had left San Miguel County with the church vestments and other things, of which he had certain knowledge; others had dug up the dead to bury them elsewhere, as had happened in Taos County, and Bishop Lamy seemed to be condoning all this.[12] The next tract, as of September 22, 1860, is entitled "Reflexions on the Ministers of the Gospel," and meant as a general slap at the greedy ones now coming to New Mexico. Here is where the writer mentions the identity as a whole body of these tracts as a "literary periodical" being published in Taos.[13] He does not give the actual title, but this could well be the publication which Pedro Sánchez many years later recalled as Padre Martínez' paper named *El Crepúsculo*, whether it bore this title or not.

There follows another tract on "The Christian Church," without date or else one which the transcriber failed to copy. The essay is built on the once famous Spanish Catechism of Ripalda, but it soon strays into an outlandish use of similes. Speaking of Taos, the writer says that there exist two parties. One is the *Católicos Coludos*, which the copyist mistranscribed as "Caludos." (The meaning is a New-Mexicanism for the *ratón coludo*, or ground squirrel, and here with reference to the foreigners with wider bottoms). The other party is the *Protestantes* (as Lamy's partisans were now dubbing Padre Martínez, actually Vicente Ferrer Romero and his own followers). Both are then compared to church edifices. The first broad-beamed party under Lamy demands money instead of payment in kind, and therefore is practicing simony; the second party consists of the faithful who follow genuine priests (Martínez and Lucero) who render their services for Christ and are content with free-will offerings, never denying any ministrations when these cannot be paid for. In short, the Coludos Party is the Religion of Money while the other is the Religion of Christ.[14]

Here especially, neither the style of writing nor the thought processes are those of Padre Martínez himself, but more like those of that anonymous fellow who had addressed himself to Griñé and Medina. Hence both seem to have come from the pen of Vicente Ferrer Romero, who again finds mention in the last tract that we have. This one, dated simply 1861, is now identified as coming from the same press, the sole owner and director being Romero himself. Entitled "Religious Exhortations to Christians," it starts out by quoting First Peter 5:1-2, about the feeding of flocks. Regarding the sacrament of Confession, it says, anyone can hear confessions in extreme necessity, referring to James 5:6. But now, says the writer, the sacraments and funerals belong to a Monopoly, hence in such cases the faithful need not worry if they are denied these services when they cannot pay. As a final note, he declares that genuflexion is due to God alone, and that bishops demanding the gesture toward their own persons are just feeding their pride.[15]

Of course, this is not Martínez doctrine at all, nor is the style his. That matter of having to pay for confession, along with the one about genuflecting before a bishop, point to some Protestant minister in town behind Romero, feeding him with biblical verses besides. In brief, all of these publications do seem to be the product of Vicente Ferrer Romero who, using Padre Martínez' own writings of the times for his own ends, was promoting a sort of religious cult of his own, part Protestant and part Catholic in concept. Bishop Lamy, assuming all this to be the Taos padre's own propaganda, would naturally judge it as having the elements of a real schism.

It was in this same year of 1861, dated May 4, that a *Historia Consisa del Cura de Taos Antonio Jose Martinez* was printed in Taos. The anonymous author refers to himself simply as *El Historiador*. Henry R. Wagner, in his article on the first New Mexico press, said that he had a copy of it, ascribing the authorship to Padre Martínez himself. But from its very title (without *Presbítero*), as well as the author's anonymity, and no less the padre's physical and mental state at this time, one can safely say that it was not his own work. Nor would he have mispelled the adjective "concise." Again, under the circumstances, one can conclude that Vicente Ferrer Romero was the author. Moreover, the biographical data used by Wagner from this book are similar to those in Padre Martínez' own *Relación de Méritos* of 1838, hence Romero had merely made a brief or "concise" adaptation of it. [16]

Death and a Testament / 22

T he foregoing tracts are the last published activities we have in connection with the Padre of Taos. How long this went on we have no way of knowing at present. But from them, and the other attending circumstances, one can conclude that he was no longer active in politics as he kept on tormenting his soul with his double ecclesiastical fixed idea about tithing and his inviolate status as *cura propio*. If Romero reflected his feelings in some way, his attacks on Bishop Lamy and his foreign clergy had been becoming more direct and pronounced, and yet he never denied his prelate's legitimacy as the Bishop of Santa Fe. Much less did he ever for one moment deny the Catholic Faith of his forefathers.

But his mania was steadily taking its toll, and this became more evident toward the end of 1862 when, for a short spell, he deluded himself by thinking that he still enjoyed the five-year episcopal faculties granted by Bishop Zubiría long ago to administer the sacrament of Confirmation. In his little baptismal book of 1859-1867, we find that on December 7, 1862, he confirmed a number of infants, and several more on Christmas Day, noting down at the bottom of the page: "*con autoridad pontificia hice estas confirmaciones.*" There is also something like it at the top of the page. Some six other confirmations appear on the very last page for December 25, 1865, although unsigned and with no other comment.[1] His vaunted expertise in Canon Law could have told him that his privileges to confirm back in those days had been for a restricted period. At least during this month of December, and in that of 1865, brief spells of delusion had made him believe that he enjoyed permanent faculties by no less than direct papal authorization – while we also recall that tract in which he held that Confirmation was not strictly of obligation. Perhaps this is why he performed no other ministrations of this sort.

In the same delusions of grandeur, harking back to his title of Ecclesiastical Judge and Vicar under Bishop Zubiría, he dispensed a nephew and niece of his, who were first cousins, from their close degree of consanguinity before he married them. These were José Leandro Martínez and Soledad Martínez, the children of his brothers Pascual and José María respectively.[2]

Beyond his many other sacramental ministrations recorded in his private registers until his death, we have one more sally of his into the outside world of secular affairs. On July 23, 1865, he submitted his views to a Doolittle Committee on the sad plight of the nomadic Indians, exactly as he had done to the Mexican federal government far back in 1843. Little had changed in this regard, he wrote, and in fact their condition was worse under the American government. Next he described the wars which had been waged against the Navajo since 1800, between intervals of truce which lasted from two to five years, and similar clashes with the Utes and Comanches who used to sell captive females and children to the Hispanic folk. Now he lashed out again at the frequent sales of liquor to these wild tribes, and again proposing their assemblage into towns whereby they could be taught that all people came from the same Creator. As a result there would be no further need for martial laws.[3]

This suggests a very lucid interval of his at this time, but one nonetheless suggestive of his living in the past a good part of the time. Nor must it have taxed the old man's physical and mental energies too much, since in substance it was the very same document which had elicited the praise and approval of Mexican President López de Santa Ana many years before. But it does show that the poor fellow, while regressing more and more into the past – and doing "crazy" things like the sacramental confirmations and marital dispensations just mentioned – still had at heart the welfare of the poor and downtrodden, even those hostile Indians who had raided his people for centuries and which in recent times had made off with his livestock.

Almost exactly two years later he died, on July 27, 1867, after having received the last rites from his faithful but sometimes vacillating disciple, Padre Lucero. As the latter recorded it, he buried him on the 29th inside his private oratory of Guadalupe on the Plaza of Don Fernando.[4] When Willa Cather was preparing her now classic novel about Lamy, she picked up a piece of Taos gossip of those days, to the effect that the dying Martínez had said to Lucero at his bedside: "*Lucero, cómete tu cola!*" This was a Spanish scatological profanity, the equivalent of the more curseful American-English "Go to hell!" – by which he evidently meant that Lucero should quit bothering him. On the other hand, Pedro Sánchez wrote that the good Padre Martínez had died, while surrounded by his brothers and many friends, with these words on his lips: "Lord, may your Will be done."[5] Cather's version reflects the cynical view which had come down from the padre's foes, the one of Sánchez the wishful tradition among those who still remembered him with love and admiration. Whichever one might be authentic or false, they both fall within the province of legend and not history.

When the news of his death reached Santa Fe, a new local newspaper published a very brief notice on his passing, as that of a person greatly loved by all who knew him. *De mortuis nil nisi bonum,* we might say. A week later it carried a long obituary by Pedro Sánchez which reviewed his entire life and accomplishments – with some inaccuracies peculiar to Sánchez and his *Memorias* – and promising a full biography in the near future. More than two thousand persons had attended the funeral, wrote Sánchez, among whom were three hundred members of "*la fraternidad piadosa de Taos.*" Obviously this meant the Penitentes, while we must not exclude the cultist followers of Vicente Ferrer Romero. Among the dozen honorary pallbearers whom Sánchez named were seven with *americano* surnames.[6]

As for his erstwhile ecclesiastical adversaries, we have two references in which Bishop Lamy made the following comments. On September 6, 1868, when writing to the Roman Curia, he mentioned that an unfortunate Mexican priest had created a schism in an important parish for some ten years, and had taken it upon himself to judge all cases requiring marital dispensations; he had also married couples who were related in the first degree (not brothers and sisters!), and since his death several months ago (well over a year) people had been waiting to be reconciled with the Church. For the new priest in Taos (Ussel) had requested the proper faculties to remedy the situation.[7] On February 3, 1869, Lamy wrote to Bishop Purcell that a Jesuit father was preaching a mission in Taos (more than one according to others), where the unfortunate Martínez had effected a schism until he passed away on July 28, 1867. The man had ended as he had lived, Lamy went on to say, but most of the people, except for his own relatives, were coming back to obedience, and the Jesuit mission which had been producing much fruit would leave very few remnants, if any, of this sad episode.[8]

According to the Jesuit weekly at Las Vegas, when Bishop Lamy visited Taos in 1879, the former adherents of the old *zizania* (the biblical tares) had come to greet him with the rest of the ever faithful parishioners.[9] The fact is that most of Padre Martínez' relatives and close friends did reconcile themselves with the Church through the influence of the zealous Neapolitan Jesuits whom Lamy had introduced into the diocese, and who were the best of orators in Spanish besides. But Father Gabriel Ussel also deserves a compliment for having called them in to do the job. Those few individuals who failed to come under their spell became the foundation for Spanish-speaking Presbyterianism in New Mexico, not from any grasp of Calvin's abstruse theories of predestination as from seeing one way of carrying on a bitter partisanship which had become deeply ingrained.

But of considerably greater interest than the minutiae of Padre Martínez' death and funeral, and its immediate aftermath with regard to the people's different reactions, is his last will and testament. Written in 1865, it had been revised by him on June 27, exactly a month before his death.[10] His progressive dementia, we must say, while operative when it came to his ecclesiastical *idée fixe*, was suspended for the nonce when it came to purely mundane matters, as it had previously done when the Utes and Apaches made off with his livestock. The will and testament started out with the standard Hispanic Catholic invocation to the Holy Trinity, which he ended with a specific request to be buried in his oratory of *la Purísima Concepción*, and laid out in his silk cassock and biretta. Then he mentioned that he had once been married to María de la Luz Martín back in 1812, from whom he had a daughter who had died in 1824. Next he disposed of his property in favor of several individuals, the details of which need not concern us here.

He went on to say that after forty-two years of parochial administration, and revoking all previous wills, he had signed this one in his Taos residence on July 9. This was just two weeks before he died. The executors he named were Santiago Valdez and Pedro Sánchez, his now all-too-familiar biographers. But now two things stand out among his legacies and final declarations: One, that he was ready to die at peace with himself after an entire life dedicated to God and to his fellowmen; two, that Santiago Valdez was to inherit, besides part of his estate, all of his papers. As one of his household who had been under his care since childhood, and whom he had adopted and educated with all the rights of inheritance, Valdez had recognized no other father or mother than himself and had obeyed him completely. Therefore he had been like a son to him. Furthermore, the padre stipulated that Santiago's children were to assume and carry on his own surname – which we know they did.

Finally, what interests us still more in connection with this declaration is not only the curious fact that Padre Martínez made no mention at all of his having had children by Teodora Romero, but his bland declaration that he was at peace with himself after having dedicated his entire life to God's honor and the welfare of his fellowman. There is not the faintest hint of humility in a man who, for example, had betrayed some of his fellow padres during most serious crises in the past, besides having for a period violated his sacred sacerdotal state. One does not expect a public confession, of course, but at least some sort of general expression which others often used in their wills – such as "having been a sinner during my life."

But of such a stamp had been his entire life's outlook, his sights ever set on the polar star of eventual personal greatness through his most laudable dedication to the poor and the downtrodden, when all the while he unwittingly kept letting his inordinate pride – not to mention some other grave faults – cooperate fully with time and chance in bringing on his downfall both as a leader and within his own personality. While one has to retract for this very reason, and with sore regret, a statement made in a previous book that Padre Martínez was New Mexico's greatest son, one can still say that he was her major genius in his own century as well as those before and after his time. He was indeed her most prominent player on the historical stage, both on the civil and the ecclesiastical scene in a most colorfully dramatic bygone era.

NOTES / BIBLIOGRAPHY

NOTES

PART ONE

Genesis of a Gifted Soul / 1

1. AASF, B-10, Abiquiú.
2. Valdez, *Biografía*, p. 98.
3. Martínez, *Relación*, *N.M. Hist. Rev.*, vol. 3, pp. 328-29.
4. N.M. State Record Center, Surveyor Gen. Report No. 116.
5. Twitchell, *Leading Facts*, vol. 2, p. 337n, *Mil. Occupation*, p. 134.
6. Chavez, *N.M. Families*, pp. 71-73, 222-26.
7. Chavez, "Genízaros," *Handbook Am. Indian*, pp. 198-200.
8. AASF, M-1, B-10, Abiquiú.
9. *Ibid.*, B-10 Abiquiú; Loose Docs. 1754, no. 3.
10. *Ibid.*, B-10, Abiquiú.
11. *Ibid.*, Loose Docs. 1804, no. 12.
12. Chavez, *N.M. Families*, these surnames; AASF, B-34, M-29 Sta. Cruz, M-8 Cochiti.

Precocious Lad of Abiquiú / 2

1. Martínez, *Relación*, *N.M. Hist. Rev.*, vol. 3, pp. 325-46.
2. Romero, *Hist. Consisa*, cf. Wagner, *N.M. Hist. Rev.*, vol. 12, pp. 4-6.
3. Valdez, *Biografía*, p. 97.
4. Sánchez, *Memorias*, p. 11; Read, *Hist. Ilustr.*, p. 343.
5. Cf. Chavez, *Archives*, Education in Index.
6. AASF, M-37, Taos.
7. *Ibid.*, B-38, Taos.
8. *Ibid.*, M-1 Abiquiú.
9. Romero, *loc. cit.*, pp. 4-6; Valdez, *op. cit.*, p. 97; Sánchez, *op. cit.*, pp. 11-12; AASF, B-38 Taos.

The Young Presbítero / 3

1. Chavez, "Vicario Roybal," *El Palacio*, vol. 55, pp. 231-52.
2. Cf. Chavez, *Archives*, places and clergy in Index.
3. AASF, General, *Historical*, Ranchos Church.
4. Cf. Chavez, *Oroz Codex*, Index, *Archives*, pp. 43-46, 61-62, 82, 94, 97.
5. Chavez, *Archives*, p. 97; AASF, Loose Docs. 1826, no. 6.
6. *Ibid.*, pp. 150-52 on Patentes IX (1817); pp. 189-90 on Accounts LXII (1817).
7. Martínez, *Relación*, *N.M. Hist. Rev.*, vol. 3, pp. 329-34.
8. *Ibid.*, pp. 334-35.
9. Valdez, *Biografía*, pp. 99-103; Martínez, *loc. cit.*, pp. 335-36.
10. Martínez, *loc. cit.*; Valdez, *op. cit.*, pp. 106-09; Romero, *Hist. Consisa*, *N.M. Hist. Rev.*, vol. 12, pp. 4-6.
11. Martínez, *loc. cit.*, p. 336.
12. *Ibid.*, p. 328-29; Valdez, *op. cit.*, p. 110.
13. Valdez, *op. cit.*, pp. 110-23.
14. Valdez, *loc. cit.*, pp. 113-28, *Notes I*, p. 17; Martínez, *loc. cit.*, p. 336-37.
15. Martínez, *loc. cit.*, p. 337; AASF, B-71 Tomé; Valdez, *Biografía*, pp. 129-31; Romero, *loc. cit.*, pp. 4-6.
16. *Old S.Fe*, vol. 1, pp. 162, 173.
17. Valdez, *op. cit.*, p. 97; Romero, *loc. cit.*; Sánchez, *Memorias*, p. 12.
18. Martínez, *loc. cit.*, p. 337; Valdez, *op. cit.*, pp. 131-36; Romero, *loc. cit.*
19. Chavez, *Archives*, pp. 190—93 on Accounts LXIII-LXVI (1825).
20. AASF, Loose Docs. 1826, no. 7.
21. Martínez, *loc. cit.*; Valdez, *Notes I*, p. 17, following pp. not numbered.
22. Martínez, *ibid.*; Valdez, *ibid.*

Padre of Taos at Last / 4

1. Valdez, *Biografía*, pp. 136-37, *Notes I*, p. 16-17.
2. *Ibid.*
3. AASF, Loose Docs. 1819, no. 11.
4. Valdez, *Notes I*, pp. 16-17.
5. Chavez, *Archives*, p. 156 on Patentes XV.
6. Chavez, *N.M. Families*, pp. 21-22.
7. Valdez, *1903 Biography*, pp. 302-07.
8. Chavez, *Archives*, p. 156 on Patentes; Adams-Chavez, *Missions 1776*, pp. 102-13.
9. AASF, Loose Docs. 1827, nos. 8, 9.
10. *N.M. Hist. Rev.*, vol. 9, p. 96.
11. Valdez, *Notes I*, unpaged; Chavez, *Archives*, p. 196 on Accounts LXXVI.
12. AASF, Bur-39 Taos.
13. *N.M. Quarterly* (Spring 1963), pp. 33-42; Warner, *Archb. Lamy*, pp. 84-88; AASF, B-10 Abiquiú, B-38 Taos, M-53 Sta. Fe.
14. AASF, B-47 Taos.
15. *Ibid.*, Bur-39 Taos.
16. Chavez, "Doña Tules," *El Palacio* vol. 57, pp. 227-34.
17. AASF, Loose Docs. 1827, nos. 18, 19.
18. *Ibid.*, 1828, no. 4.
19. Valdez, *Notes I*, unpaged; Martínez, *Relación*, *N.M. Hist. Rev.*, vol. 3, pp. 337-38; AASF, B-47, B-48, M-39 Taos.
20. Martínez, *loc. cit.*, pp. 338-39; Sánchez, *Memorias*, p. 14.
21. Valdez, *loc. cit.*, unpaged.
22. *Ibid.*; Sánchez, *op. cit.*, pp. 17-19.
23. *Ibid.*
24. *Ibid.*
25. *Ibid.*
26. Valdez, *Notes I*, unpaged, *Drafts*, p. 21; AASF, B-48, Bur-39 Taos.
27. AASF, B-47 Taos.
28. *Ibid.*, M-41, B-55 Taos.
29. Anon., *Ill. Hist. of N.M.*, p. 337; AASF M-(1877) Taos; Read, *Hist.Ilustr.*, pp. 495, 531, 543.
30. Cf. Bibliography, Huntington Library.

Penitentes and Paternity / 5

1. *Old. S.Fe*, vol.1, pp. 27-72; *N.M. Hist. Rev.*, vol.12, pp. 107-08; Martínez, *Relación*, *N.M. Hist. Rev.*, vol. 3, p. 340; Valdez, *Notes I*, unpaged.
2. Chavez, *Archives*, p. 154 on Patentes LXX (1829).
3. *Ibid.*
4. Chavez, "Penitentes," *N.M. Hist. Rev.*, vol. 29, pp. 97-123, *My Penitente Land*, passim.
5. Huntington Library, *Ritch Coll.*, Memo Book No. 4, p. 325.
6. AASF, B-48 Taos.
7. *Ibid.*, B-38 Taos.
8. Anon., *Ill. Hist. of N.M.*, p. 374.
9. AASF, B-58 Taos.
10. *Ibid.*, B-49 Taos.
11. *Ibid.*, B-50 Taos.
12 Census 1850, Ter. of N.M., Taos Co., nos. 1451, 1452.
13. AASF, Bur-42A Taos.

Father Also of Padres / 6

1. Valdez, *Notes I*, unpaged, *Drafts*, pp. 21-22; cf. note 18, chap. 3 *supra*.
2. Sánchez, *Memorias*, p. 20.
3. Martínez, *Relación*, *N.M.Hist.Rev.*, vol. 3, p. 340; Valdez, *Notes I*, unpaged.
4. Valdez, *Notes I*, unpaged, *Drafts*, pp. 22-28.
5. AASF, B-49 Taos.
6. Valdez, *Notes I*, unpaged, *Drafts*, pp. 28-30; Martínez, *loc. cit.*, p. 339.

7. Martínez, *loc. cit.*, pp. 341-43; Valdez, *Notes I*, unpaged, *Drafts*, p. 30.
8. Valdez, *Notes, I*, unpaged, *Drafts*, p. 30.
9. Valdez, *ibid.*

Penitentes Again and a Press / 7

1. Valdez, *Notes I*, unpaged, *Drafts*, p. 30.
2. *AASF, Patentes* LXXIII (1833).
3. *Ibid.*, several copies; cf. Chavez, *Archives*, p. 182.
4. Chavez, *op. cit.*, pp. 260-61, p. 66 on Loose Docs. 1803, no. 14.
5. Cf. Borhegyi, "Esquipulas," *El Palacio*, vol. 61, pp. 387-98.
6. AASF, *Patentes* XXVIII (1833-1872).
7. Valdez, *Notes, I*, unpaged, *Drafts*, p. 31; AASF, M-21, Bur-20, 21, Picuris.
8. Valdez, *ibid.*, *Drafts*, p. 31-32; Chavez, *op. cit.*, p. 182 on *Patentes* (1833).
9. Valdez, *ibid.*; Martínez, *Relación*, *N.M. Hist. Rev.*, vol. 3, pp. 339-40.
10. Chavez, *op. cit.*, p. 156 on *Patentes* XV (1833, 1835); Valdez *Notes (Engish)*, p. 70, *1903, Biography*, p. 310.
11. AASF, *Accounts* LXXVI (1834).
12. Valdez, *Notes I*, unpaged, *Drafts*, pp. 34-35.
13. Wagner, "Spanish Press," *N.M. Hist. Rev.*, vol. 12, pp. 15-16.
14. *Ibid.*, pp. 1-40; McMurtrie, "Hist. of Printing," *N.M. Hist. Rev.*, p. 372-410.
15. Wagner, *loc. cit.*, p. 6.
16. McMurtrie, *loc, cit.*, pp. 380, 384.

War of the Chimayoses / 8

1. Valdez, *Notes I*, unpaged (1837).
2. Chavez, *Archives*, p. 178 on *Patentes* (1822).
3. *Old S.Fe*, vol. 1, p. 10.
4. Valdez, *loc. cit.*
5. AASF, B-72 Tomé; Sánchez, *Memorias*, p. 43.
6. Sánchez, *op. cit.*, pp. 21-22.
7. Read, *Hist. Ilustr.*, p. 239.
8. Valdez, *loc. cit.*
9. Martínez, *Relación*, *N.M. Hist. Rev.*, vol. 3, p. 339.
10. Valdez, *loc. cit.*
11. *Ibid.*; Sánchez, *op. cit.* p. 23; Read, *op. cit.*, p. 240.
12. Chavez, "Genízaro Gov.," *N.M. Hist. Rev.*, vol. 30, pp. 190-94.
13. *Ibid.*
14. Valdez, *loc. cit.*
15. *Ibid.*; Sánchez, *op. cit.*, pp. 21-23.
16. Valdez, *loc. cit.*
17. *Ibid.*
18. Read, *op. cit.*, p. 249.
19. Valdez, *loc. cit.*
20. Martínez, *loc. cit.*, pp. 340-42.
21. Sánchez, *op. cit.*, pp. 13, 23-25.
22. AASF, Bur-40 Taos.
23. *Ibid.*, M-40 Taos.

War's Results, A New Decade / 9

1. Valdez, *Notes I*, unpaged (1838).
2. *Ibid.*
3. *Ibid.*
4. *Ibid.*
5. AASF, *Accounts* LXXVI (1838).
6. Cf. Note 11, Chap. 7 *supra*.
7. Cf. Note 5 *supra*.
8. Valdez, *loc. cit*; Martínez, *Relación*, *N.M.Hist. Rev.*, vol. 3, p. 327.
9. *Ibid.*; cf. Bibliography, Valdez and Huntington Library.

10. Valdez, *loc. cit.* (1840).
11. *Ibid.*
12. *Ibid.*
13. AASF, Bur-40, B-50 Taos.
14. Valdez, *loc. cit.* (1841).
15. *N.M. Hist. Rev.*, vol. 17, pp. 313-14.
16. Valdez, *loc. cit.*
17. *Ibid.*, here paged, 56.
18. *Ibid.*, p. 57.
19. *Ibid.*, p. 58.
20. AASF, Loose Docs. 1842, no. 4.
21. Valdez, *loc, cit.*, pp. 59-61.
22. *Ibid.*, p. 61.
23. Chavez, "Mora Valley," *El Palacio*, vol. 62, pp. 318-23.

A Dirtier War of Politics / 10

1. AASF, Accounts LXXVI (1834).
2. *N.M. Hist. Rev.*, vol. 30, p. 19.
3. Valdez, *Notes I*, unpaged (1843).
4. Valdez, *loc. cit.*; Read, *Hist. Ilustr.*, pp. 261-66; Keleher, *Turmoil*, pp. 66-71.
5. Valdez, *loc. cit.*; Sánchez, *Memorias*, p. 27.
6. Valdez, *loc. cit.* (1844), *Notes II*, p. 296.
7. *Ibid.*
8. *Ibid.*
9. AASF, Accounts C-1, LXXVI (1844).

The Padre and The Americanos / 11

1. Chavez, *Archives*, p. 185 on Patentes (1845).
2. *Ibid.*, p. 184 on Patentes (1840-1845).
3. AASF, Loose Docs. 1841, no. 5.
4. Martínez, *Relación*, *N.M. Hist. Rev.*, vol. 3, p. 340.
5. Chavez, *op. cit.*, p. 184 on Patentes (1843).
6. Valdez, *Biografía*, unpaged, *Notes I*, (1845).
7. Chavez, "New Names," *El Palacio*, vol. 64, pp. 291-318, 362-380.
8. Howlett, *Machebeuf*, p. 213.
9. Chavez, *loc. cit.*
10. *Ibid.*
11. *Ibid.*
12. Valdez, *Notes I* (1845); AASF, M-40, B-52, Bur-41 Taos.
13. Valdez, *Notes (English)*, pp. 72-74.
14. Valdez, *Notes I*, unpaged.
15. *Ibid.*
16. *Ibid.*, *Notes II*, pp. 294-98.
17. *N.M. Hist. Rev.*, vol. 30, pp. 340-41.
18. Read, *Hist. Ilustr.*, p. 253.
19. Cf. Note 17 *supra*.
20. Valdez, *Notes II*, pp. 297-99.

1846 – The United States / 12

1. Read, *Hist. Ilustr.*, pp. 263-74; Twitchell, *Mil. Occupation*, pp. 49-86.
2. *Old S. Fe*, vol. 2, p. 252.
3. Valdez, *Notes (English)*, pp. 76-80.
4. *Ibid.*, pp. 80-82.
5. Keleher, *Turmoil*, p. 9.
6. AASF, Accounts C-1 (1851).
7. Emory, *Notes*, pp. 38-43; Twitchell, *op. cit.*, pp. 74-75.
8. Valdez, *loc. cit.*, p. 88.
9. Emory, *loc. cit.*; Twitchell, *op. cit.*, pp. 84-86.

10. Valdez, *loc. cit.*, pp. 87-88.
11. Emory, *loc. cit.*; Gibson, *Journal*, pp. 216-74.
12. Twitchell, *op. cit.*, pp. 122-23; Read, *op. cit.*, pp. 280-81.
13. Twitchell, *ibid.*, pp. 125-28; Read, *ibid.*, pp. 281-82.
14. Valdez, *loc. cit.*, pp. 90-92; AASF, B-52 Taos.
15. Valdez, *ibid.*
16. Twitchell, *op. cit.*, pp. 127-28.
17. Valdez, *loc. cit.*, pp. 92-94.
18. Twitchell, *op. cit.*, pp. 129-32; Read, *op. cit.*, pp. 282-83.
19. Valdez, *loc. cit.*, pp. 96-98; Sánchez, *Memorias*, pp. 34-36.
20. Valdez, *ibid.*, pp. 100-02.
21. *Ibid.*, pp. 102-04.
22. *Ibid.*, pp. 112-16.
23. Twitchell, *op. cit.*, p. 133.
24. Sánchez, *op. cit.*, p. 32.
25. Twitchell, *op. cit.*, pp. 155-56; Read, *op. cit.*, pp. 287-98; Valdez, *loc. cit.*, pp. 116-18.
26. Valdez, *ibid.*; *N.M. Hist. Rev.*, vol. 8, pp. 98-129.
27. Twitchell, *op. cit.*, pp. 176-77.
28. Valdez, *loc. cit.*, pp. 106-12.
29. *Ibid.*, pp. 118-22; AASF, B-54 Taos.
30. Valdez, *loc. cit.*, pp. 70-72.
31. AASF, Patentes XIX (1845).
32. *Ibid.*, Patentes XI (1850); cf. Chavez, *Archives*, p. 186 on Patentes.
33. Cf. Chavez, *op. cit.*, pp. 151-52, 154, 186.
34. *N.M. Hist. Rev.*, vol. 16, pp. 368-78, vol. 12, pp. 4-6; Keleher, *op. cit.*, p. 124.
35. Read, *op. cit.*, p. 294.
36. Valdez, *loc. cit.*, pp. 123-26.
37. *N.M. Hist. Rev.*, vol. 17, pp. 125-27.

PART TWO

A Friendly French Bishop / 13

1. Chavez, *Archives*, p. 186 on Patentes XI, etc. (1851).
2. AASF, Lamy File, Aug. 15, 1851, no. 12; Horg. Coll., Aug. 28, 1851, no. 10, Machebeuf. Letters, Sept. 29, 1851; Ellis, "New Notes," *El Palacio*, vol. 65, pp. 26-75.
3. Salpointe, *Soldiers*, p. 196; cf. also, Howlett, *Machebeuf*, p. 178.
4. AASF, Martínez File, no. 1; Lamy File, 1851, no. 7.
5. *Ibid.*, Lamy File, *Bullae* 1850; cf. Horgan, *Lamy*, p. 73.
6. Cf. Adams, *Tamarón Visitation*, Introduction.
7. Cf. Chavez, *My Penitente Land*, pp. 222-26.
8. AASF, Horg. Coll., Aug. 28, 1851, nos. 9, 10; Machebeuf Letters, Sept. 29, 1851.
9. Cf. Horgan, *Lamy*, pp. 12-18.
10. AASF, Horg. Coll., Machebeuf Letters, 1839-1886, Prop. Fide 1856, nos. 12, 17.
11. Cf. Horgan, *Lamy*, pp. 19-110.
12. *Ibid.*, pp. 89-93.
13. AASF, Lamy File, June 29, 1851, no. 8.
14. *Ibid.*, Horg. Coll., Machebeuf Letters, Sept. 29, 1851.
15. Cf. Ellis, *loc. cit.*; AASF, Clergy Card File, *Pinard*.
16. Keleher, *Violence*, p. 180; AASF, Lamy File, Mar. 15, April 12, 1851, nos. 5, 7.
17. AASF, Lamy File, Aug. 15, 1851, no. 12.
18. *Ibid.*
19. *Ibid.*, Horg. Coll., Machebeuf Letters, Sept. 29, 1851.
20. *Ibid.*, Prop. Fide, 1856, nos. 12, 12a, 17.
21. *Ibid.*, Lamy File, Nov. 1, 1851, no. 17.
22. *Ibid.*, M-41, Bur-54 Taos.
23. *Ibid.*, Horg. Coll., Prop. Fide, 1856, nos. 12, 17; Salpointe, *op. cit.*, pp. 196-97.
24. *Rev. Catolica*, vol. 8, pp. 197-98; AASF, Clergy Card File, *Cárdenas*.

25. AASF, B-23 S. Felipe, B-7 S. Miguel.
26. *Ibid.*, Lamy File, Feb. 1, 1852, no. 1.
27. *Ibid.*, Clergy Card File, *Valencia.*
28. *Ibid.*, Patentes XIX (1852).
29. *Ibid.*, Lamy File, April 10, 1853, no. 6, Aug. 6, 1853, no. 7a.
30. *Ibid.*, B-1, Bur-6, Arroyo Hondo.
31. Chavez, *Archives,* p. 121 on Loose Docs. 1855, no. 11, p. 122 on same, 1856, nos. 16-19.
32. AASF, Clergy of Archd. I, no. 2.

Grey Eminence of Taos / 14

1. AASF, Lamy File, Aug. 15, 1851, no. 12; Horg. Coll., Machebeuf Letters, Sept. 29, 1851.
2. *Ibid.*, Horg. Coll., Machebeuf Letters, May 31, 1852.
3. *Ibid.*, Prop. Fide, Mar. 7-9, 1853, no. 5.
4. *Ibid.*, Jan. 5, 1853, no. 6.
5. Cf. Horgan, *Lamy,* p. 165; Defouri, *Sketch,* p. 41.
6. *Horgan, Lamy,* p. 164.
7. AASF, Horg. Coll., Prop. Fide, Mar. 3, 1853, no. 9.
8. *Ibid.*, Jan. 5, 1853, no. 6.
9. *Ibid.*, Feb. 3, 1853, no. 3.
10. *Ibid.*
11. *Ibid.*, M-55 Sta. Fe.
12. *Ibid.*, Lamy File, Pastorals.
13. *Ibid.*
14. *Ibid.*, Horg. Coll., Prop. Fide, Jan. 5, 1853, no. 6.

The Seal of Confession / 15

1. AASF, Horg. Coll., Prop. Fide, Feb. 3, 24, 1853, nos. 3, 4.
2. S. Fe *Gazette,* Jan. 8, 1853.
3. AASF, Horg. Coll., Prop. Fide, Jan. (13), 1853, no. 1.
4. *Ibid.*, 1856, nos. 12, 17.
5. *Ibid.*, Jan. (13), 14, 16, 18, 1853, no. 1.
6. *Ibid.*, Feb. 3, 1853, no. 3.
7. *Ibid.*
8. *Ibid.*, Feb. 24, 1853, no. 4.
9. *Ibid.*
10. *Ibid.*, Jan. 28, 1853, no. 2.
11. *Ibid.*
12. *Ibid.*
13. *Ibid.*
14. *Ibid.*, Feb. 22, 1853, no. 2.
15. *Ibid.*

Still the Amicus Curiae / 16

1. AASF, B-9, B-10, Abiquiú.
2. *Ibid.*, Horg. Coll., Machebeuf Letters, Jan. 22, 26, 1854.
3. *Ibid.*, M-6 Albuquerque.
4. *Ibid.*, Horg. Coll., Prop. Fide, Mar. 3, 15, 1853, no. 9.
5. *Ibid.*, Mar. 17, 1853, no. 9.
6. *Ibid.*, Lamy File, Mar. 31, 1853, no. 4.
7. *Ibid.*, B- and M- (1853) Sta. Fe.
8. *Ibid.*, Clergy Card File, *J.F. Ortiz.*
9. *Ibid.*, Horg. Coll., Prop. Fide, 1856, no. 17.
10. *Ibid.*, Clergy Card File, *Otero.*
11. *Ibid.*, *Cabeza de Baca.*
12. *Ibid.*, Horg. Coll., Prop. Fide, 1856, no. 17.

13. *Ibid.*, April 2, 1853, no. 2a.
14. *Ibid.*, Lamy File, April 10, 1853, no. 6.
15. *Ibid.*
16. *Ibid.*
17. *Ibid.*, Horg. Coll.,Machebeuf Letters, Jan. 22, 26, 1854.
18. *Ibid.*, Lamy File, April 15, 1853, no. 7b.
19. *Ibid.*, May 3, 1853, no. 9.
20. *Ibid.*, cf. Note 18 *supra.*
21. *Ibid.*, Bur-1 Arroyo Hondo.
22. *Ibid.*, Lamy File, *Bullae;* Horg Coll., Prop. Fide, Aug. 5, 1853, no. 14.
23. *Ibid.*, Martínez File, Dec. 17, 1853, no. 2.

Back to the Public Forum / 17

1. AASF, Clergy of Archd. I, nos. 1-3.
2. *Ibid.*, Lamy File, Pastorals, no. 3.
3. *Ibid.*, J.F. Ortiz File, July 21, 1853, no. 3.
4. S.Fe *Gazette*, July 15, 1854.
5. AASF, Martínez File, Oct. 14, 1854, no. 3.
6. *Ibid.*, Horg. Coll., Prop.Fide, July 29, 1854, no. 7, Machebeuf Letters, Nov. 30, 1854.
7. *Ibid.*, Martínez File, May 28, 1855, no. 4.
8. Cf. Note 6 *supra;* Salpointe, *Soldiers*, p. 207.
9. AASF, Clergy of Archd. I, nos. 3, 8.
10. *Ibid.*, Horg. Coll., Machebeuf Letters, Nov. 30, 1854.
11. Cf. Chavez, *Archives*, p. 124, no. 38 (now missing from archives).
12. AASF, Horg. Coll., July 24, 1855, no. 10.
13. *Ibid.*, Bur-42 Taos, Bur-6 Arroyo Hondo.
14. *Ibid.*, Martínez File, Nov. 29, 1855, no. 4a; Horg. Coll., 1855, no. 11.
15. S.Fe *Gazette*, May 31, 1856.
16. AASF, Clergy Card File, *Gallegos.*
17. *Ibid.*, Horg. Coll., Prop. Fide, Jan. 1, 1856, no. 16.
18. Cf. Davis, *El Gringo*, pp. 95, 186, 228-38, 267-70.
19. Cf. Note 13 *supra.*
20. AASF, Horg. Coll., Prop. Fide, April 24, 1856, no. 3.
21. *Ibid.*, Machebeuf Letters, April 12, 1856.
22. *Ibid.*, Prop. Fide, 1856, no. 12a.
23. *Ibid.*, no. 18.
24. *Ibid.*, no. 17.
25. *Ibid.*
26. *Ibid.*, no. 12.

Lamy versus Martínez / 18

1. Cf. Chavez, *Archives*, p. 122, 1856, nos. 16-18; AASF, Clergy of Archd. I, nos. 2, 4.
2. Cf. Chavez, *op. cit.*, p. 122, 1856, no. 20 (now missing).
3. S.Fe *Gazette*, May 31, 1856.
4. *Ibid.*, May 3, 1856.
5. AASF, Lamy File, April 22, 1856, no. 21; Horg. Coll., 1856, no. 2.
6. *Ibid.*, May 5, 1856, no. 22; Horg. Coll., 1856, no. 4.
7. *Ibid.*, Mar. 29, 1854, no. 4.
8. S.Fe *Gazette*, May 24, 1856, reprinted May 31.
9. *Ibid.*; AASF, B-55 Taos.
10. Cf. Chavez, *op. cit.*, p. 123, 1856, no. 25 (now missing).
11. *Ibid.*
12. AASF, Lamy File, June 7, 1856, no. 26.
13. Cf. Chavez, *op. cit.*, p. 123, 1856, no. 27 (now missing).
14. *Ibid.*, 1856, no. 28 (now missing).
15. *Ibid.*, 1856, no. 29 (now missing).

16. AASF, Horg. Coll., Oct. 1, 1856, no. 7.
17. *Ibid.*, Lamy File, Oct. 23, 1856, no. 32.
18. Cf. Note 16 *supra*.
19. *Ibid.*
20. Howlett, *Machebeuf*, p. 233.

Man of La Mancha / 19

1. S.Fe *Gazette*, Oct. 25, 1856.
2. AASF, Horg. Coll., Nov. 12, 1856, no. 10.
3. *Ibid.*, Lamy File, Oct. 23, 1856, no. 32.
4. *Ibid.*, Bur- (1856) Taos.
5. Cf. Note 3 *supra*.
6. Cf. Chavez, *Archives*, p. 123, 1856, no. 31 (now missing).
7. Cf. Note 3 *supra*.
8. AASF, Horg. Coll., Nov. 12, 1856, no. 10.
9. *Ibid.*
10. *Ibid.*, B-72 Tomé, M-41a Taos.
11. Cf. Chavez, *op. cit.*, p. 123, 1856, no. 34 (now missing).
12. S.Fe *Gazette*, Nov. 22, 29, 1856.
13. *Ibid.*
14. AASF, Martínez File, Nov. 14, 1856, no. 4b.
15. *Ibid.*, Lamy File, Mar. 3, 1856, no. 6.
16. *Ibid.*, Horg. Coll., April 13, 1857, no. 12.
17. *Ibid.*
18. *Ibid.*
19. *Ibid.*, Martínez File, May 2, 1857, no. 5; Horg. Coll., 1857, no. 3.
20. *Ibid.*

Schism and Excommunication? / 20

1. AASF, B- (1857) Taos.
2. *Ibid.*, Martínez File, June 22, 1857, no. 6.
3. *Ibid.*, J.E. Ortiz File, July 23, 1857, no. 1.
4. *Ibid.*
5. *Ibid.*, Martínez File, Oct. 21, 1857, no. 7.
6. *Ibid.*, Nov. 12, 1857, no. 8.
7. *Ibid.*
8. *Ibid.*
9. *Ibid.*, J.E. Ortiz File, Nov. 12, 1857, no. 2.
10. S.Fe *Gazette*, Aug. 15, 1857.
11. *Ibid.*
12. *Ibid.*, Aug. 22, 1857.
13. *Ibid.*, Sept. 30, 1857, Mar. 27, 1858.
14. *Ibid.*, Oct. 30, 1858.
15. AASF, Horg. Coll., May 13, 1859, Prop. Fide, 1859, no. 3.
16. *Ibid.*, Martínez File, Mar. 29, 1858, no. 9.
17. Howlett, *Machebeuf*, pp. 232-33.
18. AASF, Bur-42 Taos.
19. *Ibid.*, B-1 Arroyo Hondo.

Last Gasps, An Old Press Again / 21

1. AASF, Martínez File, 1859-1861, no. 10.
2. *Ibid.*, pp. 1-3.
3. *Ibid.*, pp. 12-14.
4. *Ibid.*, pp. 29-32.
5. *Ibid.*

6. *Ibid.*, pp. 4-7.
7. *Ibid.*, pp. 3-11.
8. *Ibid.*
9. *Ibid.*, pp. 19-22.
10. *Ibid.*
11. *Ibid.*, B-58 Taos, rear cover.
12. Cf. Note 9 *supra.*
13. AASF, cf. Note 1 *supra,* pp. 26-28.
14. *Ibid.*, pp. 15-18.
15. *Ibid.*, pp. 22-25.
16. Cf. *N.M. Hist. Rev.*, vol. 12, p. 6.

Death and a Testament / 22

1. AASF, B-58 Taos, p. 115.
2. *Ibid.*, M-41a Taos.
3. Keleher, *Frontier*, pp. 362-64.
4. Bur-42a Taos.
5. Sánchez, *Memorias*, p. 40.
6. S.Fe *New Mexican*, August 3, 17, 1867.
7. AASF, Lamy File, Sept. 6, 1868, no. 11.
8. *Ibid.*, Horg. Coll., Feb. 3, 1869, no. 8.
9. *Rev. Catolica*, vol. 3, p. 484.
10. Warner, *Archb. Lamy*, pp. 84-88.

BIBLIOGRAPHY

(Only of sources referred to)

AASF. Archives of the Archdiocese of Santa Fe. These consist of two main sections.

    I. MISSIONS: Loose Documents (1680-1850), Diligencias Matrimoniales (1678-1869), Patentes (copied official letters, 1697-1853), Accounts (1710-1855), Books of Baptisms, Marriages, Burials of various missions, varying dates. – All of these were calendared in Chavez, *Archives of the Archdiocese of Santa Fe, 1678-1900.* (Diocesan material, 1851-1900, has been transferred to Persons and Places in second Diocesan Section.)

    II. DIOCESAN: Loose or bound records from 1851 to the present, filed according to Persons and Places, such as Archbishops, Clergy, Chancery, Parishes, etc. – A special file, *Horgan Collection,* consists of Lamy-Machebeuf papers (from U.S., France, Vatican Propaganda Fide) which Mr. Paul Horgan kindly donated to Archbishop Sanchez. – A Clergy Card File is in process of compilation from these archives and other sources.

Adams, Eleanor B. *Bishop Tamaron's Visitation of New Mexico, 1760.* (Albuquerque, 1956).

Anonymous. *An Illustrated History of New Mexico, Its Sources and People* (Los Angeles, Chicago, New York, 1907).

Borhegyi, Stephen F. de. "The Cult of Our Lord of Esquipulas in Middle America and New Mexico," *El Palacio,* vol. 61 (1954).

Cather, Willa. *Death Comes for the Archbishop* (New York, 1927).

Census of 1850, Territory of New Mexico. Library of Congress microfilm, courtesy of Virginia L. Olmsted.

Chavez, Fray Angelico. *Archives of the Archdiocese of Santa Fe, 1678-1900* (Washington, 1957).

_____. *Missions of New Mexico, 1776,* with E.B. Adams (Albuquerque, 1956).

_____. *My Penitente Land* (Albuquerque, 1974).

_____. *Origins of New Mexico Families in the Spanish Colonial Period* (Santa Fe, 1954).

_____. *The Oroz Codex* (Washington, 1972).

_____. "Doña Tules, her Fame and her Funeral," *El Palacio,* vol. 57 (1950).

_____. "Early Settlements in the Mora Valley," *El Palacio,* vol. 62 (1955).

_____. "El Vicario Don Santiago Roybal," *El Palacio,* vol. 55 (1948).

_____. "Genízaros," *Handbook of North American Indians,* vol. 9 (Washington, 1979).

_____. "José Gonzales, Genízaro Governor," *New Mexico Historical Review,* vol. 30 (1955).

_____. "New Names in New Mexico," *El Palacio,* vol. 64 (1957).

_____. "The Penitentes of New Mexico," *New Mexico Historical Review,* vol. 29 (1954).

Davis, W.W.H. *El Gringo* (New York, 1857).

Defouri, James H. *Historical Sketch of the Catholic Church in New Mexico* (San Francisco, 1887).

Ellis, Bruce T. "New Notes on Bishop Lamy's first years in New Mexico," *El Palacio,* vol. 65 (1958).

El Palacio. Museum of New Mexico, Santa Fe.

Emory, Lt. W.H. *"Notes of a Military Reconnaisance, 1846-1847* (Washington, 1848).

Gibson, Geo. Rutledge. *Journal of a Soldier under Kearny and Doniphan, 1846-1847* (Glendale, 1935).

Handbook of North American Indians, vol. 9 (ed.) Wm. C. Sturtevant, Alfonso Ortiz (Washington, 1979).

Horgan, Paul. *Lamy of Santa Fe* (New York, 1975).

Howlett, W.J. *Life of Bishop Machebeuf* (Pueblo, 1908).

Huntington Library, microfilm of Santiago Valdez, *Biografía* of Padre Martínez and assorted MSS, nos. RI 2209-RI 2211. Contents in sequence: 1) Copied sections (1826-1845), unpaginated except for initial pp. 16-17, and referred to here as *Notes I*. 2) Some drafts (1830-1835), referred to here as *Drafts*, pp. 21-35. 3) The 1877 Biography proper, ornate title-page and neat text (1793-1826) apparently unfinished, and referred to here as *Biografía*, pp. 92-141. 4) Copied sections again (1845) and referred to here as *Notes II*, pp. 294-300. 5) Different Biography, formal title-page dated 1803 (1801-1818), but dealing only with Taos church, and referred to here as *1903 Biography*, pp. 301-310. 6) English translations by Larkin G. Read of separate Martínez documents and Valdez' commentary (1845-1851), and referred to here as *Notes (English)*, pp. 70-128.

Keleher, William A. *The Fabulous Frontier* (Santa Fe, 1945).

_____. *Turmoil in New Mexico, 1846-1868* (Santa Fe, 1952).

La Revista Católica, Jesuit weekly (Las Vegas, 1875-1900).

Martínez, Antonio José. *Relación de Méritos del Presbítero Antonio José Martínez, Domiciliario del Obispo de Durango, Cura Encargado de Taos en el Departamento de Nuevo México* (Taos, 1838). Poor but adequate English translation in *New Mexico Historical Review*. See: Romero, Cecil V.

_____. *Historia Consisa del Cura de Taos Antonio José Martínez* (Taos 1861). Attributed to him, but evidently composed by someone else. See: Romero, Vicente Ferrer, and Wagner, Henry R.

_____. Letters and articles in the Santa Fe *Gazette*.

_____. His material in Tracts of Taos publication. See: Romero, Vicente Ferrer.

McMurtrie, Douglas C., "The History of Early Printing in New Mexico," *New Mexico Historical Review*, vol. 4 (1929).

New Mexico Historical Review, Historical Society of New Mexico, Santa Fe, and University of New Mexico, Albuquerque.

New Mexico Quarterly, University of New Mexico, Albuquerque.

New Mexico State Record Center, Santa Fe.

Old Santa Fe, 3 vols. (1913-1916), Santa Fe.

Read, Benjamin M. *Historia Ilustrada de Nuevo Mexico* (Santa Fe, 1911).

Romero, Cecil V. "Apologia of Presbyter Antonio J. Martinez," *New Mexico Historical Review*, vol. 3 (1928). Translation of *Relación de Méritos* of Padre Martínez.

Romero, Vicente Ferrer, most probable author of *Historia Consisa del Cura de Taos Antonio José Martínez* (Taos, 1861). Also of Tracts as editor of Taos periodical (1859-1861).

Salpointe, J.B. *Soldiers of the Cross* (Banning, 1898).

Sánchez, Pedro. *Memorias sobre la Vida del Presbítero Don Antonio José Martínez* (Santa Fe, 1903).

Santa Fe *Gazette* or *Weekly Gazette*, also bilingual as *Gaceta de Santa Fe*.

Santa Fe *New Mexican* or *The New Mexican*, *Weekly New Mexican*, *Daily New Mexican*, also bilingual as *El Nuevo Mejicano*.

Twitchell, Ralph E. *The Leading Facts of New Mexico History*, 5 vols. (Cedar Rapids, 1911-1917).

_____. *The History of the Military Occupation of New Mexico, 1846-1851* (Denver, 1909).

Valdez, Santiago, *Biografía del Rev. P. Antonio José Martínez, Cura-Párroco del Curato de Taos, N.M. A.D. 1877, Comenzada a Copiar el dia 20 de Enero. A.D. 1877*. MS of unfinished work with original or copied sections for same. See: Huntington Library.

Wagner, Henry R., "New Mexico Spanish Press," *New Mexico Historical Review*, vol. 12 (1937).

Warner, Louis H. *Archbishop Lamy an Epoch Maker* (Santa Fe, 1936).